To Charles and Sue - I hope you will find this text useful in your Christian walk.
With best wis
From Hilton.

An active Christian for many years, Hilton McCann is a keen observer of human behaviour and a student of psychology. His particular interest is attitude – which he regards as the bridge between stimulus and action. In this book, he describes what attitude is, why it matters and its transformational potential.

Hilton's first book reflected his 45-year career in financial services. He has gleaned rich life experiences working abroad in different cultures, traditions and corporate scenarios.

Now retired, Hilton lives in rural England with his wife. He is a member of a local church where he worships regularly.

All royalties earned on the sales of this book will go to
Médecins Sans Frontières

To Braden, Esmé and Jonah – crowns to their grandparents (Proverbs 17:6) – and blessed reminders that God is good.

Hilton McCann

The Psychology of Attitude

A Christian Perspective

Austin Macauley Publishers™
London • Cambridge • New York • Sharjah

A CIP catalogue record for this title is available from the British Library.

ISBN 9781528963244 (Paperback)
ISBN 9781528963626 (ePub e-book)

www.austinmacauley.com

First Published 2021
Austin Macauley Publishers Ltd®
1 Canada Square
Canary Wharf
London
E14 5AA

In completing this text, it would be remiss of me not to mention the on-going support from my mentor and long-time friend Pastor Randy Trail – who encouraged me to keep going and finish the task I had begun. I am also grateful to all those who took the time to talk to me about what I was thinking and writing and enquiring about progress along the way. Above all, I want to record my love and gratitude to Lynn – my wife and friend of many years – the person who knows better than anyone else the attitudinal deficiencies of the author.

Table of Contents

Teach Me Your Way, O Lord
Psalm 86:11

Preface

Background

The title chosen for this text is 'Psychology of Attitude' – considered appropriate because psychology is the scientific study of the human mind and its functions – especially those affecting behaviour. In addition, philosophy has to do with the nature of knowledge. The Stoic Epictetus believed that "...one becomes a philosopher when they begin to exercise their guiding reason and start to question the emotions and beliefs and even language that others take for granted...".[1] In short, this text combines elements of Psychology and Philosophy in its consideration of the role of attitude in determining behaviour.

While a number of published works refer to stimulus and response with respect to behaviour, this text identifies a third element (attitude) that links the other two and which determines an individual's response to a particular stimulus in a particular set of circumstances. Therefore, attitude exerts a huge influence – because if individuals can control their attitudes, they will be better able to control their behaviour. Accordingly, this text concerns the definition and characteristics of attitude and how the human mind chooses its response to a stimulus.

Attitude is a significant element in the psychological makeup of humankind and is therefore as prevalent as humankind itself. It is intangible and although present in all of us all of the time and everywhere (whether in an active or a passive form) it is only observable some of the time. In influencing how human beings make decisions and take actions, attitude can be a positive force sometimes or a negative force at other times. Despite all this – and even though it is an integral part of defining who each of us is as individuals – attitude appears not to be well understood or to stimulate much interest.

---

[1] Ryan Holiday and Stephen Hanselman; The Daily Stoic; Profile Books; Pg 71; 2016

This text postulates that if humankind could understand attitude, we might be able to learn how to control our attitudes positively. If we were able to do so, we would be one step closer to knowing how to control the effects of those stimuli that give rise to attitudes that prompt responses. The quantum of potential for empowerment that arises from being able to control our own behaviour is transformational. Accordingly, the thesis of this book is that the person who understands and can positively control the influences that shape his/her attitude will be empowered to make positive things happen not only in his or her own life – but also in the life of others.

While this pursuit of understanding is a worthy one – like all other worthy pursuits – this one requires energy and diligence to pursue it to a meaningful conclusion – because inter alia, psychological, social, theological, behavioural and philosophical imperatives impinge upon attitude – each overlapping the other – producing myriad permutations.

Objectives

This text has four objectives:

The first objective is 'to ground' the entire discussion set out in the text upon Holy Scripture – by reference to the central role of Almighty God. Since our Lord created humankind with the amazing capacity to generate attitudes in the first place, He must have had a purpose in doing so. Thus, Scripture has been used extensively to understand the role of attitude – and to explore the relationship between God's plan for humankind and His provision to achieve that plan.

Secondly, while everyone may be aware of attitude at a subliminal level, it seems that few human beings are conscious at a meaningful level of the significance of attitude in the whole scheme of human endeavour. Accordingly, this text will attempt to make readers more aware of the breadth and depth of the meaning of attitude – pointing to its universality, its potency and the multiple forms in which attitude manifests itself. A working definition is provided.

The third objective is to consider the dynamics of attitude within our human frame – describing its hierarchy, its linkages to character formation and ultimately, to behaviour.

The fourth objective is to demonstrate: (1) why control of our attitudes creates the potential for transformational change not only within the life of individuals but also within the lives of those people around us and (2) how to compile a plan designed to help develop attitudes that will culminate in making positive things happen in individual lives.

Ironically, although attitude has been part of our humanity since the day each of us was born, we understand it poorly. Therefore, we refer to it loosely and we treat it peripherally. The text will demonstrate that this is inappropriate because character, behaviour, choices, conscience, sensitivity, discipline, humility and discernment are all predicated upon attitude.

The text is divided into five sections. Section 1 comprises the 'The Platform' – so called because it provides the introduction to the text that follows. The Platform initiates discussion on how attitude works and how it arises in the first place. In this respect, the word 'stimulus' is introduced. When a stimulus combines with an attitude, there is a response. The response may be positive or negative – seen or unseen – but real. Stimulus is the catalyst, attitude is the 'driver' and action is the output – for good or ill – passive or active – immediate or delayed – obvious or hidden. Section 1 refers to what we know about attitude – based on both personal and general experiences – comparing negative and positive attitudes. Importantly, all this is contrasted with Christ's attitude. An initial working definition is suggested.

Attitude defines who I am. Therefore, to understand who I am, I need to understand my attitudes and to be able to distinguish my real attitudes from what I think my attitudes are. Having done so, I will be in a better position to consider whether my attitudes enhance or impair my attempt to be the best I can be in life. Understanding one's attitude involves a journey of self-discovery – and Section 2 starts that process by introducing a model ('The Composition of Mankind') that – over 7 chapters – identifies and describes the 'components' in the hierarchy of attitude. Each line of the model presents 3 factors that are described in dedicated chapters. Components are linked both horizontally and vertically. The model's components describe what make us human – and one of the most basic factors that makes us human is our mortality – so chapter 2 embraces a discussion about mortality and immortality – because the distinction between the two has a fundamental effect on our attitude to life.

This leads into chapter 3 and to a description of the tri-partite nature of humankind – spirit, soul and body. Spirit and soul are by definition 'immortal' while body and mind are 'mortal'. The significance of spirit and soul is described in terms of their eternal existence.

In expanding the discussion in the previous chapter, chapter 4 identifies the linkage between: (1) our in-born spirit and conscience, our soul and sensitivity and (2) how personal discipline is necessary to control our physical body/mind. The Christian needs an acute conscience, highly tuned sensitivity and substantial discipline to do the right thing – and to do the thing right.

Chapters 5 and 6 revolve around character – because character is at the core of the Christian experience. Humility is foundational to character – and humility is a very significant component in the consideration of attitude of mind. This discussion forms part of chapter 5 – which demonstrates that humility is a pre-requisite to understanding and thereby to character formation. The text sets out the intrinsic link between humility and character. In turn, this leads to a description of how all this affects discernment in making choices. Since we make so many choices every day of our lives – this is a significant part of attitude of mind.

In light of its importance with respect to attitude formation, chapter 6 takes a deeper look at character by reviewing types of: (1) principles, (standards, values, and virtues); (2) traits and habits (including a positive disposition) and (3) qualities (such as integrity, honesty, trust and gratitude) that comprise character. Successful adoption of principles, traits and qualities is an important step in adopting the right attitude – they are transformational.

The next chapter (7), is the final chapter in section 2. Chapter 7 concludes this part of the discussion and provides a brief overview of some additional influences on attitude. These include environment, expectations, perceptions and other stimuli that have a bearing on the attitudes we adopt and the behavioural implications. The model is now complete.

By this stage, readers will have been presented with a working definition of attitude and a description of many factors that impinge upon human beings in the formation of their attitudes. The material in chapters 2-7 will enable readers to take a good hard look at their own attitudes and by addressing some of the questions posed, help them to tease out the sources and acceptability of their own attitudes and behaviours – in their own objective view.

Section 3 (comprising Chapters 8, 9 and 10), changes the focus in 2 ways – firstly from humankind's attitude to God's attitude and secondly, from putting people in touch with their inner selves by examining their attitude – to an exploration of the wider environment in which attitude comes into play.

Chapter 8 considers God's person. This chapter sits at the core of the text – because it provides the answer to the question – as to why attitude is important. The chapter provides some comments on the deity and purity of God with reference to His attributes and His holiness. Comments on the eternal dimension of our God and His perfection, patience and grace are included. However, it has to be made clear that in reality, Almighty God is beyond description – His ways are infinite and His knowledge is beyond our comprehension.

Chapter 9 is somewhat of a shock after the glory of God described in the preceding chapter – because the focus in chapters 9 and 10 is on how far humankind has slipped from the perfection associated with God's original creation in the Garden of Eden. This analysis serves to indicate how badly humankind has wilfully worsened what originally began as a perfect environment. Chapter 9 explores the status of humankind and couples this exploration with a description of the worth of a Christian's soul – and considers what God expects of His creation. Some thought is given to the status of non-Christians. The chapter ends with some comments on 3 requirements that are fundamental to the adoption of appropriate attitudes in Christian service: love, awe and faith.

Chapter 10 provides an indication of humankind's attitude to humankind – and presents some of the challenges arising for Christians. Chapter 10 refers to certain fundamental human weaknesses that are common in human beings – including insensitivity, duplicity, indifference, and indiscipline – and not least – unacceptable behaviour. These are amongst the important hurdles that present themselves in Christian living.

The focus of Section 4 (comprising 4 chapters) is application. This Section includes some reflections (chapter 11) on areas the text has covered thus far – and that are relevant to Christian living. Chapter 12 includes comments on communication and scriptural guidance on attitude. This is followed by some further thoughts on living daily as a Christian – with particular reference to prayer, Scripture per se and meeting with other believers. Chapter 13 is an introspective chapter that invites readers to do some 'soul-searching' in considering their attitude towards certain fundamental matters in life – how we use our time, energy and money. Chapter 13 addresses the question – what is my attitude to the things that make life worth living for me? These matters are considered to be amongst the most important for consideration in anticipation of preparing a plan of action.

The last chapter in the text (14) offers some prompts for action. It includes a summary outline of the text (intended as an aide memoire) – and then a guide to compiling an action plan – the purpose of which is to encourage the adoption of attitudes that lead to changes in lives. The chapter includes an additional aid in this respect – in the form of an analysis of key sentences from the text. (It should be noted that the intention is not to provide a 'let-out' for those who don't want to read the whole text. Instead, the purposes are to facilitate quick reviews of the text and the compilation of the action plan.) Section 5 contains five appendices.

Holy Scripture has been cited extensively throughout the text. The purpose is to provide a meaningful foundation to the discussion. In this respect, one author has usefully pointed out "...We do not believe in Christ because we believe in the Bible; we believe in the Bible because we believe in Christ...".[2] That is to say, Jesus Christ is our foremost example in word and in deed – and what we read in Scripture attests to what we believe. Accordingly, the significance of Scripture cannot be overemphasised and this explains the inclusion of so many quotes from Scripture. Unless otherwise stated, all Scriptural references are taken from the New International Version of the Holy Bible; International Bible Society; Zondervan Publishing House. Scripture taken from the HOLY BIBLE, NEW INTERNATIONAL VERSION®. NIV®. Copyright © 1973, 1978, 1984 by International Bible Society. Used by permission of Zondervan. All rights reserved worldwide.

Lastly – out of thesis comes antithesis – so I invite you to test the thesis that I presented at the beginning of this Preface – and to help develop an antithesis. Subsequent thought might help those interested to conclude Hegel's dialectic with the construction of a synthesis. Simply stated, don't just take my word for the veracity of what I have written – test it and see for yourself – because failure to accord attitude its rightful place in the whole scheme of things will lead to sub-optimisation on a grand scale. I have quoted widely from the work of people involved in psychological, social, theological, behavioural and philosophical disciplines. My objective is to provide a grounded approach – based on the citations of experts in these disciplines. Having done so, I believe there is so much more that could have been added – so I encourage you to supplement what you read in this text by researching these matters more widely.

---

[2] A Reasonable Response; Quoted by William Lane Craig and Joe Gorra; Pg 107; Moody Publishers; 2013 – as quoted by Peter May; The Search For God & The Path To Persuasion; Pg 106; Malcolm Down Publishing; 2016

Lastly, we should be aware that attitudes are often formed unintentionally. It is possible to be completely unaware that we have adopted an attitude – so we must keep challenging ourselves if we are to understand more fully the type of person we are – as opposed to the type of person we believe we are. I encourage you to take active steps in understanding, enhancing and developing your attitudes for your own personal development and that of others.

Section One
The Platform

Chapter One

Introduction

1.1 "I Don't Like Your Attitude!"

As one author has pointed out "...the interpretation of a remark or word has an immense amount of power...".[3] I wonder what came to your mind as you read the sub-title of this paragraph? You may have been reminded of circumstances when you heard these same highly emotive words being spoken. Perhaps they were spoken to you – or perhaps it was you who spoke them! However, even if you have not been physically present when an exchange like this took place, what do you imagine could have been behind an 'outburst' like this? Here is a scenario that these words conjure up in my mind as I think about them.

I imagine a highly charged environment where hostility underlies the words being spoken. The speaker's tone is not friendly and in fact, may be somewhat haughty. The speaker's expression is somewhere between withering and contemptuous – a raised eyebrow perhaps. Whether there is further invective, disrespect and insults accompanying these words depends upon the reply of the person to whom these words were addressed (the addressee). The prevailing mood is at best negative and entirely disagreeable at worst. This is not a nice place to be.

Now consider some of the many possible reasons why the speaker is so displeased that (s)he considers it necessary to speak in this pejorative manner. The speaker's attitude reflects not only his/her strong adverse emotions but maybe even disappointment and anger. Here are a few of the many possible explanations why the speaker is so annoyed:

[3] Ryan Holiday and Stephen Hanselman; The Daily Stoic; Profile Books; Pg 119; 2016

- maybe the speaker (reasonably) allocated an important task to the addressee but despite placing trust in the addressee and supporting him/her with resources and assistance, the addressee has failed to deliver what was required;
- maybe the speaker would have been more tolerant if the addressee had worked harder to achieve the goal or had been more apologetic at not having achieved it – but instead the addressee has accepted little or no responsibility for the failure – with a carefree shrug of the shoulders or folded arms indicating total indifference;
- maybe the speaker is a nasty person – and has not provided any meaningful support or assistance to the addressee – who despite gargantuan efforts, could not have achieved the objective because it was unreasonable in the first instance;
- maybe, despite the significance the speaker attached to the objective – which had been explained to the addressee – the latter's failure will have serious, adverse consequences for the speaker;
- maybe the speaker is a parent who has exercised great patience with an uncooperative adolescent son or daughter who simply refuses to pull their weight;
- maybe the speaker over-reacted and abused their authority in a vitriolic outburst – deliberately trying to demean the credibility and status of the addressee;
- maybe the speaker has acted abnormally and out of character and wished the words had never been spoken.

Notice how many possibilities there are with respect to different attitudes and how they might/might not apply in all the scenarios considered. Clearly, my imagination created a scenario that does not fit all the scenarios considered – so one point to note is that an open mind is helpful in forming attitudes. (In this respect, one author has pointed out "When a person says 'No' and really means it, he or she is doing far more than saying a word of two letters. The entire organism – glandular, nervous, muscular – gathers itself together into a condition of rejection. There is, usually in minute but sometimes an observable degree, a physical withdrawal or readiness for withdrawal. The whole neuromuscular system, in short, sets itself on guard against acceptance. When, to the contrary, a person says 'Yes', none of the withdrawal activities takes place. The organism is in a forward – looking, accepting, open attitude. Hence the more 'yeses' we can, at the very outset, induce, the more likely we are to succeed in capturing the attention for our ultimate proposal…".[4]) Maybe the speaker had some justification or maybe (s)he had none. Maybe the addressee deserves empathy or maybe (s)he deserves strong words in the circumstances.

Here is a totally different scenario – in which the addressee may not have achieved the outcome anticipated – but nevertheless managed to achieve something of note – through diligence, effort and personal discipline. In such circumstances, the speaker might say to the addressee, "I like your attitude." This sentence infers approbation – it is an endorsement of the addressee. What type of scenario do you imagine this time?

In this case, I imagined a positive environment where encouragement underlies the words being spoken. The speaker's tone is friendly and may be somewhat compassionate. The speaker's expression reflects approbation and underlies the relaxed tone used in speaking. The speaker and the addressee may have an exchange – in which case the tone will be affirmative and pleasant for both. The prevailing mood is entirely positive. This is an encouraging environment.

Now consider some of the many possible reasons why the speaker feels it appropriate to speak in this manner. The speaker's attitude reflects his/her positive approval. Here are a few possible explanations as to why the speaker is so much at ease:

- maybe the speaker is extremely pleased that the task allocated has been achieved to the extent that it has;
- maybe the speaker is extremely pleased that (s)he has been proved right in allocating the task to the addressee;
- maybe – despite a huge amount of time and energy having been invested by the addressee, the intended goal was not achieved – but by dint of the commitment and effort invested, the addressee has proved him or herself to be worthy of the trust placed in him/her;
- maybe the speaker recognises the potential of the addressee and is attempting to use this exchange to encourage the addressee to do even bigger and better things in future.

---

[4] Dale Carnegie; How To Win Friends And Influence People; Pg 159; 2006; Vermilion

Although these two scenarios are very different, they have at least one common feature – they reflect attitudes. The first scenario is totally negative and the second is totally positive. Consider which of the two scenarios is more common in your experience (whether as a participant or an observer)? One author believes that there is only one thing that is more contagious than a good attitude – and that is a bad attitude.[5] Even in our disparate environments, most of us will have opportunities to encourage someone – whether we realise it or not. Take a moment to consider how often you encourage positive behaviour – looking for positive aspects in negative scenarios? For example, when you speak, do you consider not only what you are saying but the tone of voice you are using? In addition to the words you are speaking, do you consider what message your body language is conveying? In this respect, one author wrote "…Letting one save face! How important, how vitally important that is! And how few of us ever stop to think of it! We ride roughshod over the feelings of others, getting our own way, finding fault, issuing threats, criticising a child or an employee in front of others, without even considering the hurt to the other person's pride. Whereas a few minutes' thought, a considerate word or two, a genuine understanding of the other person's attitude, would go so far toward alleviating the sting…". [6]

Considering the scenarios above from the perspective of the addressee, when you have been allocated a task, what is your attitude in approaching it – total commitment or non-committal or outright uncooperative? Do you consider whether your attitude is obvious to other people – and if so – how do you think this affects you, the person who allocated the task to you and those around you?

1.2 How Attitude Is Manifested

Firstly, it should be said that attitude is often personified – that is to say – it's easier to talk about attitude as if it had a form or substance of its own – as if it was tangible. So, when we refer to attitude being obvious, we mean to say that the external manifestation (for example – physically or verbally) of a certain attitude is obvious. Attitude is not tangible – clearly, we cannot touch it or see it per se. This manifestation may take the shape of words used but it may also emanate from the expression on a person's face or in their body language. Similarly, we talk often about attitude in the singular whereas we might more

---

[5] John C Maxwell; Attitude 101; Pg 7; 2003; Maxwell Motivation

[6] Dale Carnegie; How To Win Friends And Influence People; Pg 228; 2006; Vermilion

correctly refer to 'attitudes' – in the plural. Here are some comments on the manifestation of attitude:

1.2.1 Obvious Manifestations of Attitude

Words and behaviour reflect attitude – and sometimes we choose to reveal our attitudes by what we say, by our behaviour and by our body language. Examples of attitude being obvious include: when someone hugs someone else; when a child throws a tantrum; when someone is nasty to someone else or when someone gives way to someone else etc.

Even if our attitude is obvious – say by way of a verbal reaction – we might not use words that reflect what we deeply and truly believe (for example, more praise may be due than what we are prepared to acknowledge). Alternatively, we might try to convince anyone nearby that our attitude is different from what we are actually feeling inside (for example, we might feel angry but make every effort not to show it). On the other hand, the attitude we reveal might be genuine – but overdone at the same time – especially if we speak in anger or when influenced by a highly charged atmosphere. Attitude is very sensitive to influence.

However, while attitude is not visible per se, emotions arising from attitude (such as anger, happiness, strain) or body language (raised eyebrows, a smirk, a scowl, or embarrassment) may be visible. These visible signs sometimes give away an underlying attitude.

While we can control 'expressions of attitude' to an extent, in the heat of the moment, we sometimes give the game away and blurt out something – which on reflection – we would have preferred not to have said – or to have said differently. Similarly, when we become embarrassed – or uncomfortable – this is often reflected in unintended body language which may be obvious to people around us.

1.2.2 Covert Attitudes

The manifestation of attitude is not necessarily visible per se. While we often choose to reveal our attitudes, we sometimes prefer to hide or disguise both our behaviour and body language in order to reveal nothing about the attitude of our mind. So, attitude need not be obvious – consider for example when someone forms a view in their own mind but neither their outward behaviour nor speech gives any hint that this – or any other view – has been formed. Some of us are able to internalise what we are thinking and/or feeling without revealing any trace of emotion whether as a facial expression or as body language. In such circumstances, people may still be feeling emotion – anywhere along the spectrum from happiness to hate – but making a conscious effort not to let anyone else see or know that. This 'cover-up' might reflect a person's personality – but sometimes people make conscious efforts to hide their attitude and thereby do not reveal who they really are. It has been said "…The vices are often very hard to detect since clever people who have them can still act just like the virtuous do in public. What is in a person's heart is what really matters to character, not how she presents herself to the world…".[7] Consider which of all these many permutations might apply to you.

Apart from tell-tale signs (such as facial expressions and body language), at the point in time when a person adopts a certain attitude, sometimes the consequences of adopting that attitude might be latent – replete with potential for action but deferred until some future time. So, an attitude need not only be displayed in what is said or done – but may also be hidden by what is not said or not done – with consequential action (or words) being deferred for the time being. Withholding words – or not taking action immediately might be deliberate – resulting for example from what conscience might dictate as appropriate in the circumstances – or resulting from a person's view that a deferment of action or words is in her or his best interests – or because we prefer not to make our attitude obvious at that point in time for whatever reason. Sometimes, it is better to remain quiet in order to avoid the risk of worsening or complicating a situation – but at other times, remaining quiet may be unhelpful or even misleading. Sometimes, inaction is the best course of action – but at other times, inaction may be dishonest, disastrous – or even cowardly.

1.2.3 Attitudes Revealed Unintentionally

In between revealing and hiding our attitude, there is at least one more permutation – and that is while sometimes we would prefer that our attitude was not obvious – we reveal it unintentionally. In certain circumstances, many of us find it difficult to obscure our emotions. Consider, for example, displays of effusive happiness when someone meets someone else at an airport – or someone crying at a funeral or at a moment of great happiness such as at a wedding.

---

[7] Christian B Miller; The Character Gap; Pg 19; Oxford University Press; 2018

1.2.4 Some Attributes of Attitude

Clearly, there are very many permutations of stimuli, attitudes and responses. This is a dynamic and constantly changing process that involves a huge range of variables. Here are some comments that describe the phenomenon that we call attitude:

- Attitude is sensitive to influence – good or bad;
- Attitude reflects not only who we are but sometimes also who we would like others to think we are;
- Attitude is very powerful and may be deceptive;
- Attitude is neither tangible nor measurable;
- Attitude may or may not be visible;
- Attitude is multi-faceted and ubiquitous – it exists everywhere human beings exist;
- There are innumerable permutations of stimuli, attitudes and responses;
- Attitude is sometimes a force for good – as demonstrated in acts of kindness or generosity – and at other times it is a negative force – such as in displays of bad temper or violence;
- Even when attitude has been stimulated, its manifestation may or may not be obvious to people around. Often that stimulation gives rise to a prompt to take action – but unless action is actually taken at that point in time – nobody around need have any indication of the attitude that has been adopted – and this is also the case when the stimulus does not prompt an action – nobody around need be aware that an attitude has been adopted in the first place;
- There is a dichotomy between the attitude that prompts a person to do the right thing for the right reason and the attitude that prompts a person to do the right thing for the wrong reason;
- In the same way that the end does not justify the means, attitude does not justify the action;
- One author believes that "…Our character appears to be very complex, and given the available evidence, it does not lend itself to being labelled as either virtuous or vicious. Instead, we seem to have powerful capacities for good, sitting side by side with powerful capacities for

bad…”. [8] (Character and attitude are intrinsically linked. This relationship will be explored in a subsequent chapter.) The Garden of Eden provides an example of good and evil sitting side by side. If I was asked to describe the Garden of Eden in one word – I might say “perfection” – but the perfection that once obtained infers perfect attitudes – which existed at one time. However, these (better than good) attitudes were soon influenced and subverted by evil – producing not only bad attitudes – but also consequent negative actions.

The next paragraph considers some of the factors that influence the attitudes we adopt in certain circumstances – and which create a plethora of permutations.

1.3 What Gives Rise to Attitude?

Attitude has internal roots – it emanates from all those factors within us that combine to make us who we are. At the outset, something stimulates it – but that something can be almost anything. For example, the sound of a very young child laughing innocently and uncontrollably might be the stimulus that provokes an attitude of happiness and enjoyment for all within hearing of the chuckling and gurgling – to which hearers might respond by feeling uplifted and encouraged and grateful for that experience. One fact is clear – when an attitude is adopted (whether obvious or not), there is a reason for it. Something amongst myriad external possibilities has stimulated an internal part of us as human beings – and this stimulus gives rise to a response.

The diagram below shows something stimulating the human body/mind – and this stimulus leads to an attitude being formed. The attitude reflected by that stimulus creates a response – which can be positive or negative. It is important to understand this chain reaction in order to appreciate that attitude does not just happen. The next questions are what are the stimuli and where do they originate. The fact is that the stimuli differ for each of us – and depend on a number of factors – such as the environment – or when the stimulus happened – or the people around – and much more. The important point is that the form of response to the attitude created by the stimulus reflects our character. This is a critical point – about which more will be said later.

[8] Christian B Miller; The Character Gap; Pg 121; Oxford University Press; 2018

Figure One	Stimulus/Attitude/ Response

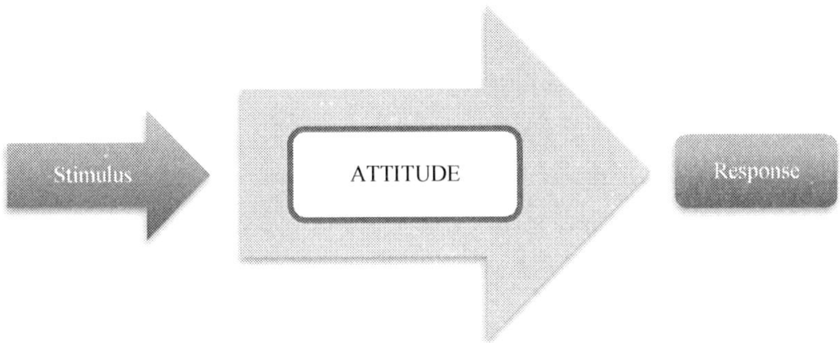

1.4 Attitude in Practice

Someone has said that "attitude is everything". (In fact, one author from whose work I quote elsewhere has used these words as the title of his book). This statement is replete with food for thought. Some of us will know from our respective individual experiences that if we start any day in a negative frame of mind – dreading what might happen – we are more likely to interpret everything that happens subsequently as negative. On the other hand, if we start a day in a positive frame of mind, discouraging events may still happen – but we will be in a better frame of mind to deal with them. People who see glasses half-full rather than half empty are much better equipped to deal with whatever life throws at them. There are many people around who have few resources (whether money or other assets, or influence or power or prestige) but who are making substantial contributions to their community and are leading happy and fulfilled lives despite their circumstances. Arguably, attitude is the determining factor.

Sometimes, in 'extreme scenarios' – attitude can make a huge difference. In such circumstances, some people act extremely courageously – demonstrating physical and mental strength they never knew they had. Medically, it is said that those people who – despite the odds – can summon sufficient will power and inner resources of courage to fight their medical problem – have a better chance of surviving longer. This does not mean that those who fight their problems in this way always win – it means that those who adopt a more positive and courageous attitude are likely to have a much better chance of achieving a successful outcome. "...Things turn out best for people who make the best of the way things turn out...".[9] The opposite applies also. Those people who (for

[9] John Wooden

whatever reason) are unable to draw upon inner resources of resolve and tenacity have a much lower chance of achieving a happy outcome. One question that might be beneficial for each of us to consider is what would my attitude be in such circumstances? One study "...the largest of its kind, tracked over 2000 adults over the age of 65 in the south-western United States. Optimistic people – faith filled people – had better health habits, lower blood pressure, and feistier immune systems and were half as likely to die in the next year as negative people. If you have a positive attitude, you are likely to live a decade longer than people with a negative attitude. Are you happy to hear that? If not, you could be in serious trouble...".[10]

1.4.1 Resilience

One author has suggested, "...What we really need is resilience: the capacity to face up to failure and to learn from it. Ultimately, that is what growth is all about...".[11] Elsewhere, it has been said that "...psychological resilience is the ability to successfully cope with a crisis and to return to pre-crisis status quickly. [1] Resilience exists when the person uses "mental processes and behaviours in promoting personal assets and protecting an individual from the potential negative effects of stressors". [2] In simpler terms, psychological resilience exists in people who develop psychological and behavioural capabilities that allow them to remain calm during crises/chaos and to move on from the incident without long-term negative consequences. Psychological resilience is an evolutionary advantage that most people have and use to manage normal stressors...".[12]

Further "...Psychologists have identified some of the factors that make someone resilient, among them a positive attitude, optimism, the ability to regulate emotions, and the ability to see failure as a form of helpful feedback. Even after misfortune, resilient people are blessed with such an outlook that they are able to change course and soldier on...".[13] It is important to note that Scripture never promises a trouble free life for Christians – in fact Scripture anticipates that life will not be easy – one apostle has written "...consider it pure

[10] Martin Seligman; Learned Optimism: How to Change Your Mind and Your Life; New York; Simon & Schuster/Free Press; 1998: 7ff – As Quoted by John Ortberg; The Me I Want to Be; Pg 248; Zondervan; 2010

[11] Matthew Syed; Black Box Thinking; Pg 292; John Murray (Publishers); 2016

[12] enwikipedia.org

[13] Psychologytoday.com

joy, my brothers and sisters, whenever you face trials of many kinds, because you know that the testing of your faith produces perseverance…"[14] and again "…blessed is the one who perseveres under trial…"[15] and "…being strengthened with all power according to His glorious might so that you may have great endurance and patience…".[16]

Elsewhere, another author has said that "…despair equals suffering without meaning. When people can find some meaning in their suffering, they can avoid falling into despair, and they can find strength and resolve to overcome the suffering. When people feel there is no meaning, they succumb to despair and hopelessness…Through sharing, people are supported as they move through their grief journeys. Growing one's spirit and then ensuring that the wisdom gleaned throughout a lifetime is passed on is among life's most powerful and spiritually enlightened activities…".[17]

Like so many other good disciplines – the values of resilience should not be separated from the effort and strong attitudes of mind that are required to turn resilience into practical applications. Resilience reflects an attitude of courage and determination – but it's perhaps easier said than done. The story that follows presents an appropriate balance.

1.4.2 Resilience

– A Practical Example of What This Means In Practice

In a very relevant article published in Psychology Today, the authors recounted a story about Asha Mevlana. This story helps define what resilience is in practice. In summary Mevlana's story is as follows. When she was 24, Mevlana discovered a lump in her breast. Unlike the experiences of many others, this diagnosis was not the moment that changed her life. Nor was that moment when she had a biopsy or when she underwent eight months of chemotherapy or the consequent baldness, or any of the other effects that were caused by her illness. In fact, the life-altering moment was when her doctors announced that she was cancer-free. This was when she became aware of a fundamental change

---

[14] James 1:2-3

[15] James 1:12

[16] Colossians 1:11

[17] Diana Boufford; Exercise for Spiritual Fitness As included In Shannon Polly & Kathryn Britton; Character Strengths Matter; Pgs 169-170; Positive Psychology News LLC; 2015

within her. Although she was not religious, she prayed for an opportunity to change her life.

"Mevlana isn't alone. Each year, some 13 million people around the world are diagnosed with cancer, 10 million suffer brain injuries, and 50 million survive car wrecks. One in three women will be beaten, raped, or abused in her lifetime." The article referred to comments made by Judith Herman (a Harvard Medical School professor and author of *Trauma and Recovery*) who pointed out that "traumatic events are extraordinary not because they occur rarely, but because they are so overwhelming when they do happen". The article referred to a material percentage of survivors having to deal with post-traumatic stress disorder or serious depression or anxiety – but on the other hand, there are survivors of trauma who recover – some of whom demonstrate meaningful resilience by using their experience to move forward – in a new direction and on a different path. The article refers to such people as super-survivors. Mevlana is one such super-survivor.

Having been diagnosed with cancer, Mevlana took violin lessons – and was asked to play music that demonstrated how she felt at the onset of her treatment. Mevlana said she "played the anxiety that I felt when they injected me with chemo, and I played how I tried to be strong for everyone else when I was terrified".

Prior to becoming ill, Mevlana was not motivated to try to build a career in music – but this changed. She started practising in a disciplined way and began playing electric violin in some rock bands. Visiting a friend in Los Angeles, she was persuaded to search out opportunities to play for fees. She was in her own view an amateur violinist without a job or income or anywhere to live. She had never taken a risk like this before – but in 2007 she moved to Los Angeles. Whilst there, she left her violin in a repair shop and when she went to collect it, the shopkeeper told her about an opportunity with Twisted Sister – whose lead singer he knew. She got the job – and moved on from strength to strength. The article said that "she was soon playing with other musicians, including Alanis Morissette, Jay Z, and Mary J. Blige; she played at the *Grammy Awards*, on *The Tonight Show*, and with the band on *American Idol*."

Mevlana fundamentally changed her life after a crisis. She and others like her are very much out of the ordinary. They deal with the same problems as everyone else and then some. The article says "We're not praising the bright side of tragedy. No trauma is good. Every trauma involves suffering. There's nothing inherently positive or indispensable about atrocities, violence, disasters, or illness. But it's important to understand that resilience is possible." The fundamental lesson here is that despite tragedy, people whose attitude is appropriate can not only survive – but come out the other side of a major trauma positively changed with potential to influence people near and far in ways that were previously unimaginable.

This is a very meaningful story that precisely demonstrates the significance of a resilient attitude in practice! (Summarised and included here with kind permission from the authors – Dr David Feldman and Lee Daniel Kravetz.)[18]

Elsewhere, some of the many other examples of people dealing with adversity have been pointed out – for example "...Robinson Crusoe was written in prison. John Bunyan wrote Pilgrim's Progress in the Bedford jail..." and so on.[19]

1.4.3 Some Other Examples

So far, we have considered the significance of positive attitudes as reactions to stimuli such as events or circumstances – but what about the effects of attitude in pro-active circumstances. Take employment for example. Employers customarily look for people who have what might be described as a 'can do' attitude – that is to say – people who are willing to do everything they can to make a success of whatever task is allocated to them. (The opposite course is to concede before one even starts that a proposed task is impossible. In this circumstance, failure is probably inevitable.) In his book, 'Black Box Thinking', Matthew Syed provides valuable examples of learning from mistakes in the healthcare industry – and describes failure as follows "...progress in most human activities depends, in large part, on our willingness to learn from failure. If we edit out failure, if we reframe our mistakes, we are effectively destroying one of the most precious learning opportunities that exists...".[20]

Andrew White provides another example of the application of using attitude proactively. In one of his books, he points out "...Whenever I encounter a person who is difficult to love, I pray 'Lord, help me to love them!' In my experience, this never requires a miracle, just a change of attitude and an act of will. Often,

---

[18] David B. Feldman PhD, Lee Daniel Kravetz, published July 1, 2014 – as quoted in psychologytoday.com; July 2014

[19] John C Maxwell; Attitude 101; Pg 18; 2003; Maxwell Motivation

[20] Matthew Syed, Black Box Thinking; Pg 94; John Murray (Publishers) 2016

people who seem 'unlovable' begin to change when they are loved...".[21] Note from this example that the other person (or circumstance) hasn't changed. The only thing that has changed is the author's attitude to the other person or circumstance. It has to be said that this is much easier to describe than to achieve in practice because our nature leads us to believe that when something is amiss, it is the fault of someone else. If you read no further (although I very much hope you will keep on reading), reflect for a moment on how much your attitude inclines you to overlook your own shortcomings by apportioning blame to others. Is the answer never, sometimes or frequently? Lord – help us to see our attitudes more clearly for what they really are. Help us to learn from failure and to develop resilience and fortitude – humbly.

1.5 A Personal Example

By way of a follow up to this point, I want to share a personal anecdote that helped me understand a simple but very valuable lesson about the significance of attitude. Married, with two young children, my wife and I bought a small plot of land many years ago. We built a house there – where we anticipated that all being well – we would live out our lives. We had spent as much money as we had – and could borrow – on this project leaving little to furnish the house in the way we would have liked. This was not considered to be a problem at the time since we anticipated being able to buy more of what we wanted over the years to come DV. We watched on as the house was built – but it seemed to take a very, very long time. We checked on progress regularly – that is to say – every day. We simply couldn't wait for the day when we could move in. Eventually, the building work was finished and we moved in – almost penniless – but very happy. Within 15 months of that very happy day, the Bank for which I worked at the time made some noises about re-locating me to the Isle of Man. While this was a re-location by definition, the Isle of Man was only thirty minutes flying time from where we lived at that time (Northern Ireland) – so it was not exactly the other side of the world. Nevertheless, I declined the offer – politely. Time passed by and this matter was raised again. The suggestion was made that I should go and have a look around and review my original decision. I went – but declined once again. The Bank then said we should go as a family and have a look because the move was considered to be in all our interests. We went, looked

[21] Andrew White; Faith Under Fire; Pg 54; Monarch Books; 2011

around and while we believed the Island would be a good place to live and to raise a young family, we did not consider the advantages to be strong enough to tempt us to sacrifice our new home, our Church connections – and all the friendships we had built since our early childhood in Northern Ireland. The Bank was not best pleased to hear that we preferred to stay where we were – so an offer was made that I couldn't refuse!

Some months later, we moved from Northern Ireland – leaving behind all our friends and family – and our much-loved and long-awaited new home. I have to admit that our attitude about every aspect of this change was negative. We were insufficiently wise or mature at the time to understand that: (1) we had a skewed attitude in the first place – we were not being objective; (2) because our attitude was negative, we were not considering this opportunity objectively, (3) our negative attitude was prejudicial to our future happiness and the well-being of our children and (4) our attitude needed to change if we were to make a success of the opportunity we had been given – we needed to understand this was an opportunity – not a threat.

Time teaches us many things – and as we become older, we have a better understanding why it was Solomon asked for wisdom – for its worth is truly greater than silver and gold.[22] As it turned out, we lived very happily in the Isle of Man for the following 9 years. In addition, if we hadn't moved, I would not have been able to gain the experience that proved necessary in being offered other, more senior positions further afield.

What had changed between when the offer was first made to go somewhere else to live and when we arrived at our new home? All the physical features were the same. The countryside, the weather, the houses, the people and everything else were all the same. We realised when we thought about it that the only thing that had changed was our attitude. We didn't want to leave Northern Ireland at the outset and our views during the exploratory visits were influenced by our negative attitude. When we were obliged to go there to live, our attitude became much more positive. We saw everything through a different lens that created the perspective we lacked so badly at the beginning. Someone has said "...sometimes the difference between a good day and a bad day is just your attitude...". Attitude is so potent – and we must not under-estimate it!

There may be an application for you here. If you are considering a future course of action – you may be praying for guidance. I recommend that your

[22] Proverbs 3:14

prayers include a request that Almighty God will enable you to approach your decisions with an appropriate attitude – because this is where enlightenment begins.

1.6 Christ's Attitude

Jesus Christ is THE role model for all Christians. Jesus taught many principles – simply and innovatively. The Beatitudes are a case in point. In Matthew's gospel, the writer records eight Beatitudes that Jesus taught in the 'Sermon On The Mount'. In summary, the Beatitudes focus on virtues such as humility and love that flow out of salvation and which lead to the transformation of a person's innermost being. The Beatitudes present the new way – it is not just murder that is wrong, the very attitude that prompts a person to consider the act of murder is wrong also. The attitudinal implication is striking. The Sermon on the Mount represents attitude in action.

"...Blessed are the poor in spirit, for theirs is the kingdom of heaven. Blessed are those who mourn, for they shall be comforted. Blessed are the meek, for they will inherit the earth. Blessed are those who hunger and thirst for righteousness, for they will be satisfied. Blessed are the merciful, for they will be shown mercy. Blessed are the pure of heart, for they will see God. Blessed are the peacemakers, for they will be called sons of God. Blessed are they who are persecuted because of righteousness, for theirs is the kingdom of heaven...".[23]

The sermon on the mount [24] presents a Scriptural obligation for believers to follow Christ's example. We are encouraged to "...be perfect, therefore, as your heavenly Father is perfect...".[25] An appropriate attitude will help us understand what this means – thereby guiding us how we should live and behave as Christians.

In His teaching, Jesus referred often to the experiences of people in their daily lives. He asked many open-ended questions – because generally speaking, the best way to learn how to apply what we know is to test it in our everyday experience. That daily living experience is real and therefore meaningful – much more so than someone simply telling us – but Jesus is not only a teacher, He is also our Example and Saviour. He took upon Himself (voluntarily) the form of sinful man – with all that that entails – but without succumbing to wrongdoing

[23] Matthew 5:3-10
[24] Matthew – Chapters 5-7
[25] Matthew 5:48

of any nature at any time. As a human being, He was subject to all the vagarious circumstances of life – so it's relevant to consider Jesus' attitude. For example, He was compassionate[26] and loving. No one then or since has or could merit or win His love. He made the supreme sacrifice for all mankind. Despite this sacrifice, He was treated as if He was a criminal – and eventually He was cruelly killed. His reaction to how He was treated is totally remarkable – He said "…Father forgive them for they do not know what they are doing…".[27] This is a fundamental example of attitude in action. However, to be clear – salvation by attitude is not possible. An appropriate attitude will neither replace nor be any substitute for acknowledgement of Jesus Christ as Lord of our lives. It is important to note that attitude is influenced by salvation. "…When I started counting my blessings, my whole life turned around…"[28]

When we consider our human nature – being gracious in what we do and say is a particularly difficult standard to maintain. If we are able to step back and objectively examine our own lives, we will perhaps have clearer insight into how we act and re-act as part of the process of daily living. The question is whether or not we are sufficiently sensitive in our behaviour to even begin to think about the attitudes we adopt in the process of living? I identify with the apostle Paul when he says "…For what I do is not the good I want to do; no, the evil I do not want to do – this I keep on doing…". [29] The question I find I need to ask myself often is what prompts me to adopt an inappropriate attitude? Even if my attitude does not give rise to an unworthy action per se – it often stimulates a negative thought. If I keep questioning my attitudes, I might benefit by way of learning how to improve. The Japanese use a management process called Kaizen – which the Kaizen Institute defines as "…the practice of continuous improvement…".[30] This is a truly aspirational concept that has many applications (see Appendix 4).

1.7 A Personal Perspective

My approach to 'attitude' is based upon my understanding of Holy Scripture. Accordingly, it is important to clarify that I write as a practising Christian – that is to say, I believe God is Lord and Creator of mankind. I believe that He is from

---

[26] Matthew 14:14 and Matthew 15:32
[27] Luke 23:34
[28] Willie Nelson
[29] Romans 7:19
[30] www.in.kaizen.com

everlasting to everlasting and that Jesus Christ His only Son was born to a virgin and that Jesus lived a sinless life on earth. I believe that Jesus took upon Himself the form of sinful men, and died on the cross at Calvary so that all those who accept Him by faith as Saviour – could be redeemed – "…For God so loved the world that He gave His one and only Son that whoever believes in Him shall not perish but have eternal life…"[31] I believe that I have been made in the image of God and that one day I will be with my resurrected Saviour in Heaven – made possible only by Christ's supreme sacrifice at Calvary and through God's grace and mercy. I am merely a sinner saved by grace. I am quick to add (in the words of another pilgrim) that "…the system of ethics that my Christian faith gives me is formidable, since it is constantly showing me the gap that exists between what I am doing and what I should be doing…".[32] I am not a Christian because I am good – I am a Christian because I am aware how much I fall short of being good.

That being so, I am very conscious of Paul's words concerning those who do not recognise Christ as Lord. Paul said "…the god of this age has blinded the minds of unbelievers, so that they cannot see the light of the gospel of the glory of Christ, who is the image of God…".[33] Notwithstanding this fearful text, I dare to hope that people who are non-Christians will be motivated to consider this text – and that in doing so, their openness of mind will be rewarded. If you consider yourself to be in this position, please read on. In particular, if you are a non-Christian who is persuaded that science leaves no room for God, please consider Para 8.5. Lee Strobel's text is really well informed and presents meaningful arguments that you may care to consider. In any event, I hope non-Christians will find words in this text that stimulate them and encourage them to ponder their eternal welfare and significance in the eyes of Almighty God.

The society in which we live has no moral standards by which to monitor its own behaviour. In general, we live substantially without discipline – moral and otherwise – without caring overly about the needs of other people and often without respect towards each other. As a result of all this, we have defaulted to the lowest common denominator – which is that anything goes – just don't involve me or ask me to do anything that requires commitment – and especially not Spiritual commitment! If we look around this world we inhabit, we cannot

---

[31] John 3:16

[32] Edouard Michelin – as quoted by Theodore Roosevelt Malloch; Practical Wisdom In Management; Pg 28; Greenleaf Publishing; 2015

[33] 2 Corinthians 4:4

but fail to notice that it is broken. This suggests that the current prevalent 'anything goes' approach does not work – and this time in which we live is not the first time it has been tried – consider "...In those days, Israel had no king; everyone did as he saw fit...".[34] One does not need to be a Christian to recognise the chaos this attitude brings in its wake. I hope that the text that follows resonates with you – whatever your beliefs.

Having provided some background to attitude, it might be useful to try to define what attitude is – although I do so with respectful temerity.

1.8 Definition

Not unlike the proverbial elephant, 'attitude' is hard to describe – but often obvious when and if one sees it in action. One writer says that "...attitude is an inward feeling expressed by behaviour...".[35] For example, consider a child stomping his or her feet in temper because (s)he did not get their own way. Perhaps a less obvious but a more meaningful example is where someone remains calm when everyone around him/her is losing their cool – with all that this entails. This too is attitude in action. Of course, as stated above, sometimes attitude is not obvious – for example when someone internalises their attitude to the extent that doing so becomes a part of their nature – as happens when people demonstrate patience. It so happens that when attitude is translated into (especially bad) behaviour, we seem to be more sensitive to displays of attitude by someone else than we are to similar displays of our own attitude – especially if that display includes adverse behaviour.

Psychology provides a number of technical definitions of attitude – and while such definitions have substantial academic value – they may not provide the same sort of insight for people whose interests are more practical than academic. Since this is not a textbook, a simple 'working definition' is offered to provide a context for our preliminary thoughts on attitude. Therefore, initially it is suggested that attitude might be described <u>as a pattern of thought that stimulates or prompts[36] an individual to think, act or to react in a particular way – in a particular set of circumstances.</u> (This definition is described as 'initial' because it is refined later in the text.)

---

[34] Judges 21:24

[35] John C Maxwell; Attitude 101; Pg 13; 2003; Maxwell Motivation

[36] In this context, prompts may be considered as triggers (see below)

The stimulus referred to in the definition might be (for example) a communication or an experience or an event or even a circumstance while the 'prompt' referred to above might be a frame of reference or a paradigm.[37] Note that the focus here is on individuals in general and upon the attitude of individuals in particular. It might be (reasonably) argued that 'attitude' can be manifested by groups of people (such as crowds or protesters or supporters etc.) as opposed to individuals. This is very true and so it would be inappropriate to interpret this as meaning that 'communities' are unimportant in this respect. One writer has said "…no matter how smart or gifted a person is, if his attitude is not what it should be, it affects the entire team…".[38] Further, ethnicities and countries and even sports teams are sometimes described in terms of their cultural attitude – or by the actions that arise from their attitude – such as 'aggressive' or 'bad sports'. Since human beings regularly behave in non-rational ways, it is considered that the discussion that follows is already sufficiently myriad without inclusion of consideration of the complexities arising from group/community behaviour. Accordingly, consideration of the culture of groups will not form part of the general discussion on attitude that follows.

1.9 'Trigger' Events

It's important when considering attitude to bear in mind the wide range of possibilities and permutations that exist – because <u>attitude is a complex phenomenon – activated by a vast number of external 'triggers'.</u> Triggers include (for example) communication, an experience, an event or a circumstance. A trigger for one person may act as a trigger in one scenario only (e.g. an insult where the person insulted has no opportunity to reply) or the trigger might apply in all circumstances for that person (e.g. where despite being able to reply, the insulted person remains offended). Further, the trigger for one person might (or might not) be a trigger to people generally in such circumstances. Further still, the potential for a trigger to stimulate an attitude will depend on the effect of the trigger on the person involved in the circumstances that obtain. (For example – sometimes, we are not embarrassed because we are alone when the trigger event takes place – but if others had been present our reaction might have been

---

[37] Covey defines a paradigm as "…a model, theory, perception, assumption or frame of reference … the way we see the world…" – Stephen Covey; The 7 Habits Of Highly Effective People; Pg 31; Simon & Schuster; 1989

[38] John C Maxwell; Be A People Person; Cook Ministries; 1994

different). When a trigger event occurs (see Figure 1 above), it will be a stimulus to the formation of an attitude that produces a response in the form of an action or a reaction – and actions/re-actions may be immediate or may be deferred. If there is a re-action – it may be passive (a re-action not to take any action). Actions/re-actions may be visible (such as words or deeds) or not visible (such as thoughts or opinions) and may be positive or negative. As individuals we adopt attitudes – but we are not always aware that we have done so.

Despite all the permutations, one fact remains as described in the quote that follows – "…[Earl] Nightingale found that all of the great writers, philosophers and religious leaders have agreed that our thoughts determine our actions…" [39] – and in this respect, another writer believes that "our attitude at the beginning of a task will affect its outcome more than anything else…".[40]

With respect to circumstances, there are so many permutations that it is not possible to identify for each person those stimuli that give rise to that person's individual attitudes. Instead, it might be helpful to try to identify some of the factors that are relevant to attitude for people generally – and these are considered in subsequent chapters. These factors are important for everyone – but especially so for people with religious beliefs. For Christians, Holy Scripture tells us explicitly that our attitude should be "…the same as that of Jesus Christ…".[41] This is such a fundamental and comprehensive statement that there can be no doubt – in principle – as to what is expected from each of us. However, we need to understand not only what this means in principle – but also what it means in practice. Scripture helps us by providing some detail about application of the principle – so that on a day-to-day basis – situation by situation – circumstance by circumstance – we have some understanding as to what approach is expected of us as Christians. We will consider these matters further in due course – but since every individual human being has capacity to demonstrate attitude, it might be interesting to consider where attitude comes from. Is there something within us that creates this innate capacity to stimulate attitude? This is taken up in subsequent chapters.

---

[39] As quoted in Attitude Is Everything; Pg 20; Attitude Is Everything Inc; Jeff Keller; 2012

[40] John C Maxwell; Attitude 101; Pg 18; 2003; Maxwell Motivation

[41] Philippians 2:5

1.10 Summary

This first chapter noted that attitude is not well understood or widely considered – despite the fact that attitude plays a part in every human being's life – every day. To try to counteract this approach, chapter one seeks to draw attention to the unique and potent nature of attitude. In so doing, chapter one has attempted to identify some of the characteristics of attitude before attempting to create an initial definition. It was pointed out firstly that 'attitude' is a collective term because in the business of living, human beings experience many attitudes. Secondly, attitude is ubiquitous – every human being has attitudes so 'attitude' is part of the experience of every human being – and while the physiognomy of attitudes can be categorised, not every human displays all attitudes – and certainly not at the same time – nor even in the same circumstances. Thirdly, attitude is intangible – and because it is so difficult to define, we often (wrongly) attest to observable actions emanating from attitude being stimulated as the structure of how we define it – losing sight of the fact that not every manifestation of attitude is observable in the first place (e.g. hidden grief or a thought). Fourthly, attitudes may be positive or negative – and this has a direct effect on reaction – and behaviour. That said, not every negative attitude leads to a positive reaction – and not every positive attitude leads to a negative reaction.

More generally, attitudes do not appear in isolation. An attitude is prompted by a stimulus and gives rise to a reaction (see Figure One). As inferred above, the complicating and amazing factor is that the stimuli are different for each person – as are the circumstances in which people find themselves in living their lives. That means that attitude extends to how we reach conclusions and the decisions we take. These fundamental life matters do not just happen, they are part of a process over which each of us as individuals exercise control.

Lastly in this chapter, in light of all of the above, it will be no surprise that we discovered the permutations of attitude are myriad.

Attitude is an integral part of defining who we are. It has been noted that "…when people put forward an argument, you cannot separate what they say from whom they are…" [42] and Scripture tells us that we should "…be very careful, then, how you live…" [43]

[42] Philosophy Brief – The Brains Trust; The Economist; Pg 12; 04 August 2018
[43] Ephesians 5:15

One of the objectives of Chapter One was to point to the significance of attitude in our make up as human beings. It is suggested that attitude is worthy of our attention because if we can understand it, we will be one step closer to controlling our attitudes and therefore ourselves. The text that follows attempts to help readers to consider the implications as we live day by day. In the next chapter, a model will be introduced to facilitate this process and to create a road map through at least some of the significant matters that impinge.

Section Two
A Model for Consideration

Chapter Two
Composition of Humankind

2.1 Introduction

Chapter One provided the context for the expansion of the text that follows. We know already that attitude is a complex phenomenon – not least because each of us has capacity to adopt attitudes but we do so in different ways at different times – prompted by different stimuli – and producing different reactions. We cannot rely on patterns of behaviour or uniformity to predict outcomes because the permutations are beyond quantification. That said, it is possible to categorise some parts of the process that produce responses to attitudes that have been formed by relevant stimuli. In order to provide a framework for that discussion, a model will be created incrementally – beginning in this chapter.

Once complete, the model will provide an overview of the 'superstructure' of attitude formation within humankind. It has to be said that herein lies more than one challenge – for example, there is no general consensus about two fundamental elements in particular. Firstly, the building blocks (that will be introduced over the next few chapters) that form the structure of the text that follows represent the author's view. Secondly, it is not even clear what constitutes being human. (Why there should be any uncertainty about this is amazing not least because this very matter has been the subject of research since classical scholars debated it in Greece thousands of years ago.) In any event, we will begin considering what it means to be human with reference to anthropology. '*Theological anthropology*' is the investigation of the relationships between the soul, mind, and body – and that is the area of focus in this chapter – beginning with consideration of mortality and immortality. The diagram below shows the first 2 levels of the model.

Figure Two	Model 1

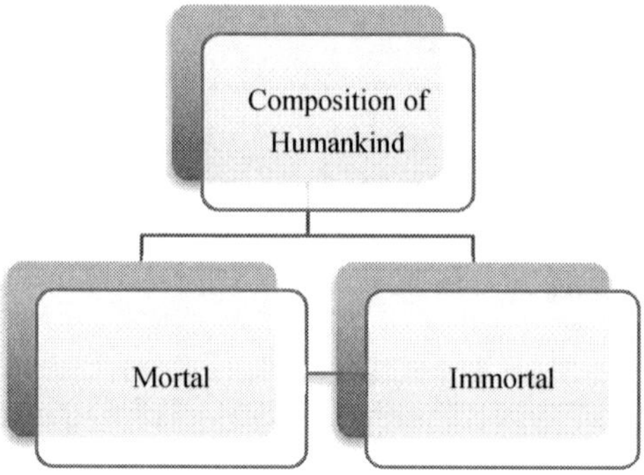

One writer has pointed out that "…three interrelated issues have long challenged the discipline of theological anthropology: the relationship between the soul and the mind, the relationship between the soul and the image of God and the relationship between the soul, or mind and body…". [44]

2.2 Mortality

Considering merely the external shell of our body, we can't fail but appreciate what the Psalm writer meant when he wrote that we are fearfully and wonderfully made. [45] We marvel at the complexity of our heart and brain, the sensitivity of our skin – enabling us to feel the movement of a single hair moving over it, the significance of our organs, limbs, sight, hearing and the ability to smell. The functions of kidneys, livers, bladders and our intestines. The list is endless. However, the perception gained by considering how all these parts of our body function and co-ordinate – miraculous though they are – gives only an inkling of the complexity and intricacy of the human body. It is estimated that the global population is something like 7.2 billion people in the world today. While there are differences between us for all sorts of reasons, our bodies work according to principles that are common to all of us. One such common feature of our humanity is that our life span is finite. We are ephemeral creations by definition. Clearly then, someday, each of us will die – a salutary reminder if we needed one that human beings are mortal. Many important scientific advances have been made in recent years that allow people in general to live longer – for

[44] C Marvin Pate; From Plato To Jesus; Pg 213; Kregel Publications; 2011
[45] Psalm 139:14

example Wikipedia says that "...Japan has the highest life expectancy of any country: 90 for women and for men, 84. Compare this to America where the average life expectancy for women is 81 years, and 76 for men...". Despite the fact that generally, people are living longer than previously, Scripture makes it clear that ordinarily, our life span is around 70 years – "...or eighty, if we have the strength; yet their span is but trouble and sorrow, for they quickly pass, and we fly away...". [46] Further "...You have made my days a mere handbreadth; the span of my years is as nothing before You. Each man's life is but a breath. Man is a mere phantom as he goes to and fro: He bustles about, but only in vain; he heaps up wealth, not knowing who will get it...". [47] This is endorsed by a non-Biblical resource that says that "...life expectancy has reached 71 years...". [48] Accordingly, although there is greater longevity in at least some countries – we remain mortal – and thereby – subject to death.

While some people might find this type of discussion morbid, it is factual nevertheless – and importantly – it is fundamental to the human 'superstructure' that we are modelling. However, death is not a morbid topic for the Christian – because Christians believe that our mortality as humans points us to a better place – reserved for those who believe in God. Our life span reflects time within our physical nature – while our faith points us to eternity within our spiritual nature. Christians understand that the time allocated to us human beings on earth is only a part of eternity – death is not the end. Consequently, Christians believe that only those things that have eternal significance have meaningful value. Consider Matthew 6 (19-21) – which speaks to creating treasure in heaven. Elsewhere, scripture says "...So we fix our eyes not on what is seen, but on what is unseen, for what is seen is temporary, but what is unseen is eternal...".[49] We frequently are unable to distinguish the wood from the trees in this respect – especially so when we are younger.

Since death is 'natural' nature has a procedure for dealing with it. Once a person dies, the corpse that remains is merely a shell that will begin to deteriorate immediately upon the death of the body – and in due course only the basic physical elements will be left behind. Christians believe that when the body dies, the soul leaves the body – and goes to be with the Lord – for the rest of eternity.

---

[46] Psalm 90:10
[47] Psalm 39:5-6
[48] Within Reach – Leader; The Economist; Pg 9; April 28-May 4, 2018
[49] 2 Corinthians 4:18

The words of the English Burial Service (that include inter alia "ashes to ashes, dust to dust") reflect this. In fact, these words are an adaptation of a verse found in Genesis that refers to the fact that mankind was originally created from the dust ("...the Lord God formed the man from the dust of the ground and breathed into his nostrils the breath of life, and the man became a living being...". [50]). After death, the human body reduces to its basic elements meaning that it will return to the dust from which it was originally formed – "...all come from dust, and to dust all return...". [51] Accordingly, Scripture provides that "...In the sweat of thy face shalt thou eat bread, till thou return unto the ground; for out of it wast thou taken: for dust thou art, and unto dust shalt thou return...". [52]

2.3 Immortality

A synonym for immortality is timelessness. In light of the comments in the previous paragraph regarding mortality, immortality is of fundamental significance – which ironically is not much talked about. As human beings, we are much more likely to be interested in 'the here and now' or the near future rather than dwell upon death and beyond. "...I know that one truth about us is that we forget that we are going to die..."[53] As stated above, those of us who serve Almighty God and who recognise Him as He who was and is – and evermore shall be – we have a hope that non-believers cannot enjoy. <u>God is infinite – existing before what we recognise as time (but which is actually part of eternity) – and will continue living forever.</u> This is the source of the Christian's hope. I have this hope – which I believe in faith and in reliance upon the Scriptures. Needless to say, the hope of immortality is of utmost significance – and I urge you to stop and consider the implications of eternity if you have not done so already.

All other things being equal, we know that our bodies will last around 70 years but not so our souls. <u>Our souls pre-date our birth and will exist after our lives expire.</u> The irony is that we are prepared to spend so much time, effort and resources in maintaining a body that we know is finite – and which from an early age begins to show the effects of wear. The corollary is that we are willing to

---

[50] Genesis 2:7

[51] Ecclesiastes 3:11

[52] Genesis 3:19 – King James Version

[53] John Ortberg; When The Game Is Over It All Goes Back In The Box; Pg 154; Zondervan; 2007

devote much less effort and resource nurturing our spirit and soul – that are eternal. Is this not a clear example of the irrationality of humankind?

Here are some mundane examples of our irrationality in living. We know beyond any shadow of doubt that smoking kills. That being so, why do so many of us want to kill ourselves by smoking? Further, we know that an unhealthy diet is likely to cause a range of medical problems. That being so, why do so many of us continue to eat what we know is not good for us – and refuse to eat what we know is good for us? In addition, we know that our bodies need exercise to keep them 'operational' and to help to prevent problems arising. Therefore, why are so many of us so lazy? The answer to each of these questions is obvious. Despite knowing what is good for us, we choose a short-term advantage and ignore the long-term consequences. Note – these decisions are not imposed upon us – we make them deliberately and in full knowledge of the potential consequences. Totally irrational! It is so easy to miss the wood for the trees.

Although the Bible does not state explicitly that the soul is immortal, there are a number of references in Scripture that endorse the fact that it is. For example – way back in the Old Testament we are told, "...He has made everything beautiful in its time. He has also set eternity in the hearts of men; yet they cannot fathom what God has done from beginning to end..."[54] Elsewhere Scripture says "...God, the blessed and only Ruler, the King of kings and Lord of lords, who alone is immortal...".[55] Significantly, Jesus said "...For my Father's will is that everyone who looks to the Son and believes in Him shall have eternal life, and I will raise them up at the last day...". (John 6:40.) Paul told the members of the congregation in Rome to 'seek' immortality (Romans 2:5-7). He taught Christians at Corinth that they must be changed and 'put on' immortality (1 Corinthians 15:51-55).[56] (Additional references include: "...The eternal God is your refuge...; [57] ...the Lord is the true God; He is the living God, the eternal King [58] and ...He is the true God and eternal life..."). [59] Such passages infer that the soul continues to exist after death. Note also that human beings "...are destined for the grave...But God will redeem my life from the

---

[54] Ecclesiastes 3:11
[55] 1 Timothy 6:15/16
[56] Gary Petty; What Does The Bible Say About The "Immortal Soul"?; https://www.ucg.org/user/gary-petty; United Church Of God
[57] Deuteronomy 33:27
[58] Jeremiah 10:10
[59] 1 John 5:20

grave; He will surely take me to Himself...". [60] There are many more passages in Scripture that show the soul (whether righteous or wicked) survives death. (for example: Matthew 10:28; Luke 23:43; John 11:25; John 14:23; 2 Corinthians 5:1 and Romans 2:6-8.)

The question is – what more has Almighty God to do to get our attention? Even the sacrifice of His Son has not been sufficient to draw the attention of humankind to the fact that there is more than 70 years of time to take into account – there is the rest of eternity. In short, "...We are all capable of fighting for what has little value while forgetting things of transcendent value...".[61]

2.4 The Historical Context

The belief that humankind comprises two parts – body and soul – is referred to as Dualism. One writer notes that "...throughout church history, the vast majority of Christian thinkers have correctly understood Scripture to teach that ...the soul/spirit is an immaterial component different from the body (Eccles 12:7; Mt 10:28), that death involves the soul leaving the body (Gen 35:18; 1 Kings 17:21,22) and that after death, the soul continues to exist in a disembodied intermediate state while awaiting the resurrection of the body (Heb 12:23; Lk 23:46; 2 Cor 5:1-10; Phil 1:21-24)...". [62] (Note that when this writer referred to 'immaterial', he did not mean unimportant. Rather, he meant that the soul is spiritual – i.e. not physical.)

Scripture distinguishes body and soul – for example Jesus said "...Do not be afraid of those who kill the body but cannot kill the soul...".[63] Where then did the dualistic interpretation of Genesis 2:7 (that the human is composed of a body and soul) come from? "...The answer is the Greek translation (the Septuagint, LXX) of Genesis 2:7, which renders *nepesh* as *psyché* (soul), thus imparting into that word the anthropological dualism that goes back as far as Homer (900 BC) and is championed by Plato. To put it another way, Plato's separation of the body and the soul...and his merger of mind and soul set the Greek Old Testament on a different trajectory of interpretation than originally envisioned by the Hebrew Bible. That trajectory included the New Testament, which essentially presents

---

[60] Psalm 49:14-15

[61] Paul David Tripp; A Quest For More; Pg 26; New Growth Press; 2007

[62] William Lane Craig – as quoted by C Marvin Pate; From Plato To Jesus; Pg 218; Kregel Publications; 2011

[63] Matthew 10:28

humans as a composite of mind, or soul, and body...But for the moment, it will suffice to say that the New Testament, like classical Greek philosophy, essentially equated the mind (reason) with the soul (cf Rom.12:2, the renewal of the mind, with Col. 3:10, the renewal of the image of God [soul]), which in turn seems to be synonymous with the 'heart' (see Matt.11:29; Mark12: 29-30 and parallels; Rom. 1:21, 28). So, mind, reason, and heart appear to be interchangeable with soul in the New Testament...". [64]

Many of the world's religions embrace a belief in a form of life after death – so it will be no surprise that discussion about theological anthropology – as has been referred to above – has gone on for many years. For example, Plato [428-348 BC] was a student of Socrates – so perhaps it is not surprising that Plato – like Socrates believed that human existence does not end in death. "...According to Plato, a human being is the combination (or unity) of a body and a soul..." [65] Later, "...Augustine subscribed to Platonic theory that man is a union of body and soul and that the body is a prison to the soul ..." [66]

2.5 Implications Arising

As has been pointed out already, there are many critically important implications arising from a consideration of mortality and immortality – but I want to consider two a little further.

Firstly, as stated above, for Christians, life is eternal – and does not end with death. Death is merely a stepping-stone in the journey of immortality. The apostle Paul said "...I want to know Christ and the power of His resurrection and the fellowship of sharing in His sufferings, becoming like Him in his death, and so, somehow, to attain to the resurrection from the dead...". [67] Now we know that "...God has given us eternal life, and this life is in His Son...".[68] Elsewhere, John says "...We will be resurrected some-day, as Jesus was, with a new, glorified body, into a new birth and hope of an inheritance that is eternal life which has been divinely set apart for us...". [69]

---

[64] C Marvin Pate; From Plato To Jesus; Pg 215; Kregel Publications; 2011
[65] C Marvin Pate; From Plato To Jesus; Pg 119; Kregel Publications; 2011
[66] C Marvin Pate; From Plato To Jesus; Pg 37; Kregel Publications; 2011
[67] Philippians 3:10-11
[68] 1 John 5:11
[69] David P McCarthy; "I am Living in The Eternity of The Eternities"; Word Alive Press; 2012

Secondly, if there is more to us than merely 'the here and now' and if our spirit and soul live forever, these fundamental truths should so influence our mind-set[70] and world-view that how we live must reflect their significance in every part of us – both external and internal. Attitude impinges upon the way we live – the way we think and what prompts us to think in that way, the way we act – what we choose to do and which actions we will find unacceptable, whether we speak or whether we remain silent – and if we speak how we will do so.

More generally, it has been said that "...The immortality of the soul is foundational in Western thought, both philosophical and religious...". [71] That being so, it merits attention.

2.6 Summary

In this chapter, we have level one of the model of the superstructure of humankind referred to above. We looked at two foundational facts of life that have been the focus of intellectual discussion for many, many years – time and eternity. These matters are at the core of what influences the development of human attitudes. We distinguished that part of humankind that is mortal – the body and compared it with the parts that are immortal – spirit and soul. We recognised how skewed our approach to life is – in that we allow 'here and now' type matters to influence us disproportionately. Simultaneously we relegate matters of eternal consequence to a secondary level in our approach to how we should live our lives. The next chapter (3) will introduce spirit, soul and body – all of which emanate from immortality and mortality. This will be the third level of the model.

---

[70] That is to say, our world view, see also index for other references;

[71] Gary Petty; What Does The Bible Say About The "Immortal Soul"?; https://www.ucg.org/user/gary-petty; United Church Of God

Chapter Three

Spirit, Soul and Body

3.1 Introduction

In the last chapter, we presented the first layer of the model that describes our human framework. Having considered the significance of the dichotomy between mortality and immortality – which elements contribute to our definition of ourselves as human beings, this chapter focuses firstly on our immortal spirit and on our soul – and then on our mortal physical body and mind – as shown in level 3 of Figure 3 below.

Paul referred to this tri-partite structure when he said "…May your whole spirit, soul and body be kept blameless at the coming of our Lord Jesus Christ…" [72] (2 Corinthians 4:16 and 5:10 refers also).

Figure Three	Model 2

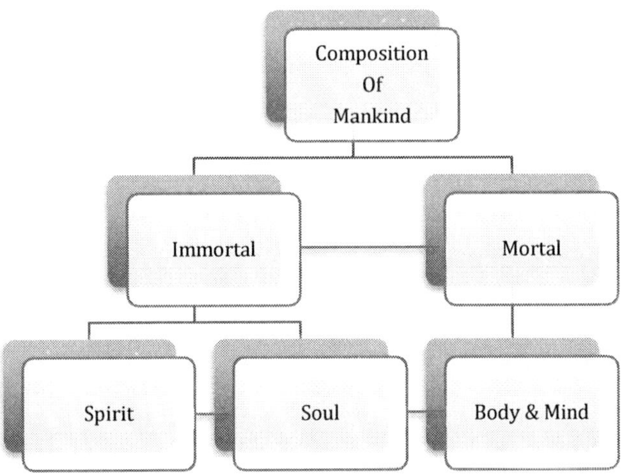

[72] 1 Thessalonians 5:23

3.2 Tripartite

One writer has pointed out that since God is a Trinity (Scripture says "...May the grace of the Lord Jesus Christ, and the love of God, and the fellowship of the Holy Spirit be with you all..." [73]) – and since mankind is made in God's image ("...Then God said, 'Let us make mankind in our image...'" [74]), therefore mankind must be triune as well – "...He has a spiritual nature that is separate and distinct from the body in which it dwells..." [75] In this respect, Holy Scripture refers to humankind being a tripartite being. Further, in writing to the Hebrews, Paul said "...For the word of God is living and active. Sharper than any double-edged sword, it penetrates even to dividing soul and spirit, joints and marrow...". [76] [In this respect, 'joints and marrow' may be considered as a reference to humankind's physical body.] Accordingly, humankind comprises: (1) spirit, (2) soul and (3) body. Remember however that as we discovered in the last chapter, our spirit and soul are immortal – they will never die whereas our body is physical – it will die. ("...Western philosophy sees a distinction between mind and body. And while in other cultures the heart is often viewed as the central organ, Western societies emphasise the importance of the mind, for which the brain is used as a proxy...". [77])

One writer puts it like this "...There is an outer you – your body – that is being shaped all the time by the way you eat, drink, sleep, exercise, and live. You may do this well or poorly, intentionally or not, but it *will* happen. Then there is an inner you – your thoughts, desires, will and character. This is being shaped all the time by what you see, read, hear, think and do. We can call this inner you the spirit. *Spiritual formation is the process by which your inner self and character are shaped...Everyone* has a spirit. *Everyone's* inner life is being formed – for better or worse...".[78] We have already considered the trouble to which we go to look after our finite bodies and compared that with how little we do to 'maintain' our soul and our spirit in respect of their eternal existence – but before we go any further, we should clarify what we mean by spirit, soul and body. A few words about each:

---

[73] 2 Corinthians 13:14

[74] Genesis 1:26

[75] Lehman Strauss; Man A Trinity (Spirit, Soul, Body); From The Series – Death And Afterward; Bible.org

[76] Hebrews 4:12

[77] "No End In Sight"; The Economist; Pg 55; 28 April – 04 May 2018

[78] John Ortberg; "The Me I Want to Be"; Pg 29; Zondervan; 2010

3.3 Spirit

It is important to distinguish between God's Holy Spirit (written in upper case) and 'spirit' – which in this text means the spirit within us as individuals. One writer points out "…The spirit and the space most familiar to each of us are contained in our own personality. The necessary path of understanding lies in reflecting on our own make-up…".[79]

The part of theology concerned with the Holy Spirit is referred to as Pneumatology. Pate refers to four functions being associated with the Holy Spirit in the Old Testament:– (1) involvement in creation (Gen 1:2; Job 26:13); (2) empowerment of the Israelites to perform certain tasks such as: building the tabernacle (Exod. 31:3-5), leading re administration (Gen. 41:38; Num. 11:25), anointing the judges for war (Judg. 3:10;6:34; 14:19); (3) association with God's prophecies (1 Sam.10:6, 10; Ezek. 2:1-2; 8:3) and (4) the Spirit will be the end-time gift that engenders obedience to God (Isa. 11:2-5; Jer. 31:33-36; 26-28; Joel 2:28-29). The same author refers to two functions of the Holy Spirit in the New Testament: (1) sanctification (or prophecy, holiness and creation) and (2) service.[80]

Dallas Willard says that "…The function of the Holy Spirit is, first, to move within our soul, and especially our minds, to present the person of Jesus and the reality of His kingdom…After we receive the new life, the Spirit continues to move upon and within us to enable us to do the kinds of works Jesus did (through 'gifts of the Spirit') and to grow the kind of inward character that manifests itself in the 'fruit' or outcome of the Spirit in our outward life: love, joy, peace, long-suffering and similar traits of Christ (Gal 2:23-25)…".[81] Paul said that "…the body without the Spirit is dead…".[82]

J I Packer says that "…the Spirit is given to Christians as 'the Spirit of *adoption*' and in all His ministry to Christians He acts as the Spirit of adoption. As such, His task and purpose throughout is to make Christians realise with increasing clarity the meaning of their filial relationship with God in Christ, and to lead them into an even deeper response to God in this relationship. Paul is

---

[79] Dallas Willard; The Divine Conspiracy; Pg 86; William Collins; 2014
[80] C Marvin Pate; From Plato To Jesus; Pg 263; Kregel Publications; 2011
[81] Dallas Willard; The Divine Conspiracy; Pg 381; William Collins; 2014
[82] James 2:26

pointing to this truth when he writes, 'Ye have received the Spirit of adoption, whereby we cry Abba, Father' (Rom. 8:15, KJV)…".[83]

The spirit within mankind may be considered as the umbilical cord between the Holy Spirit and the intrinsic nature of mankind. One writer has said "…I believe the 'spirit' part of us is that which is created most pointedly in God's image. The spirit – when distinguished in Scripture from the soul – is the part of each human being that has the capacity to know and have a relationship with God. Our Maker literally equipped us with an inner longing to find Him. In his first letter to the Corinthians (6:17), Paul says that "…he who unites himself with the Lord is one with Him in spirit…". When we accept the offer made to each of us by Jesus our Saviour to accept His Lordship of our lives, our spirit or the part of us with the capacity to know God unites with the Holy Spirit and they become one…".[84] It has been said elsewhere that "…The human spirit requires 'the spark of regeneration' before there is an understanding of the things of God. Man's spiritual nature must be renewed before there is a true conception of Godliness. Only one thing stands as a guard at the door of man's spirit, and that is his own will. When the will is surrendered, the Holy Spirit takes up His abode in the spirit of man…". [85]

Another writer explains it this way – "…For it is in persons, or 'selves' – and their experiences of feeling, thought and will – that we primarily come to know what the spiritual is. 'Spiritual' is not just something we ought to be. It is something we are and cannot escape, regardless of how we may think or feel about it. It is our nature and our destiny…".[86]

Dallas Willard has said "…The heart, or will, simply is spirit in human beings. It is the human spirit, and the only thing in us that God will accept as the basis of our relationship to Him. It is the spiritual plane of our natural existence, the place of truth before God, from where alone our whole lives can become eternal [87]…remember that our heart is our will, or our spirit; the centre of our being from which our life flows. It is what gives orientation to everything we do.

---

[83] J I Packer; Knowing God; Pg 248; Hodder & Stoughton; 2013
[84] Beth Moore; "The Beloved Disciple" Pg 214; Broadman & Holman Publishers; 2003
[85] Lehman Strauss; Man A Trinity (Spirit, Soul, Body); From The Series – Death And Afterward; Bible.org
[86] Dallas Willard; The Divine Conspiracy; Pg 90; William Collins; 2014
[87] Dallas Willard; The Divine Conspiracy; Pg 93; William Collins; 2014

A heart rightly directed therefore brings health and wholeness to the entire personality…”.[88]

“…The Spirit Himself testifies with our spirit that we are God’s children…”.[89] Further, “…God is spirit and His worshippers must worship in spirit and in truth…”.[90] It is when the Holy Spirit convicts men and women of their sin that the spirit within each of us as human beings, has the opportunity to respond and to accept the redemption offered to us. Until this point – that is prior to redemption – mankind is unable to “…accept the things that come from the Spirit of God, for they are foolishness to him, and he cannot understand them, because they are spiritually discerned…”.[91] Without the Holy Spirit, mankind is entirely unable to exercise any spiritual discernment. This is confirmed in Job – where Scripture says “…But it is the spirit in a man, the breath of the Almighty that gives him understanding…”. In verse 15 of 1 Corinthians 2, Paul reminds us that “…the spiritual man makes judgments about all things…”. One writer has said that Satan “…does not care if a man goes to Church where the Spirit of God is not in evidence. He knows that his victim is a creature of emotions, and it matters not if the emotions are attired to sentimentalism or even to tears, just so long as man’s spirit does not come in contact with God’s Holy Spirit…”.[92]

It was stated above that our spirit is the part of us with the capacity to know God. That being so, our spirit is that component of our being that is super sensitive to God’s influence. In fact, the spirit is that part of our human framework that controls the mechanism that we call our conscience (see Para 4.2 below). As we progress through the hierarchy of the components of attitude, we will see that our spirit, soul and body and mind underpin and contribute to the formation of the values and standards (see Para 6.2 below) that are foundational in the formulation of our character

3.4 Soul

It has been said that “…It’s important to distinguish the soul from the spirit, or will, because the will or the heart or the spirit is the executive centre of the self…”.[93] Dallas Willard believes that “…The soul is that aspect of your whole

[88] Dallas Willard; The Divine Conspiracy; Pg 228; William Collins; 2014
[89] Romans 8:16
[90] John 4:24
[91] 1 Corinthians 2:14
[92] Dr Lehman Strauss; Man A Trinity; Part 2; Bible.org
[93] Dallas Willard

being that correlates, integrates and enlivens everything going on in the various dimensions of the self. The soul is the life centre of human beings…”.[94] One author has said “…Everyone has a soul. Everyone has a ‘Holy of Holies’, where only that person and God can meet. Only God can touch the deepest place of another’s soul. We may think, I can intimidate, lecture, flatter, manipulate, reason, cajole, reward, or withdraw to get the behaviour I want out of that person. And maybe I can, out on the outer edges of their personality; but I can’t touch the deepest part of another person. Only God can…”.[95]

We know that our soul is of inestimable value because Scripture says “…What good will it be for a man if he gains the whole world yet forfeits his soul? Or what can a man give in exchange for his soul?…”.[96] One of the reasons that our soul is so valuable is because it is the seat of our emotions – the source of human passion, feelings and desires.[97] Scripture warns “…Above all else, guard your heart, for it is the wellspring of life…”.[98] If Satan controls our soul/heart, he controls us entirely – and so Satan will do all that is in his power to take control of our soul. “…For from within, out of men’s hearts, come evil thoughts – sexual immorality, theft, murder, adultery, greed, malice, deceit, lewdness, envy, slander arrogance and folly. All these evils come from inside and make a man ‘unclean’…”.[99] Accordingly, Scripture has just cause in reminding us “…The heart is deceitful above all things and beyond cure. Who can understand it…”?[100] Further, we should not lose sight of our responsibilities in respect of our heart because we are warned that the Lord “…will bring to light what is hidden in darkness and will expose the motives of men’s hearts…”.[101] With respect to ‘motives’, a salutary warning has been provided by one author who reminds us that “…Our motives are complicated and they can change rapidly…”.[102] “…So if you want to know how well your soul is thriving, you will have to devote yourself to the act of reflection every once in a while. No one will pressure us to do this…there are a few mirrors and scales that we all will probably need:

---

94 Dallas Willard; As Quoted by John Ortberg; Soul Keeping; Pg 39; Zondervan; 2014
95 John Ortberg; The Me I Want To Be; Pg 205; Zondervan; 2010
96 Matthew 16:26
97 Dr Lehman Strauss; Man A Trinity; Part 2; Bible.org
98 Proverbs 4:23
99 Mark 7:23 (Compare Matthew 15:19)
100 Jeremiah 17:9
101 1 Corinthians 4:5
102 Christian B Miller; The Character Gap; Pg 151; Oxford University Press; 2018

- Self-examination and confession
- Friends who love you enough to speak truth to you
- Time to be alone and listen to God
- Examination of your calendar and cheque book
- Key questions such as: How easily discouraged do I get these days? How easily irritated am I compared to six months ago?
- Attention to your secret thought life. What is your mind drawn toward – really? Where do envy or blaming or judging or lusting rob your inner person of life and joy?…".[103]

The same author points out that "…our souls need to be fed, just as our bodies do. Bodies are fed by protein and carbs; souls are fed by words. What people need from us the most is not more information. They just need words that will feed their souls. Sometimes a word as simple as 'thank you' or 'I hope you have a really good day' can feed a soul…".[104]

The significance of our heart/soul is that it defines our whole being and is the source of every attitude and behaviour pattern that we exhibit. However, as soon as the spirit within humankind is influenced by the Holy Spirit, then the focus of the human soul veers God-wards and this in turn has an absolute influence on our passions, feelings and desires. This is why Scripture refers to us becoming new creations when we are redeemed.[105] In this respect, Willard (quoted above) has said "…Your soul is what integrates your will (your intentions) your mind (your thoughts and feelings, your values and conscience), and your body (your face, body language and actions) into a single life. A soul is healthy – well ordered – when there is harmony between these three entities and God's intent for all creation…".[106] However, the contrary position is that "…The souls of human beings are left to shrivel and die on the plains of life because they are not introduced into the environment for which they were made, the living kingdom of eternal life…".[107]

---

103 John Ortberg; When The Game Is Over It All Goes Back In The Box; Pg 51; Zondervan; 2007

104 John Ortberg; When The Game Is Over It All Goes Back In The Box; Pg 159; Zondervan; 2007

105 2 Corinthians 5:17 – English Standard Version – "Therefore, if anyone is in Christ, he is a new creation. The old has passed away; behold, the new has come."

106 Dallas Willard; As Quoted By John Ortberg; Soul Keeping; Pg 43; Zondervan; 2014

107 Dallas Willard; The Divine Conspiracy; Pg 68; William Collins; 2014

"...For Socrates, the soul is the seat of intelligence and character...". [108] Meanwhile, Aristotle argued that man finds happiness – the good – when he lives in accordance with the purpose or function of his soul. And the soul consists of a rational and an irrational part. When man makes a habit of subduing the irrational part of him by emphasising the rational, the cardinal moral virtues are thereby developed: courage, temperance, justice, and wisdom...Aristotle argued that man has to choose to do what he knows is the truth or virtue. [109] We will deal with character in chapter 5 because it is character that has most to do with creating the principles, standards, values, habits and choices that prompt our words and actions – and is therefore crucial in the formation of attitude. Meanwhile, in chapter 4, we will consider the link between our souls and our character – which is sensitivity.

3.5 Body and Mind

The Psalmist captures the phenomenal complexity of human beings when (as already quoted), he says to the Lord "...I praise You because I am fearfully and wonderfully made; Your works are wonderful, I know that full well...".[110] For the purposes of this discussion, we can categorise the third component of mankind – our bodies – into two parts: (1) Mind and (2) Physical. (The word 'physical' should be interpreted to mean the corpus that carries out actions and that speaks words.)

With respect to our mind, it has been pointed out that "...God's intent is that my will would be able to oversee or direct my mind and then my body. So, if everything is working right, if you are as God created you to be, then your body will be the obedient, easy servant of your mind and your will, what you choose. Your mind also will think about and feel those things you direct it to. My will exists to be surrendered to God in every way. My mind should be under the control of my will. If that were the case, I would simply be able to choose life-giving, truthful thoughts and healthy desires. In turn my body would always submit to my mind. My habits would line up with my values. My appetites would be governed by rational thought...".[111] Regrettably, many of us can testify that for us, this is not always how it works in practice. Even though our minds should

---

[108] C Marvin Pate; From Plato To Jesus; Pg 23; Kregel Publications; 2011
[109] C Marvin Pate; From Plato To Jesus; Pg 32; Kregel Publications; 2011
[110] Psalm 139:14
[111] John Ortberg; Soul Keeping; Pg 68; Zondervan; 2014

be under the control of our will, that does not always happen and the consequence is that we do not choose life-giving, truthful thoughts and healthy desires – and so our bodies do not always submit to our minds and our habits are not congruent with our values. In Paradise Lost, John Milton said that "…the mind is its own place, and in itself can make a heaven of hell, a hell of heaven…".[112] In quoting John Milton, John Ortberg said "…God's gift of your mind is unbelievably lavish. Before you were born, your body produced about 200 billion neurons, giving you the power to think and react. You had such an embarrassment of riches that by the time you were born, you had killed off around 100 billion of those neurons, and you have never even missed them. Between your second month in the womb and your second birthday, your body was producing 1.8 synapses per second. And you weren't even tired. Your thoughts have enormous power over your life. Researchers have found that tennis players can improve their backhands simply by rehearsing them mentally. Neurons that will change you are firing in your mind. Over time, these pathways between neurons were shaped in ways that are absolutely unique to you – and God has no intention of wasting them. Even twenty years ago, researchers thought the adult brain was genetically determined and structurally unchangeable. But they have since found that even into adulthood the brain is amazingly changeable – it has neuroplasticity. Which synapses remain and which ones wither away depends on your mental habits. Those that carry no traffic go out of business – like bus routes with no customers. Those that get heavily trafficked get stronger and thicker. The mind shapes the brain. Neurons that wire together fire together. In other words when you practice hope, love or joy, your mind is actually, literally, rewiring your brain…".[113] Clearly, we need to exercise extreme care over what we allow to influence our minds. Why do we need to exercise care – because as another writer reminds us "…We are simply not aware of all the influences on our moral behaviour that could arise in a given situation. So, despite our best efforts, our choices will still often go wrong…"?[114] Further, another writer points out that "…in 2 Corinthians 3:14, Paul says the mind is 'hardened' (eporothe). In 1 Timothy 6:5, he calls the mind 'depraved' (diephtharmenon). In Ephesians 4:18, he says men are "darkened in their understanding, alienated from the life of God." In Romans 1:21, he says that thinking has become 'futile'

---

[112] As quoted by John Ortberg; The Me I Want To Be; Pg 96; Zondervan; 2010

[113] John Ortberg; The Me I Want To Be; Pg 97; Zondervan; 2010

[114] Christian B Miller; The Character Gap; Pg 207; Oxford University Press; 2018

(emaraiothesan) and 'foolish' (asunetos), because men "by their unrighteousness suppress the truth (Romans 1:18). He warns against being taken "captive by philosophy" (Colossians 2:8). And he says in 1 Corinthians 1:21, "...In the wisdom of God, the world did not know God through Wisdom..." [115]

Our character links up with our mind, our conscience and with our sensitivity to determine the attitudes that underlie the actions and words that we consider appropriate in daily life. When all these attitudes are collated in our mind, they represent our personal credo – which is at the kernel of how we live our lives. The Old Testament tells us "...Blessed is the man who does not walk in the counsel of the wicked or stand in the way of sinners or sit in the seat of mockers, but his delight is in the law of the Lord, and on His law he meditates day and night. He is like a tree planted by streams of water, which yields its fruit in season and whose leaf does not wither – whatever he does prospers...".[116] Meanwhile, in the New Testament, we are reminded that "...whatever is true, whatever is noble, whatever is right, whatever is pure, whatever is lovely, whatever is admirable – if anything is excellent or praiseworthy – think about such things...".[117]

With respect to our bodies per se, John Ortberg points out that "...God loves it when you enjoy stretching or training your body in new skills, or when you enjoy what your eyes see, your ears hear, your mouth tastes and you skin feels. The physical is not separate from the spiritual; it is the Spirit who makes our bodies come to life...". (John Ortberg; The Me I Want To Be; Pg 86; Zondervan; 2010). It has been suggested that "...The human face, and especially the eyes, are not just additional physical objects in space. We say that the eyes are the windows of the soul, and there is much truth to it. They and the face and hands are areas in space where the spiritual reality of the person becomes present to others. There the inmost being of the individual pours forth...".[118] Elsewhere it has been said "...The largest organ in the human body is an interface. Every square millimetre of our skin is connected to the nervous system and receives constant feedback through our sense of touch: friction from our clothes, breeze on our face, the press of gravity against our bodies when we lie down. It's the only sense we can't switch off. You can wear a blindfold or plug your ears – but

---

[115] John Piper; Thinking. Loving. Doing; Rick Warren; Francis Chan; and John Piper; Inter Varsity Press; Pg 123; 2011

[116] Psalm 1:1-3

[117] Philippians 4:8

[118] Dallas Willard; The Divine Conspiracy; Pg 87; William Collins; 2014

you can't stop feeling…".[119] We cannot appreciate just how wonderfully made we are.

Clearly, we need to maintain our physical bodies and in doing so, most of us establish certain routines. The objective is to make sure that we nourish our bodies, we rest, we attend to hygiene requirements, we exercise and we feed our minds. We carry out all these 'maintenance' functions almost automatically because we know that it would be foolish to do otherwise. The objective is to protect our bodies so that they remain in good condition – because we want them to last us as long as possible. (In passing, it has to be said that some of us go to extraordinary lengths in this respect because we don't stop at the basic maintenance functions – but often go to the extent of pampering ourselves. "…I go around doing nothing but persuading young and old not to care for your body or your wealth in preference to your soul…".[120] Notwithstanding the experience of Socrates, the quantum of money spent annually on cosmetics, clothes, hair-styling, grooming and gym memberships etc. is staggering. Each of us needs to determine how much is enough? Despite all this on-going care, we remain vulnerable to injury and illness – and ultimately as discussed in a previous chapter – our life span is finite.

It's important to remember that whoever we are – and whatever our circumstances – our experience is limited. No matter how long we have lived – and despite how widely travelled and educated we may be, our life span is infinitesimally small relative to eternity. Accordingly, we need faith to believe that beyond the finite existence of our body/corpus and mind, our soul and spirit will continue to exist – throughout eternity. Scripture tells us that "…faith is being sure of what we hope for and certain of what we do not see…".[121]

3.6 The Significance of Soul and Spirit

By extension, the significance of our immortal soul and spirit cannot be over emphasised. Scripture warns "…Above all else, guard your heart, for it is the wellspring of life…".[122] We have noted already that Scripture sometimes refers to the 'heart' when referring to the soul. Elsewhere Scripture reminds us "…The

---

[119] "Beyond Human Touch"; 1843; Pg 38; August/September 2019

[120] Socrates; The Trial And Death Of Socrates; 30 a-b; Translated By GMA Grube; Indianapolis: Hackett; 1975

[121] Hebrews 11:1

[122] Proverbs 4:23

Lord does not look at the things man looks at. Man looks at the outward appearance, but the Lord looks at the heart…"[123] This is a significant warning about two important matters. Firstly, the approach of mankind is often superficial. Scripture anticipates that we will be more likely to look after our physical bodies – especially what is on the outside – than we are to look after the more significant parts of our make-up that are on the inside – our heart and soul. The second point is the need to take care of our heart (soul) because that is the source of every aspect of our being! This is worthy of further consideration. Everything we do emanates from deep within our being – from our everlasting soul.

According to the Westminster Catechism, "…The chief object and purpose of man is to glorify God and to enjoy Him forever…".[124] If we have not accepted the Lordship of Christ in our lives, our soul's eternal purpose is diverted from its original purpose. How does this work? After Jesus was crucified, He overcame death and is now seated at the right hand of God – interceding for humankind – "…Christ Jesus, who died – more than that, who was raised to life – is at the right hand of God and is also interceding for us…". [125] Meanwhile, in anticipation of His resurrection, Jesus told His disciples that He was leaving them – and that this was necessary in order for the Counsellor (the Holy Spirit) to come. Jesus said "…if I go, I will send Him to you. When He comes, He will convict the world of guilt in regard to sin and righteousness and judgement…". [126] The Holy Spirit in-dwells every believer. We need to be aware of the affinity between the Holy Spirit and the spirit that resides within each of us as human beings. J I Packer says "…the Spirit teaches the mind of God, and glorifies the Son of God, out of the Scriptures; also, that He is the agent of new birth, giving us an understanding so that we know God and a new heart to obey Him; also, that He in-dwells, sanctifies, and energises Christians for their daily pilgrimage; also, that assurance, joy, peace and power are His special gifts…". [127] The relationship between the Holy Spirit and the spirit attains its ultimate potential when God's Holy Spirit is married to our human spirit. When an individual accepts the Lordship of Christ in their life, that person's physical body is imbued by the Holy Spirit – and everything changes.

---

[123] 1 Samuel 16:7
[124] Westminster Larger Catechism
[125] Romans 8:34
[126] John 16:7-8
[127] J I Packer; Knowing God; Pg 247; Hodder & Stoughton; 2013

For example, the Holy Spirit alters our approach – away from I, me and mine towards God. In turning our mind and intellect to serving God, we become more sensitive to the needs of our fellow human beings and more sensitive to our need to be humble and to praise God continually. This becomes possible through a re-prioritisation as the Holy Spirit implants new values and standards within our human spirit. These new values and standards very much influence our conscience.

What about those who do not believe? The difficulty is that because the soul of mankind in general has not allowed God's Holy Spirit to influence it, non-Christians are not aware of their purpose in life – or if they are aware, they have not absorbed this fact to the extent that they have allowed it to direct their lives ("…Unless the Lord builds the house, its builders labour in vain…". [128]) The soul of a non-Christian is separated from the Holy Spirit's direction and influence – and instead, defaults to serving the needs and whims of the body that contains it. This is no surprise because if we do not have a higher and greater purpose outside ourselves, we will naturally consider the preservation of self to be our highest and most significant objective and priority. This perhaps explains why there is so little humility amongst humankind. The prevalent view is that there is not enough to go around so I must struggle to accumulate all that I can get to make my life as easy and as comfortable as possible for as long as I can enjoy it. Dr Covey refers to this as a "scarcity mentality".[129] No one needs to be reminded of the futility of this approach because we are all aware (whether by our own experience or first-hand knowledge of others or through what we read in newspapers and magazines) that no matter how much we have or obtain, it is never enough. We have an insatiable desire for more. Many wealthy people accumulate more than they could ever need – or spend – but seem to be driven for some illogical reason to want or to need to keep generating more and more – and so it goes on. It's not that they are greedy necessarily – because they recognise that it is unlikely they will spend all they have – but they just need more anyway. Humankind cannot optimise its potential by merely accumulating assets – or indeed by anything else that can be bought. That is just not how life

[128] Psalm 127:1

[129] Steven Covey; The 7 Habits Of Highly Effective People; Pg 230; Simon & Schuster; 1989

is. "…Economists typically treat rational self-interest as the lode-star of human behaviour…". [130]

3.7 Summary

In this chapter we extended our discussion on the fundamental distinction between immortality and mortality introduced in chapter 2. We noted that our spirit and our soul are timeless whereas our body is finite by definition. We noted also that since God is a Trinity and since humankind is made in God's image, then we should not be surprised that Holy Scripture refers to humankind being a tripartite being. In describing what spirit and soul mean, we emphasised the eternal significance of each. On a more mundane level, we considered the irrationality of pandering so much to our physical needs relative to the eternal needs of spirit and soul – which receive so much less attention. This chapter prompts some questions about our attitude to life. For example – how much thought have we given to the significance of our spirit and soul? If our spirit and soul are timeless, how should this affect our body and mind? Do our attitudes – and by extension, our behaviour – sufficiently reflect the eternal nature of our spirit and soul? Are our attitudes weighted overly towards our respective body and mind – that by definition – are finite?

The next chapter continues consideration of spirit, soul and body – and introduces level 4 of the model – which refers to conscience, sensitivity and discipline and their linkages to spirit, soul and body.

---

[130] "Free Exchange – The Uncultured Science"; The Economist; Pg 64; 27 July 2019

Chapter Four

Conscience, Sensitivity and Discipline

4.1 Introduction

In Chapter Three, we considered the significance of immortality and mortality per se – and with respect to the attitude of mind that is produced by awareness of mortality. In this chapter, level 4 of the hierarchy is introduced. Level 4 focuses on 'conscience' 'sensitivity' and 'discipline'. It is suggested that conscience flows from our spirit – and sensitivity is rooted in the soul. 'Discipline' refers to control of the body and mind. Note that there is not only a hierarchical relationship between each level but there is also a horizontal relationship between the components. In the absence of an active conscience, sensitivity will be dulled – in which case our body and mind will default to their lowest common denominators and ultimately end in adverse attitudes.

Figure Four	Model 3

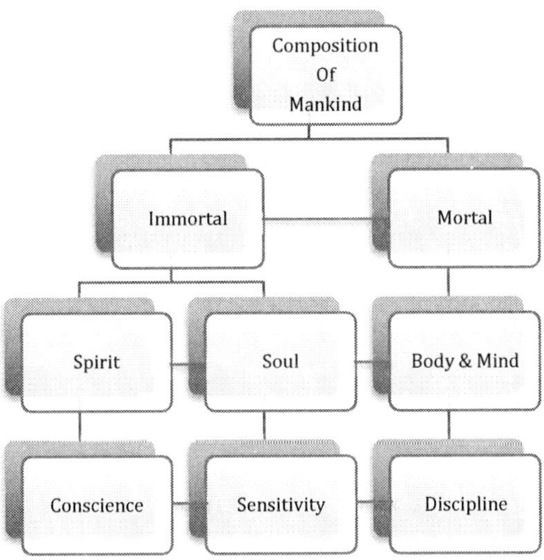

Some comments on conscience, sensitivity and discipline.

4.2 Conscience

Conscience has been mentioned more than once already. Conscience has much to do with the internal peace of mind that is the result of our behaviour being attuned to our belief system. When our credo and our actions are out of kilter then our conscience is out of kilter and peace of mind eludes us. 'Behaviour' is the action we take but before that, decision-making and choice (about which more later) must happen and so conscience affects how we make decisions before it affects behaviour. As well as our decisions and behaviour, conscience also influences our character – the seat of our affections, desires and passions. (Much more will be said about character in due course but for the time being, character (vide Para 5.3 below) is an extremely important part of our being. Amongst other things, it reflects the principles by which we live. Character may be considered as a combination of standards, values habits and choices that form our very nature. So, some of us have what are sometimes described as upright characters or dependable characters or characters that are honourable. On the other hand, some of us have what are referred to as a 'bad character'. All these descriptions mean an approach to life that is marked by certain attributes.

Sometimes referred to as the 'inner voice' or 'voice within', Wikipedia defines conscience as "…an aptitude, faculty, intuition or judgment that assists in distinguishing right from wrong. Moral judgment may derive from values or norms…". (With reference to 'values' see the corresponding text in Para 6.2.2 below.) Elsewhere – in the Cambridge Dictionary, conscience is defined as "…the part of you that judges how moral your own actions are and makes you feel guilty about bad things you have done or things you feel responsible for…". Meanwhile guilt has been described as "…an emotion we often feel whenever we do something (or do not do something) that goes against the standards we have set for our behaviour…".[131] Simply stated, conscience helps us to determine whether something is right or wrong according to our moral code. "…The problem is that our will does not allow the conscience to operate as it was

[131] Christian B Miller; The Character Gap; Pg 59; Oxford University Press; 2018

intended. We can make our conscience do what we want our conscience to do…”.[132]

Note that it is not only Christians who have consciences because non-Christians have consciences also. “…Everyone knows there are differences between right and wrong. We all experience guilt. Human beings were not left in total ignorance until they have the gospel proclaimed to them. In their consciences, they have something substantial to work on. This should stir their souls and cause them to seek after God…”.[133] Notice the relationship between conscience and soul. Speaking of Adam Smith (often referred to as the ‘Father of Economics’), a reviewer of a book about the oracle said that “…Contrary to what is often assumed, the Scot did not advocate ruthless self-interest. The very first sentence of ‘The Theory of Moral Sentiments’ reads ‘How selfish soever man may be supposed, there are evidently some principles in his nature, which interest him in the fortune of others, and render their happiness necessary to him, though he derives nothing from it except the pleasure of seeing it…’”.[134]

Unsurprisingly therefore, conscience is not something recognised by the Christian faith exclusively – it is inherent in the psyche of all human beings whether we regard it as religiously significant or not. “…This may be based on the fact that human beings, though fallen in sin, retain a semblance of the ‘image of God’ in which image they were created originally (Gen 9:6; 1 Cor 11:7)…”[135] Importantly, conscience influences our choices, our behaviour – and ultimately our actions – and it is therefore central to a discussion on attitude. It is a potent force. The extent to which conscience prevents us from pursuit of an evil action is a moot point – but there are many stories of people who years after the act that violated their conscience in the first place, testify to their conscience being salved or placated by some subsequent contrite action (such as admission of guilt) on their part. We should not underestimate the influence and strength of this force within us.

One writer has said “…Through our individual conscience, we become aware of our deeply held moral principles, we are motivated to act upon them,

---

[132] R Albert Mohler Jr as cited in Thinking. Loving. Doing; Rick Warren; Francis Chan; and John Piper; Inter Varsity Press; Pg 52; 2011

[133] Peter May; The Search For God & The Path To Persuasion; Pg 104; Malcolm Down Publishing; 2016

[134] An Enlightened Life; (Book Review Of Adam Smith: What He Thought And Why It Matters; Jesse Norman; Allen Lane); The Economist; Pg 64; 28 July 2018

[135] S Lewis Johnson; The Doctrine Of Common Grace; No other info available

and we assess our character, our behaviour and ultimately our self against those…conscience is always knowledge of ourselves, or awareness of moral principles we have committed to, or assessment of ourselves, or motivation to act that comes from within us (as opposed to external impositions)…”.[136] For the Christian, our conscience is that monitor or evaluator put in place by the Holy Spirit that sensitises us to the direction Almighty God wants us to take. How does our conscience know what is right or wrong? Our conscience knows because that is one of the roles of the spirit that God created within us. When we accept Christ as Lord of our lives – the point at which the Holy Spirit joins with our spirit, renders our conscience acutely sensitive to God’s influence. “…Those of us who are redeemed are also given what 1 Corinthians 2:16 calls the ‘mind of Christ’. Life takes on a far more accurate estimation and perspective when we learn to view it increasingly through the vantage point of the One who spoke it into existence…”.[137] This consciousness or concern for the well-being of other people that is a hallmark of the Christian emanates from the influence of the Holy Spirit in our lives. We have discovered already that until our spirit unites with the Holy Spirit, our lives cannot be what God wants them to be – nor reflect the fruits of the Spirit (vide para 3.3. above). However, when this union happens, our credo changes and we become sensitised to the plans God has for each of His children. At this stage, our conscience becomes totally active (notice that it was not totally inactive prior to this) and we are prompted to test everything against what Scripture describes and requires of a believer.

Note that “the more you obey your conscience, the more your conscience will demand of you…”.[138] Note also that “…skills are acquired by practice. No practice, no skill; much practice, much skill. Any skill will wither on the vine and gradually fade away in the degree it is starved of practice, and the same skill will increase precisely in the degree that it is given exercise in practice. The neural cell is no different from the muscle cell in this. Use it or lose it is Nature’s inviolable law…”.[139] The more one ignores conscience, the less sharp it becomes until ultimately it is virtually ineffective and no longer influences adverse

---

[136] Giubilini, Alberto, “Conscience”, The Stanford Encyclopedia of Philosophy (Spring 2016 Edition), Edward N. Zalta (ed.),
URL = <http://plato.stanford.edu/archives/spr2016/entries/conscience/>

[137] Beth Moore; “The Beloved Disciple” Pg 283; Broadman & Holman Publishers; 2003

[138] C S Lewis; Mere Christianity; Pg 196; HarperCollins; 1952

[139] David Keirsey; Please Understand Me II; Pg 39; Prometheus Nemesis Book Company; 1998

behaviour or action to the extent that it inhibits that behaviour or action. Thus, before a person accepts Christ, that person has a conscience – but in this circumstance it is frequently a blunt weapon – because of lack of usage. This was brought out starkly in an account of a North Korean who escaped from a labour camp where he had been held for years. He said that detainees were encouraged to report all sorts of things to the guards – even if these had been committed by a member of one's family. The chilling commentary made it clear that he would do this without any conscience whatsoever – that is to say without any felt concern or responsibility for the person about whom he was reporting. This was the only way of life that he had ever known. He was unable to distinguish the implications of his own actions beyond the superficial – he simply did what he was required to do.[140] Clearly, his conscience had been redundant for so long that it was rendered ineffective. On a lighter note, the story is told that in US, "...the IRS received one letter that read, 'My conscience is bothering me because of cheating on taxes, so I'm sending $10,000. If my conscience doesn't clear up, I'll send in the rest of what I owe...'".[141]

So, conscience comes into play at different levels in different people – but the important point is that the more sensitive we are, the more inclined we will be to living life in the way Christians ought. Most of us will have a conscience about what might be loosely described as 'bigger misdeeds' – for example stealing money from a bank – but would the conscience of the same people come into play if (s)he was to claim expenses dishonestly? The fundamental core of the action is the same in both examples – stealing – the only differences are the quantum and the method. Take a moment to consider what troubles your conscience – and then consider the types of things that God might expect to trouble the conscience of a Christian. For example, would your conscience trouble you if you were indiscreet – or if you broke a confidence – or if you said or thought things that were unbecoming? Would God expect your conscience to trouble you about these things? How sensitive is your conscience would you say?

The implication is that when the human spirit that has become sensitised to the influence and direction of God's Holy Spirit – through His saving grace and favour – our conscience becomes more aware of those around us and to their needs. If we have God's love in our hearts – how could it be any other way?

---

[140] Escape From Camp 14; Blaine Harden; Viking; 2012

[141] John Ortberg; When The Game Is Over It All Goes Back In The Box; Pg 114; Zondervan; 2007

"...In other words, He [the Holy Spirit] prompts our consciences about our moral failings, demonstrates to us the beauty of goodness revealed in Christ, and the inevitability that we will be held to account for our failings, when evil is eventually overthrown...".[142]

This must lead to changes in our sensitivity as that sensitivity begins to reflect principles that are new to us and that lead to changes in our attitude and our character. Our character reflects precisely who we are – by reference to what we do and how we do it. Conscience and sensitivity work hand in hand within our mind to produce our attitude. Of course, we experience many attitudes – such as an attitude to honesty or to integrity or to dignity or to racism or to extremism or to abortion or to the death penalty – and to so many more things. It is the accumulation of our attitudes to all these variables that combine to produce our credo – how we live and the actions that emanate from how we live.

4.3 Sensitivity

The word 'sensitivity' was used a number of times in the previous paragraph. Clearly, our conscience will not be pricked if it is insufficiently sensitive – and as noted above, conscience comes into play at different levels in different people. This is because the level of sensitivity that triggers the conscience reflects our attitude to what is appropriate and what is inappropriate. Consider the sensitivity of Job's friends – Scripture tells us "...When they saw him from a distance, they could hardly recognize him; they began to weep aloud, and they tore their robes and sprinkled dust on their heads. Then they sat on the ground with him for seven days and seven nights. No one said a word to him, because they saw how great his suffering was...".[143] These men were sensitive to the grief of their friend. (As an aside, I like to remember the manner in which these men comforted Job when I offer support to someone who is grieving. In such circumstances, we are often embarrassed because we do not know what to say. This story reminds us we do not really need to say anything – our presence is enough to show that we identify with our friends who are grieving. However, they ought to have remained quiet because when they spoke, their theology was all wrong - Job did not have uncommitted sin in his life for which they said he was being punished. So, we

---

[142] Peter May; The Search For God & The Path To Persuasion; Pg 137; Malcolm Down Publishing; 2016

[143] Job 2:12-13

must know not only know when to speak and when to be quiet – but when we speak – to do so appropriately and sensitively.)

We are all different people in this world – with different experiences and beliefs – and our attitude reflects (inter alia) all the things that we have discussed already. Here is one way to look at it. Let's imagine that the world's population can be divided into four main groups. For the sake of simplicity, let's exclude from this discussion the most impoverished and the super-rich groups – and focus on the other two groups. Let's call them 1 and 2.

Life is far from easy for many people – and the people in group 1 know that only too well. It's not that they have nothing – but they don't have a lot. Without a degree of resilience, not all will survive. There may not be enough to go around in terms of cash – or anything else for that matter. In fact, cash may be very limited and the environment may be hostile. Living conditions might be rough. It might be difficult to know whom to trust – so the safest course is to trust no one – and thereby protect oneself to the extent possible. Feelings of injustice or inferiority may have crept in and become aggravated over the years. Ill health or physical weakness may be the result of an inadequate or an unhealthy diet. Education may have stopped at an early age. Work might be hard to find at best and impossible to find at worst. Where people in group 1 have a job, the pay is not great so there is a need to juggle income and expenses. The spiral goes on and on. In these types of circumstances, people need resilience to survive – and that resilience might mean that there is little time to focus on anything other than what it takes to survive. Grasping whatever opportunities come along is probably taken for granted. There is little room for taking risks in addition to those that are already part and parcel of daily life. Life is tough – so take all you can get whenever you can get it. Naturally, all this has consequences and might lead to a veneer of mistrust and hardness of heart.

On the other hand, life is much easier for some. People in group 2 do not have all the luxuries that life affords – but they have a lot more than the people in group 1. Group 2 people probably will not have the same level of resilience that group 1 people need to survive. There is an adequate – perhaps even a generous supply of everything for group 2 people – including cash. Education has been completed at a secondary level at least. Employment – whilst not guaranteed – is not likely to be an insurmountable problem. The environment may not be first class but it is better than average. There is an acceptable social life leaving little room for feelings of inadequacy – so much so in fact that there is risk of a degree of arrogance. There is not a great deal of thought about those less well off. A laissez faire attitude probably prevails. Holidays are an annual event. Health is taken seriously and includes an informed approach to regular exercise and to diet. In these types of circumstances, people have not been exposed to the same rigours and disciplines and bruising that people in the first group have experienced – they have been largely cushioned and protected from what for group 1 people are the real rigours of life.

Naturally, the descriptions of these two groups are full of generalisations – but don't let that distract you from the point that is being made – because somewhere round about or in between these two groups is probably where many of the rest of us are – or would like to be. So, for the purposes of this analogy, let's imagine an intermediate group is feasible. That is to say, we would prefer to have more than very little – but we do not expect to have every luxury. The challenge for us all is to have an appropriate level of sensitivity to other people – irrespective of which group they may be in and irrespective of which group we may be in. Pondering the circumstances of people in any group – howsoever described – is a useful exercise in making clear that our attitudes reflect (inter alia) our experiences and our background – to which we must be sensitive if we are to have a dialogue with people from other groups. Why should this be our objective?

The reason is that this is the Christian way.[144] Scripture records a question posed to Jesus as follows "…Teacher, which is the greatest commandment in the Law…"? Jesus replied: "Love the Lord your God with all your heart and with all your soul and with all your mind." This is the first and greatest commandment. And the second is like it: "Love your neighbour as yourself." All the Law and the Prophets hang on these two commandments.[145] Elsewhere in Scripture we read "…My brothers, as believers in our glorious Lord Jesus Christ, don't show favouritism. Suppose a man comes into your meeting wearing a gold ring and fine clothes and a poor man in shabby clothes also comes in. If you show special attention to the man wearing fine clothes and say, "Here's a good seat for you," but say to the poor man, "You stand there," or, "Sit on the floor by my feet," have you not discriminated among yourselves and become judges with evil thoughts?…If you really keep the royal law found in Scripture, 'Love your neighbour as yourself,' you are doing right. But if you show favouritism, you sin

[144] Matthew 22:16 and Acts 9:2 refer
[145] Matthew 22:36-40

and are convicted by the law as lawbreakers…”. [146] Unless we demonstrate this sort of sensitivity in how we live, we are unlikely to have the correct attitude in living out Christian principles. In fact, we can become so wrapped up in ourselves that we can easily slip into an attitude of insensitivity towards those who have less never mind those who have nothing. (We might even begin to despise those who have more.) The World Bank's web-site says "… According to the most recent estimates, in 2015, 10 percent of the world's population lived on less than US$1.90 a day, compared to 11 percent in 2013. That's down from nearly 36 percent in 1990. Nearly 1.1 billion fewer people are living in extreme poverty than in 1990. In 2015, 736 million people lived on less than $1.90 a day, down from 1.85 billion in 1990…”.[147] What does sensitivity mean to you. If it's just feeling sorry for people who have less rather than positive action to help those in need (whatever the degree of need), nothing much will change.

The difficulty is that "…We are not born honest or compassionate – we need a catalyst to become sufficiently sensitive to be prompted to turn empathy into practical assistance. Some people might be more predisposed in this direction than others, but still, sensitivity takes both time and work to make a lot of progress. The morally best were helped along in their journey to becoming that way, either by themselves or others (or both)…”. [148] In the same way that accepting Christ as Saviour raises us to a new level of conscience, becoming a Christian is the catalyst that releases waves of sensitivity. If you are a Christian and that is not your experience, consider how you might challenge your own level of sensitivity. <u>There are at least two lessons here. Firstly, we need to be sensitive to others and secondly if we live in this way, there will be opportunities to influence others to live similarly.</u>

The Westminster Shorter Catechism's first question asks "What is the chief end of man?" and the answer provided is that "Man's chief end is to glorify God, and to enjoy Him forever." <u>As Christians, we need to be sensitive to our calling to glorify God and to enjoy Him forever. In addition, we need to be sensitive to the people around us – that is – those whom we are called to serve. How can we serve any other person if we are insensitive to their needs or condition?</u> In so saying, we should remember also that not all needs are obvious so we should not assume because we can identify no obvious need, the other person needs nothing.

[146] James 2:1-4 and 8-9
[147] Worldbank.org; Understanding Poverty; Overview
[148] Christian B Miller; The Character Gap; Oxford University Press; Pg 173; 2018

They might not need food or clothes or somewhere decent to live – but they may need someone to notice them, to encourage them or to comfort them. They might need someone to treat them sensitively.

It would be wrong to imagine that developing sensitivity always requires particular skills or special attributes. One person may need help to get across the road – or somewhere to live or a hot meal but someone else might need a shoulder to lean on or just someone to listen and to empathize with them as they recount their problems and challenges in life. Some people may really appreciate getting help in filling out official forms or getting independent advice on matters outside their experience. Whether little or no skills will be involved – or more specialist skills, as Christians we need to be sensitive to the needs of other people if we are to meaningfully serve God by serving our fellow man. Scripture says "...Each one should use whatever gift he has received to serve others, faithfully administering God's grace in its various forms ...".[149] The primary resource required for increasing personal sensitivity is frequent consideration of Almighty God's sensitivity to humankind's deepest need in sending Jesus Christ to be the propitiation for our sins. Jesus' life shows how sensitive He was to other people – such as when He told the disciples to allow children to come to Him or when He healed people or when He asked God to forgive those who were crucifying Him. There are many more examples. We need to follow Christ's example. The second resource is deep-seated humility. Sensitivity is enhanced by humility and prompted by conscience.

One of the notable features of our lives is that everyone is busy. There seems to be an inadequate number of hours in any day to fit in all that needs to be done. Naturally, there are consequences concerning what gets left out. Unless we make a conscious decision about what to include in our lives, we risk throwing out the baby with the bath water and excluding something (or someone) that ought to have been included. Remember that not thinking about what we should exclude from our lives is the same as a definite decision to include it. Either way, something is amiss – whether by design or as a result of being squeezed out by default. Accordingly, it's valuable to consider how to allocate our time – and we need to do this often. It is not only procrastination that is the thief of time – it is everything that will keep us from focusing on what is important. The King James Version of the Bible talks about "redeeming the time"[150] – which infers that as

---

[149] 1 Peter 4:10

[150] Holy Bible; Ephesians 5:16; King James Version;

Christians we should endeavour to maximise the use of our time. This involves making time for worship and for learning about our faith – for example by reading good books. In this respect, ask yourself when you last read a Christian book? Now ask yourself how many hours you spent watching television (or pursuing your hobby etc.) last week. Now compare the two figures and ask yourself what conclusions you should draw?

Consider how much you are affected by what you read and hear that is happening globally – but especially in war zones and in disaster areas. Do we care enough even to listen – and if so, do we care enough to pray for those affected or perhaps give support or practical help? The question is whether and to what extent we have become insensitive to the needs of others?

With respect to how we treat each other, it is often the case that the time devoted to relationships – like the time devoted to 'things' – has to be pared so that other things can be fitted in. The implication is that we see friends less often and we communicate with them less – both in terms of frequency and also in terms of quality. This means we don't write letters any more (can you remember the last time you either wrote or received a handwritten letter?). We reason that they take too much time – and that is true – but then anything worth doing takes time (and effort). Sometimes we telephone (frequently when we are driving (hands free) so as not to waste any time – naturally!) but more often than not, we send a text message – written in cryptic abbreviations and emojis – because we don't have time to write out words in full – and this also saves time. (By the way, note that we have created a new verb to describe this action – 'to text'). Texting was originally referred to as the short message service ('sms') – and by definition, text messages comprise as few words as possible. By extension, we exclude words altogether if an 'emoji' provides the gist. This is not the preferred medium if you want to communicate meaningfully or sensitively – it's just a short cut – to save time. Dallas Willard has a view on hurry – he says "...I believe we should never be in a hurry. But sometimes we should act quickly. Acting quickly is a form of action. Being in a hurry is a state of mind...".[151] For me, this is a really significant distinction. Another author has said "...We must ruthlessly eliminate hurry from our lives...Jesus observed a regular practice of withdrawing from activity for the sake of solitude and prayer. Jesus was often busy, but never hurried. Hurry is not just a disordered schedule. Hurry is a

[151] Dallas Willard; Becoming The Kind Of Leaders Who Can Do The Job; Cutting Edge Magazine; Summer 1999; Vineyard USA

disordered heart…”.[152] I dislike having to rush – but in order to avoid rushing, we must be prepared acting in advance of the last minute whether it is writing a note, going to Church or catching a train. This requires discipline (about which more will be said later).

Worse still, choosing not to respond to a communication (whether it is a greeting card or a letter – or even an email or a text message) is not only bad manners – it is grossly insensitive. In short, we have (substantially) lost the ability to communicate sensitively with people in general – and with our nearest and dearest in particular. Naturally, meaningless chat remains unaffected – but when we need to talk intimately or deeply with someone whose support or guidance or love we need, it is now more difficult to identify who amongst those we know will have the time and empathy and sensitivity to meet us at the point of our need. This insensitivity has permeated so many areas of daily life. Just let anyone try to get in front of us in traffic for example and we will see each other in a different light. We even have a name for traffic aberrations that involve bad temper – ‘road rage’ – not to be taken lightly.

How different all this is to the image of Christ we read about in the New Testament! Jesus always had time to communicate meaningfully – firstly with Almighty God, then with His disciples and then with the throngs of people who flocked around him unceasingly. Jesus told us to put others before ourselves and to turn the other cheek. Jesus warned us about controlling our tongues and to be careful about what we said. Plutarch said that “…In words are seen the state of mind, character and disposition of the speaker…”.[153] Remember, Christ refused to condemn the woman caught in the act of adultery and wept at the grave of His friend Lazarus. He was – and remains – sensitive – an attitude of mind.

As Christians, we must not be insensitive about sensitivity. “…We hardly notice it, but oftentimes a kind smile from a friend…or a meaningful handshake from a supportive colleague can completely change our attitudes. Such minor acts can have great effects. If we mind them, we can…prompt or lift one another toward our joint moral ends…”.[154] We must be sensitive to the demands of our calling and to the responsibilities we bear as sinners saved by grace. We must be sensitive to the fact that we serve Almighty God – and to treat our God with awe

---

[152] John Ortberg; The Life You Have Always Wanted; Pg 79; 2002; Zondervan

[153] As quoted in Attitude Is Everything; Jeff Keller; Pg 60; Attitude Is Everything Inc; 2012

[154] Hagop Sarkissian; 2010 as quoted By Christian B Miller; The Character Gap; Pg 208; Oxford University Press; 2018

and deep respect. We must be sensitive also to the people around us – and use our time and other assets carefully. "...If anyone has material possessions and sees his brother in need but has no pity on him, how can the love of God be in him..."?[155]

How will non-Christian people with whom we rub shoulders day by day begin to understand their status unless we help them to understand – and how will we even begin to understand the needs of others if we do not approach such relationships with sensitivity and humility (see Para 5.2 below)? How can we pray effectively for others unless we are sensitive to their needs – because in the absence of that sensitivity, we will not even be able to comprehend their needs? Lord – help me to be as sensitive as I need to be – to live effectively for You. However, Christians need to be careful because "...There are some people who get so busy in church worship and projects that they become insensitive to the pressing human needs that surround them, contradicting the very precepts they profess to believe deeply...". [156] We can easily lose sight of the wood for the trees.

Note that kindness and sensitivity go hand in hand. Kindness merely means doing something for someone out of the goodness of your heart not because of any compulsion. Kindness gets to the heart of being human. It's such a potent force for the Christian – often costing nothing – but creating potentially extremely positive rapport. How often do we miss the opportunity to say thank you or to hold the door open for someone or to send a card or a gift where circumstances are appropriate? When did you last express interest in someone? We have not lost the capacity to be kind but we need to practice continuously if we are to avoid losing it – as if we were learning a foreign language! At funerals, I often wonder whether all the nice things said about the deceased were said during that person's lifetime – or whether that person never heard or knew how much (s)he was appreciated, admired, respected and loved. I imagine the Lord is pleased when a Christian is sensitive to the needs of another person to the extent they offer tangible support to that person – and especially when the Christian feels no need to publicise their good deed or try to win the approbation of others. In my view, this is the right attitude.

---

[155] 1 John 3:17

[156] Stephen Covey; The Seven Habits Of Highly Effective People; Pg 125; Simon & Schuster; 1989

(Later on, we will look at some of the implications of insensitivity – vide Para 10.2 below.)

4.4 Discipline

Attitude is reflected in character – and one important component of character is discipline. "...There is no effectiveness without discipline, and there is no discipline without character...".[157] Scripture likens the Christian way to running a race "...let us run with perseverance the race marked out for us...".[158] Like athletes, Christians are in continuous training – which means certain preferences need to be foregone – and certain physical and attitudinal regimes must be adopted. It's far easier not to be a Christian than it is to assume the life practices of someone in close personal communion with God. In anticipation of human beings not realising this, Scripture advises us to "...Consider him who endured such opposition from sinful men, so that you will not grow weary and lose heart...".[159] Further we are told "...God disciplines us for our good, that we may share in His holiness. No discipline seems pleasant at the time, but painful. Later on, however, it produces a harvest of righteousness and peace for those who have been trained by it...".[160] It's important to understand that hardship and discipline are necessary parts of life. "...For God did not give us a spirit of timidity, but a spirit of power, of love and of self-discipline...".[161] While God wants us to be happy, He wants us even more to be like Him – holy. Holiness is not possible in the absence of discipline.

However, everybody knows that it's far simpler to take the easy way out – at least in the short term. For example, it's easier not to give to those in need; it's far easier to talk about people behind their back as opposed to their face; it's far easier to stand for nothing in particular; it's far easier to cut corners, to be a little dishonest, to be insincere and so on and so on – but Christians are called to discipline their lives to not only do the right thing – but also to do the thing right. This means doing the best that you can – second best is hardly appropriate in the service of Almighty God. Thankfully, God does not expect perfection but I think

---

[157] Jim Collins; Foreword to the 25th Anniversary Edition; The Seven Habits Of Highly Effective People; Stephen Covey; Pg 3; Simon & Schuster; 2013

[158] Hebrews 12:1

[159] Hebrews 12:3

[160] Hebrews 12:10-11

[161] 2 Timothy 1:7

He does expect us to use what He has given us to the best of our ability in His service.

It requires discipline to say and to do the right thing. This is because the right thing is often the hardest thing. It requires discipline to remain true to one's principles – such as endurance in the face of adversity – or calmness in the face of provocation – or resilience in the face of having to pick up oneself and to press on. It requires discipline to be faithful to other people when they are not around to hear what we are saying about them. It requires discipline to exercise humility, integrity, honesty, love and all the other principles, traits and qualities that will be described in due course.

Jesus' life epitomised discipline. He lived a simple life – without any of life's comforts – forsaking family and friends to conduct an earthly ministry for which He was often challenged and rebuked and despised. Despite that, He continued serving those around Him at great personal sacrifice. He sought no personal gain and was often hounded for doing good. One fundamental characteristic of the discipline with which He conducted himself was in respect of His attitude towards others – especially those who were doing their utmost to cause Him harm. Consider Jesus' prayer at Golgotha "...Father, forgive them, for they do not know what they are doing ...".[162] It requires discipline to put the needs of others before our own needs – but especially so for the Lord – when His own life was at stake and when He was being shamefully and brutally treated. This is attitude in action.

Jesus prayed consistently and lengthily. "...During the days of Jesus' life on earth, He offered up prayers and petitions with loud cries and tears ...". [163] Scripture refers to prayer and praying 25 times in relation to Jesus. Jesus prayed at night – and sometimes through the night ("...One of those days Jesus went out to a mountainside to pray, and spent the night praying to God...".)[164] Jesus prayed early in the morning ("...Very early in the morning, while it was still dark, Jesus got up, left the house and went off to a solitary place, where He prayed...".)[165] Jesus found it necessary to commune with God often. What does it suggest to you if you find communication with God less necessary than Jesus? If we are not in this type of relationship with God – that is to say a relationship

[162] Luke 23:34
[163] Hebrews 5:7
[164] Luke 6:12
[165] Mark1:35

where we commune with Him on an on-going basis – then we will not be as close to Him as He would like – or as we need to be. Our characters will be less influenced and our attitudes will not so closely reflect those of our Saviour. On the other hand, frequent communication with our Lord will help us to glorify Him, to mature as Christians, to encourage the development of sensitivity towards others – and to remember whose we are and whom we serve. Proximity to our Saviour brings with it a greater and deeper knowledge of Him and of His ways. Naturally, the evil one will make every attempt to prevent us praying and to create a wedge between us and our Saviour. Prayer is not easy – but often we tend to make it harder than it needs to be because of our attitude towards it. Why should we exclude something from our lives that will enhance our character and thereby influence our attitude? The answer is that we lose our objectivity sometimes. We attach too much significance to certain matters – to the extent that we waste time on things that do not matter and devote inadequate time to things that matter more. We don't have to go to 'Prayer Meetings' to pray (although doing so is a sound practice that brings with it a number of advantages not only for ourselves – but for others also). We don't have to pray in a particular way or in a particular place or in public – or even aloud – or at a particular time. What we must do is commune with our Lord – often! This will help us with the process of forming an appropriate attitude.

In order to help us, Jesus taught His disciples what we refer to as the Lord's Prayer. [166] In doing so, He left us a pattern of how we should pray. Firstly, we are addressing our Father in Heaven – which means we should pray in reverence. Then in praying this prayer, we are acknowledging that: (1) one day, Jesus' Kingdom will be established and (2) in the meantime, the Lord's will should prevail in our lives on earth – in the same way the Lord's will prevails in heaven. We are to pray to God for what we need – in reliance upon Him who provides all things that are appropriate. The Lord's Prayer reminds us of our need to ask forgiveness from God for all the wrong things for which we are responsible – and in our turn we must forgive all those who have wronged us. Lastly, we are to ask God to help us to avoid temptation and to prevent us coming under the influence of the evil one. The Lord's prayer provides a useful template that we can use in forming our own prayers – or not as the case may be. Praying methods are not prescribed.

[166] Matthew 6:9-13

Discipline – as we noted above – is not a popular word in this day and age. It seems that we shy away from discipline ordinarily. We don't like having to conform or to behave in a particular way. Instead, we want to be able to do everything we want to do – when and how we want. The danger is that we can easily adopt a perverse approach to those around us. It seems not to matter how our actions or reactions affect others – it seems that what matters is the extent to which we will be put out – and if this is to an extent that is too great, we will default to what suits us best. Naturally, there are consequences of such behaviour – that are all too evident in this broken and confused world in which we exist. As we noted above, everything that is worth doing requires energy and effort.

4.5 Summary

This chapter picked up from the central theme of chapter 3 in emphasising that spirit, soul and body each have a fundamental role to play in creating the attitudes that culminate in producing a reaction. In this respect, we considered conscience, sensitivity and discipline. Our spirit produces conscience – something that we all possess. In turn, conscience provides guidance as we decide what is right (acceptable) and what is wrong (unacceptable) behaviour for each of us. Of course, we can easily override our conscience when we want the easy way out and this is where sensitivity comes in. Each time we override our conscience, the prompt that conscience initiates is stimulated less – until it is finally rendered impotent. The opposite applies when we respond positively. Each time this happens our conscience becomes more potent, more responsive and more sensitive. The Christian way is deeply sensitive – as to how we live and how we respond to others. We cannot be effective as Christians if we are not sensitive to their needs or in response to their needs. All this does not take place in a vacuum – which is why discipline is important. Accordingly, unless we exercise self-discipline, we will always take the easy way out. Without this discipline, conscience will not have an opportunity to influence our behaviour through our attitude. Consideration has been given to the value and to the style of frequent communication with our God. Similarly, sensitivity is one of the natural outputs of our soul – that part of our innermost being that is central to the formation of character. Note that conscience and sensitivity go hand in hand. One of the reasons that conscience is so important is that it directly affects sensitivity. In the absence of sensitivity, discipline becomes redundant. The inter-connections and the complementary roles of all these elements is amazing. Conscience, sensitivity and discipline represent level 4 in the model.

In the next chapter, we will expand the model further – to show the inter-relationships between conscience and humility, between sensitivity and character and between discipline and choices.

Chapter Five

Humility, Character, Discernment and Choices

5.1 Introduction

Consideration of the immortal (spirit and soul) and the mortal (body and mind) represent the first two levels in the hierarchy of the composition of mankind. In level 3, we identified spirit as the source of conscience, the soul as the source of sensitivity and the human body/mind as the source of discipline. We recognised that our human framework already has a measure of conscience, sensitivity and discipline whether or not we have accepted God as the Lord of our lives – but we saw how these capacities are enhanced and taken to far higher levels when people become Christians. Simultaneously, we thought about both the vertical and horizontal relationships between all these components of our framework recognizing the inter-connectivity of so many factors that affect our attitudes.

Figure Five	Model 4

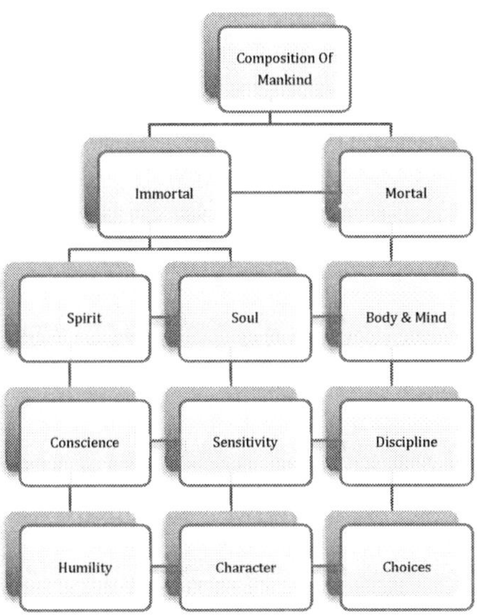

In chapter 5, we will look at three more components (level 4 in the hierarchy) – humility, character, discernment/choices to see the parts they play in how human beings form attitudes. By way of introduction, we will see that in the absence of humility, our conscience will not be as sensitive as it has been designed to be. Conscience is leveraged by sensitivity. Then alongside humility sits all those qualities that combine to form our character – emanating ultimately from our soul. Our character is a truly significant part of our make-up and is at the very core of attitude formation. This chapter ends with some words on discernment and choices – because all the elements considered so far combine to enlighten our discernment – the driver of choice. Discernment is nurtured by conscience and sensitivity and surrounded by discipline. These are endorsed and expanded by humility and character as we will see below. Let's start by looking at humility.

5.2 Humility

Firstly, it's important to understand what humility means. One writer says that it is "…the framework within which all virtue lives…".[167] One Biblical story sums up humility very clearly – here it is "…When He noticed how the guests picked the places of honour at the table, He told them this parable: 'When someone invites you to a wedding feast, do not take the place of honour, for a person more distinguished than you may have been invited. If so, the host who invited both of you will come and say to you, 'Give this person your seat.' Then, humiliated, you will have to take the least important place. But when you are invited, take the lowest place, so that when your host comes, he will say to you, 'Friend, move up to a better place.' Then you will be honoured in the presence of all your fellow guests. For everyone who exalts himself will be humbled, and he who humbles himself will be exalted.'…"[168]

Fundamentally, <u>humility is an attitude of mind</u> and the parable quoted above demonstrates clearly one of the ways that humility appears in action. Humility empowers an individual to accept an inferior outcome when that person had a legitimate right to something superior. For example, humility says: even though I was in this line before you – please go in front of me – or – even though I am an expert in what you are doing or saying – I will let you continue speaking

---

[167] Dallas Willard; Renovation Of The Heart; Pg 178; Inter Varsity Press; 2002
[168] Luke 14: 7-11

without making a big thing of my expertise or making you feel inferior – even though you appear to know less than me. Humility concedes that I have much to learn and that my mind is open to receive knowledge and not closed shut through pride. An attitude of humility empowers an individual to say – I am a sinner who does not deserve your forgiveness O God, please redeem me in Your mercy and by Your grace.

One writer's view is that "...Humility is the freedom to stop trying to be what we're not, or pretending to be what we're not, and accepting our 'appropriate small-ness'...". [169] Scripture says it like this "...Do nothing out of selfish ambition or vain conceit, but in humility consider others better than yourselves. Each of you should look not only to your own interests, but also to the interests of others. **Your attitude should be the same as that of Christ Jesus**: Who, being in very nature God, did not consider equality with God something to be grasped, but made Himself nothing, taking the very nature of a servant, being made in human likeness. And being found in appearance as a man, He humbled Himself and became obedient to death – even death on a cross! Therefore, God exalted Him to the highest place and gave Him the name that is above every name, that at the name of Jesus every knee should bow, in heaven and on earth and under the earth, and every tongue confess that Jesus Christ is Lord, to the glory of God the Father...".[170]

Scripture has much to teach us about humility with respect to our God and also about Christ as our example. Matthew records that the Lord said "...Take my yoke upon you and learn from Me, for I am gentle and humble in heart...".[171] Elsewhere, Scripture makes it clear that God "...gives grace to the humble..."[172] and again "...This is the one I esteem: he who is humble and contrite in spirit, and trembles at My word...".[173] With respect to our Heavenly Father, Scripture says "...How great is the love the Father has lavished on us, that we should be called children of God..."![174] <u>The fact of the matter is that we do not deserve any of our Lord's bounteous mercies.</u> He is our Creator – the One who was and is – and who forever will be in control. <u>We are not masters of our own destiny – we</u>

[169] John Ortberg; The Life You've Always Wanted; Pg 112; Zondervan; 2002
[170] Philippians 2:3-11
[171] Matthew 11:29
[172] James 4:6
[173] Isaiah 66:2
[174] 1 John 3:1

control nothing – and we have only what we have been given. This is aptly summarised in the title of one of Max Lucado's books – 'It's Not About Me'.

The word 'awe' has lost much of its original meaning in today's parlance. We tend to use the word loosely – often to describe the mundane – but when used properly – to describe the attitude in which we should approach our God, it means deep reverence and respect because of His love, His omnipotence, His omniscience – His grace and His favour. Our God can be truly described as The Awesome God. As we are reminded in Scripture, "…all of it belongs to You… [and]…everything comes from You and we have given You only what comes from Your hand…".[175] God is supreme!

Our God demonstrated His awesome love through Jesus Christ – His Son. Jesus is the epitome of humility. Paul says in Corinthians "…For you know the grace of our Lord Jesus Christ, that though He was rich, yet for your sakes He became poor, so that you through His poverty might become rich…".[176] Of ourselves, we are nothing – and yet Jesus Christ surrendered His place in Heaven to live amongst humankind to point us to Almighty God. During the time He lived amongst humankind, Jesus was disrespected, abused, scorned, mocked, ridiculed – and eventually murdered because of the great love that He has for every human being. In all this, Christ behaved with utmost dignity and humility. This humility is captured precisely in the lyrics of the song *He Could Have Called Ten Thousand Angels* (Loretta Lynn) as follows:

"…They bound the hands of Jesus in the garden where He prayed
They led Him thru the streets in shame
They spat upon the Saviour so pure and free from sin
They said, 'Crucify Him: He's to blame'
He could have called ten thousand angels
To destroy the world and set Him free
He could have called ten thousand angels
But He died alone, for you and me…".

The meaning of humility is eloquently summarised for us by Matthew – where he says "…You know that the rulers of the Gentiles lord it over them, and their high officials exercise authority over them. Not so with you. Instead, whoever wants to become great among you must be your servant, and whoever wants to be first must be your slave – just as the Son of Man did not come to be

[175] 1 Chronicles 29:14
[176] 2 Corinthians 8:9

served but to serve, and to give His life as a ransom for many …". [177] Matthew follows up with the following helpful words – "…The greatest among you will be your servant. For whoever exalts himself will be humbled, and whoever humbles himself will be exalted…".[178]

In quoting Paul, one author commented on the verse "…Your attitude should be the same as that of Christ Jesus: who being in very nature God, did not consider equality with God something to be grasped, but made Himself nothing, taking the very nature of a servant…". The entire life of Jesus isn't the story of somebody climbing up a ladder; it's a picture of someone coming down – a series of demotions. To begin with, Jesus was 'in very nature God'. He was at the top of the organisational chart of the universe. But He did not consider this to be 'grounds for grasping'; He gave up the right to have things His own way and became a servant. But even angels are servants, so He went lower: He became a human being. He took on flesh and blood, all our needs and limitations. This is the beauty of the incarnation – God coming down. But even on a human level, some people live as kings and celebrities, so Jesus took another demotion; He 'humbled Himself' and was born in a stable as the peasant Son of a penniless couple. But even that was not enough. He kept going by becoming 'obedient to death'. His ultimate task wasn't some glorious achievement. There was nothing glamorous about death. But His demotion didn't stop there. He went one rung lower: 'even death on a cross'… And ironically, the moment He looked most like a failure in the world scoring system was His moment of greatest triumph in the eyes of the Father. 'Therefore, God exalted Him to the highest place and gave Him the name that is above every name'.[179]

All this takes time and thought to absorb – because it is so far from our sinful nature – so far from what might be considered the norm amongst humankind – this is awesome. In this day and age, <u>we do not expect to see humility in action very often – we are more acquainted with self-esteem and arrogance</u> – yet "…Nothing has a greater, longer lasting impression upon another person than the awareness that someone has transcended suffering, has transcended circumstance, and is embodying and expressing a value that inspires and

---

[177] Matthew 20:25-28

[178] Matthew 23:11-12

[179] John Ortberg; When The Game Is Over It All Goes Back In The Box; Pg 45; Zondervan; 2007

ennobles and lifts life…”. [180] Regrettably, it seems that those with more money and more power in life often find it considerably more difficult than others to become humble – but we shouldn’t be surprised about this because Matthew has pointed out that “…Jesus said to his disciples, ‘…I tell you the truth, it is hard for a rich man to enter the kingdom of heaven’…”.[181]

Some people believe that they have ‘made it’ and – by themselves at that – without intervention or assistance from anyone – and they want everyone to know about their ‘success’. The words a ‘self-made man’ come to mind. How disappointed must our Saviour be to hear such words spoken. It is all the more obvious that when we see humility in action, we are firstly surprised but then uplifted – and often challenged. Humility requires strength of character.

It is instructive to think what the world might look like if our attitude demonstrated more humility. While no magic wands can be waved to create a humbler world than we have currently, that should not prevent us from playing our part in making things better. God has said “…If my people, who are called by My name will humble themselves and pray and seek My face and turn from their wicked ways, then will I hear from heaven and will forgive their sin and will heal their land…”. [182] This type of humility is real, it’s dynamic, it’s practical and it’s an every-day challenge as we shall see later in the text (Para 8.2) but in the meantime, we should note that if we choose to live humbly, life will not be easy – and we should not under-estimate the effort required. As we noted earlier, everything of value has a cost.

It has to be said that no matter how humble we are or might become, humility will neither replace nor become a substitute for acknowledgement of Jesus Christ as Lord of our lives. There are many non-Christians who are humble and who can inspire us Christians to try to do better – see below – but this per se cannot take precedence over the fundamental need for expression of trust in God for saving grace.

We have noted that Jesus has set us the supreme example of humility – so we should not lose sight of the fact that God expects us to emulate Christ’s example in our daily lives. We must “…live in harmony with one another; be sympathetic, love as brothers, be compassionate and humble…”.[183] Humility is

---

[180] Stephen Covey; The Seven Habits Of Highly Effective People; Pg 81; Simon & Schuster; 1989

[181] Matthew 19:23

[182] 2 Chronicles 7:14

[183] 1 Peter 3:8

a foundational element of the Christian way. Accordingly, it is an important factor in our lives as human beings – and especially so as Christian human beings. Humility is such a strong influence on our attitude that it behoves us to work harder at embedding that particular attitude deep within our being. We are told that we should "...clothe [y]ourselves with humility toward one another, because, 'God opposes the proud but gives grace to the humble.' Humble yourselves, therefore, under God's mighty hand, that He may lift you up in due time...".[184] To do so will point us in the right direction in every aspect of our lives – because we are required to "...act justly and to love mercy and to walk humbly with [y]our God..."[185]

If we think we are humble, then we may have a problem – because this mere thought shows that perhaps we aren't as humble as we might be. Note that we are required not to "...think of yourself more highly than you ought, but rather think of yourself with sober judgment...".[186] In addition, Paul urges us in Colossians "...as God's chosen people, holy and dearly loved, clothe yourselves with compassion, kindness, humility, gentleness and patience. Bear with each other and forgive whatever grievances you may have against one another. Forgive as the Lord forgave you. And over all these virtues put on love, which binds them all together in perfect unity. Let the peace of Christ rule in your hearts, since as members of one body you were called to peace. And be thankful. Let the word of Christ dwell in you richly as you teach and admonish one another with all wisdom, and as you sing psalms, hymns, and spiritual songs with gratitude in your hearts. And whatever you do, whether in word or deed, do it all in the name of the Lord Jesus, giving thanks to God the Father through Him...".[187]

This is so far from our daily experience that it might well make us gasp as we think about what these words mean. Analysing the causes and effects of the 2008 financial crisis for example, (see Para 6.4.2) one author noted "...Still missing in the current environment is a genuine sense of humility...".[188] So the attitudes described above are not what we expect to find in the people with whom we rub shoulders day by day – but just think what potentially transformative

[184] 1 Peter 5: 5-6
[185] Micah 6:8
[186] Romans 12:3
[187] Colossians 3:12-17
[188] Andrew Ross Sorkin; Too Big To Fail: The Inside Battle To Save Wall Street; Allen Lane – Penguin Group; Epilogue; 2009

words these are. Isn't it refreshing to meet someone who exhibits even some of what Paul was writing about? There are just some people around who radiate positive vibes. These are the people who make us feel better when we meet them. The components in the model have the capacity to transform us. Think what this might be like if both you and your whole family were transformed like this – and what about all your neighbours – and your whole village or town. Is it merely idealistic to imagine a whole country living according to these norms? If we believe that it is too idealistic, then I think that we are making our God appear too small. Scripture encourages us how to live "... in harmony with one another; be sympathetic, love as brothers, be compassionate and humble...". [189]

As quoted earlier, James provides that we are to "...Do nothing out of selfish ambition or vain conceit, but in humility consider others better than yourselves, not looking to your own interests but each of you to the interests of others. Your attitude should be the same as that of Christ Jesus: Who, being in very nature God, did not consider equality with God something to be grasped, but made Himself nothing, taking the very nature of a servant, being made in human likeness. And being found in appearance as a man He humbled himself and became obedient to death – even death on a cross..."![190] Further, "...Who is wise and understanding among you? Let him show it by his good life, by deeds done in the humility that comes from wisdom...".[191]

When we speak about Christianity advocating a radical approach, this is what we mean! I think we are in danger of reading Scripture too quickly (or worse still – not at all) and thereby glossing over fundamental truths and lessons – and depriving ourselves of a proper understanding of what the words are really telling us. In his letter to the Philippians, Paul says that Jesus Christ – who was by His very nature Almighty God – made Himself nothing – a servant – and allowed Himself to become subject to death – by crucifixion for your sake and for mine! The Creator did this for us. Have you ever taken a few moments to try to absorb what this means? Surely this must affect our attitude towards Almighty God – and accordingly – our attitude to humankind as well?

Naturally, we should not overlook the fact that there are many, many non-Christians who are humble – perhaps even more humble than some of us Christians. Take for example Dame Stephanie Shirley – of whom I read in a

---

[189] 1 Peter 3:8
[190] Philippians 2 v 3-8
[191] James 3:13

report published recently in a national newspaper. Dame Stephanie said that she has a "...passion in donating her wealth to good causes...the money really, has never been the thing. Rather, that the art to surviving life's cruelties and triumphs is learning to let it all go...".[192] The article goes on to say that Dame Stephanie was "...raised a Christian but no longer practises any faith...she espouses the importance of fairness, kindness and tolerance...". What a good example of attitude for us Christians if we were to accept that challenge today! I have much to learn from Dame Stephanie – and from other non-Christians whose integrity and generosity are exemplary.

5.3 Character

Thus far, we have noted that everyone has a conscience – it is innate to humankind. We noted also that conscience influences decisions and behaviour. If we have recognised Christ as our Saviour, the Holy Spirit combines with the spirit within each of us and sensitises our conscience in accordance with the Christian 'way' – our credo or world-view. The application of our world-view is a function of character – and character formation is ultimately a function of our soul – and the foundation for action – see below. Our soul creates the sensitivity required to enhance the qualities that form our character. One writer reminds us "...As the inspirational writer H Jackson Brown said in a famous quote '...character is what we do when we think no one is looking'...".[193] Elsewhere, the same author said that "...your character includes your own unique collection of characteristics or traits that are centrally important to who you are and how you act...". [194]

Accordingly, "...Character rises out of our values, the standards we set ourselves, our sacrifice and commitment and the decisions we make under pressure, but it is primarily defined by the contribution we make, the responsibility we take, the leadership we show...".[195] Character is intrinsically linked to attitude – it has been said that "...Weakness of attitude becomes weakness of character...".[196]

---

[192] The Millionaire Who Is Giving It All Away; The Daily Telegraph; News Review; Pg 33; 03 December 2016
[193] H Jackson Brown; 2000 as quoted by Christian B Miller; The Character Gap; Pg 16; Oxford University Press; 2018
[194] Christian B Miller; The Character Gap; Pg 7; Oxford University Press; 2018
[195] James Kerr; Legacy; Pg178; Constable; 2013
[196] Albert Einstein

For the Christian, character is the result of the Holy Spirit working in the human soul to produce an approach to life based on the principles (standards, values, habits and choices) that our conscience and character tell us are appropriate. One writer puts it like this – "…Character is the internal, overall structure of the self that is revealed by our long-run patterns of behaviour. It is from our character that our actions more or less automatically arise. What God gets out of your life is the person you become. That's also what you and others get…"[197] [and elsewhere] "…The deepest revelation of our character is what we choose to dwell on in thought, what constantly occupies our mind…".[198]

Dictionary.com defines character as "…the aggregate of features and traits that form the individual nature of some person or thing…" and the Merriam-Webster dictionary defines it as "…the way someone thinks, feels, and behaves: someone's personality…". The English language incorporates terms such as 'character reference' or a person of 'good character' indicating that the person described as such is a worthy individual – a person of good reputation and standing.

Character formation is a process that requires time and experience. "…You have to understand that peoples' character is not formed by decisions all at once, but by thousands of little choices they make every day without even knowing about it…"[199] "…Habits are powerful factors in our lives and because they are consistent, often unconscious patterns, they constantly, daily, express our character…".[200] There are no short cuts – and no quick fixes. The willingness to listen is an example – because listening requires patience, respect and an authentic desire to understand the other person's point of view. (Genuine listening means listening with the objective of understanding as intently as I can to what the other person is telling me – as opposed to listening merely to hear when the other person will stop speaking – probably so that I can begin to respond). One writer says "…Our lives are fashioned and shaped in the secret and private decisions that we make, in the unheard thoughts of our minds and in the everyday choices we commit to. Our character is fashioned by such choices. Our habits are formed by our daily commitment for good or bad…".[201] In his

---

[197] Dallas Willard

[198] Dallas Willard; The Divine Conspiracy; Pg 356; William Collins; 2014

[199] JP Moreland as quoted in The Case For Faith; Lee Strobel; Pg 177; Zondervan; 2000

[200] Stephen Covey; The Seven Habits Of Highly Effective People; Pg 54; Simon & Schuster; 1989

[201] Risk Takers; Malcolm Duncan; Pg 151, Monarch Books; 2013

epistle to the Romans, Paul points to suffering and perseverance as factors in character formation. He says "...we also rejoice in our sufferings, because we know that suffering produces perseverance; perseverance, character; and character, hope...".[202] Even superficial reflection points us in the direction of people we have known or perhaps read about who – despite great suffering over a protracted period – have persevered. The veracity of Paul's words reflects human experience in that people who suffer often demonstrate huge strength of character. In addition, Aristotle pointed out that "...to enjoy the things we ought – and to hate the things we ought – has the greatest bearing on excellence of character...".

Gladly, not only Christians recognise the importance of character – in fact the concept has been embraced in some schools – both as a discrete subject and as part of the curriculum. Not surprisingly, this is referred to as 'character education'. Wikipedia defines character education as an umbrella term loosely used to describe the teaching of children in a manner that will help them develop variously as moral, civic, good, mannered, behaved, non-bullying, healthy, critical, successful, traditional, compliant or socially acceptable beings. This seems like a positive approach – but the type of development referred to is not just for children – it is a lifelong process that becomes refined and refined further as children grow and develop into adults. Six 'pillars' of character have been identified – trustworthiness, respect, responsibility, fairness, caring and citizenship.

A report [203] by the Master of Wellington College describes research into character formation amongst students in 68 schools in the UK – embracing the role of teachers in developing good character and virtue amongst those students. There is even a 'Character Innovation Fund' that makes character 'awards' to schools and other organisations. In a recent article, [204] the writer pointed out that character education is far from new – referring to William Ellis – a 19th century social reformer and founder of state schools. The journalist pointed out that Ellis offered children "...a broad academic education, the ability to learn independently and the motivation to be happy, useful members of society who could mix intelligence and application with 'sympathy, kindness and humility...'

---

[202] Romans 5:3-4

[203] Professor Sir Anthony Seldon; Character Education In UK Schools; 27 February 2015

[204] A Nod Towards Character Education Is Welcome – Just Don't Start Measuring It; The Guardian; Fiona Millar; 10 March 2015

and in this respect another author has pointed out that '…Three fourths of the people you will ever meet are hungering and thirsting for sympathy…'". [205]

In an article in 2010 (just after the financial crisis), referring to Harvard Business School (HBS), The Economist identified Nitin Nohria as the 'new dean' of HBS. The article went on to say that Mr Nohria's first task was "…to try to restore faith in business generally and in business schools in particular. This means improving two things, he reckons: 'competence' and 'character'…He also wants HBS to renew its commitment to shaping its students' characters as well as their intellects…He supports a movement by students to adopt a business equivalent of the Hippocratic oath…The moral values that business people should adhere to are universal ones, not a professional code…". [206]

"…It is hard to imagine, but even economists used to see their work as being, in the end, about character. Alfred Marshall (1842 – 1924), one of the leading lights of free-market economic theory, said that one of the functions of economics was to examine 'whether the desires which prevail are such as will help to build up a strong and righteous character'. The idea of character was assassinated by woolly 20th century liberalism…". [207]

The anonymous author of Mark reminds us that "…For from within, out of men's hearts, come evil thoughts…". [208] Accordingly, displays of attitude – whether in the form of decisions, behaviour, tone of voice, words or action – reflect not only the character of the person(s) manifesting the display – but also the character of the person(s) reacting. "…It is your character, and your character alone, that will make your life happy or unhappy…if you see no reason for giving thanks, the fault lies only within yourself…". [209]

5.4 Discernment and Choices

The Psalmist prayed "…Teach me knowledge and good judgment…"[210] (which I will define as discernment). I think this is probably a valuable prayer for most of us. Discernment may be considered as the application of wisdom in

---

205 How To Win Friends And Influence People; Dale Carnegie; Pg 182; 2006; Vermilion

206 Schumpeter; A Post-Crisis Study; The Economist; Pg 53; 31 July 2010

207 Richard Reeves; The Right Kind Of Person; Management Today; Pg 23; February 2007

208 Mark 7:21

209 John McCain

210 Psalm 119:66

assessing prevailing circumstances and in deciding which course of action is optimal in those circumstances. Discernment not only points in the direction of what is best – but warns us why we should avoid other courses of action. Scripture advises us why we need discernment – "…I am your servant; give me discernment that I may understand your statutes…".[211]

Attitude is a fundamental part of every human being – not least because it affects our choices/decisions – which in turn affect whether – and if so, how we act and/or react in every circumstance in which we find ourselves throughout our lives. One of the roles of body and mind (see model) is in respect of decision-making. Every single day, we make a vast number of decisions. One author points out that "…most of us see only a tiny fraction of the choices we have…The more you become aware of how many choices are up to you, the more eagerly you embrace your turn. You can practice this today. What will you feed your mind? What thoughts will you dwell on? Whom will you have conversation with? Where will you direct your desires? How will you take care of your body? What act of service will you engage in? When will you choose to be interrupted and when will you stay on task? What will you eat? How will you spend your time? All of these calls you will make and when you add them up, they create your life…".[212]

Although we tend to make fewer important decisions than minor decisions in life, we should not lose sight of the fact that the cumulative effect of small decisions impacts our lives materially – because those decisions say so much about who we are. Accordingly, since we take so many decisions – the attitude we adopt in making them is significant. Naturally, some decisions are quite mundane (another cake?) but some are significant (will I accept this job?). Accordingly, we tend (sub-consciously) to categorise the decisions we make – allocating less time and consideration to those whose consequences are less significant. For the bigger decisions, other criteria come into play – such as whether the decisions are personal or business in nature. Some business decisions are general in nature but some are technical – thereby requiring more research and perhaps input from other specialists. In any event, there comes a point in the decision-making process when – having exhausted the research and/or all other opinions available or considered necessary – one has to choose

---

[211] Psalm 119:125

[212] John Ortberg; When The Game Is Over It All Goes Back In The Box; Pg 72; Zondervan; 2007

a course of action to adopt. Often, decision makers say that they would have liked more time or more background research or more whatever to make the decision easier. For example, consider the processes involved when one company plans to acquire another. There will never be a point in time when all possible information is to hand – because obtaining some information is a lengthy process and might involve huge expense. Therefore, sometimes estimates must be made or the preference to have the information is overtaken by the cost of obtaining it – and on top of that – circumstances change very quickly which means that a decision might have to be made right now – with or without preferred information. There are other situations when the decision point is reached much more quickly than the decision maker might choose – for example in a medical situation when sometimes decisions must be taken immediately if life is to be preserved or if injury to a patient is to be avoided or limited. Clearly, the best decisions are those based on knowledge, previous experience, wisdom and discernment. In any event, what is called for is "…a commitment to take seriously that our previous decisions and actions shape our character, as do the stories and images by which we live…".[213]

As Christians, we often pray less frequently than we ought – but then when faced with difficult decisions or when things are not going well – we pray for guidance and direction. This is not exactly what God intends. One of the ways that we can honour God is by referring all matters to Him – all of the time – whether large or small. He already knows our needs ("…your Father knows what you need before you ask Him…" [214]) – but He still wants us to consult Him – and obedience is one way we can demonstrate humility to our God. This is not least the case when decisions must be made. It is pleasing to God when we humble ourselves before Him and pray for guidance and direction – for discernment from the Holy Spirit. There are many verses in Scripture that refer – here are a few examples:

- "…I know, O Lord, that a man's life is not his own; it is not for a man to direct his own steps…". (Jeremiah 10:23)
- "…Show me Your ways, O Lord; teach me Your paths. Guide me in Your truth and teach me, for You are God my saviour…". (Psalm 25:4)
- "…The Lord will guide you always …". (Isaiah 58:11)

---

[213] James W Fowler; Stages Of Faith; Pg 105; HarperOne; 1981

[214] Matthew 6:8

- "…Trust in the Lord with all your heart and lean not on your own understanding; in all your ways acknowledge Him, and He will make your paths straight…". (Proverbs 3:5)
- "…I will instruct you and teach you in the way you should go; I will counsel you and watch over you…". (Psalm 32:8)

However, when we pray for guidance, it is not usual (although not impossible) to receive a message – verbal or otherwise – containing the Lord's response. Instead, I think the Lord expects us to use all the teaching that we have received until this point in time and to rely on inspiration from Scripture to try to understand what He wants us do in the circumstances about which we are asking for guidance. In this case, the Lord's answer to our request for discernment is to remind us to apply the experience, knowledge and common sense He has given us to do whatever is honouring to Him and in accordance with our Christian character. Scripture says "…The integrity of the upright guides them, but the unfaithful are destroyed by their duplicity…".[215]

When my grandchildren misbehave, they are told by their parents that they have made a bad choice. There is an important lesson here – which is that choice belongs to each of us. Every day we are faced with many situations in which a choice must be made. We have control of that process – but we are responsible for the consequences of the decisions made. Often, we are prone to blame other people for the consequences of our own decisions. We need to be sufficiently mature to understand the significance of this fact.

Note that our ability to make choices may be impaired – or enhanced – by external physical factors that may be significant in influencing the attitude we adopt at a decision point. For example, people who are tired normally think less clearly and have less patience than those who are fresh and well rested – so, if possible, it is better not to make important decisions (or to enter into unnecessary confrontations) when we are tired. In addition, experience tells me that I should never send an email when I am angry (leaving aside for the time being whether I have any right to be angry in the first place). Apart from that, it is preferable (if prevailing circumstances allow it) not to make decisions more quickly than necessary. Further, some people have more patience than others in dealing with difficult circumstances – but someone not so blessed might easily adopt an inappropriate attitude when stressed by people around them or by prevailing

[215] Proverbs 11:3

circumstances. The inference for those in the latter category (which includes me) is clear.

5.5 Summary

Chapter 5 is represented at level 4 of the model. In this chapter, we considered humility (a product of conscience), character (and the influence of sensitivity on character) and thirdly discernment and choices (the source of which is body and mind). Chapter 5 has shown that humility has its origins in our spirit – and is empowered by our conscience. The amount of humility that our characters manifest is dependent upon the amount of influence exerted by our conscience. Similarly, strength of character depends upon the level of sensitivity that we have allowed to be brought to bear in the level of discernment that we apply in making choices. None of this would be possible without the discipline required by human beings in forming a meaningful character. We should now be in a better position to appreciate the fundamental significance of all these components upon the attitudes we adopt in daily living. The implications and ramifications are worthy of consideration. Taking the last chapter and this one together shows something of the complexity, intricacy and quantum of factors that impinge upon attitude. The number of permutations of attitude is difficult to absorb – but the model provides a skeleton on which to focus our thoughts.

The discussion in this chapter on character will continue into chapter 6 – where we will consider what I have called 'Qualities Of Character' – that is to say, the principles, traits and qualities that cumulatively combine to create people of character.

Chapter Six

Qualities of Character

6.1 Introduction

One of the reasons why attitude is significant is that – ultimately – it determines our behaviour and reflects who we are as individuals. In our efforts to find out more about who we are, we have gone right back to the fundamentals of our humanity. We are mortal beings. Secondly, we looked at which parts of our human framework will last throughout eternity – spirit and soul and we looked also at our body/mind that will perish and return to dust. Then we considered certain components of the composition of mankind. In this respect, we looked at the role of the human spirit in creating high levels of conscience and which in turn produces humility. Secondly, we looked at the production of enhanced levels of sensitivity by the soul and lastly, discipline produced by the human body and mind and the consequent effect on discernment and choices.

In chapter 5, we pointed to the significance of character in the attitude formation process – and we want to think about that further in chapter 6 as we identify the qualities that make a character robust. Character is ultimately the product of an immortal soul and spirit working through our mind/body. Attitude is a truly accurate mirror of our innermost being because attitude influences the choices we make as a result of our humility and character – the key drivers in determining the significance we attach to discernment. The choices we make flow from this process. These choices and the discernment with which they are made emanate from our mind and reflect (inter alia) the status of our spirit and soul.

In chapter 6, we will probe character a little further by taking a look at some of the principles, traits and qualities that produce the sort of character that was described in chapter 5. The diagram of the model has been extended to include level 5. (It is worth noting that what I have referred to as 'qualities of character' have received much wider attention. For example – "...Character Strengths and Virtues: A Handbook and Classification presented the intellectual foundation, measurement strategies, and organising framework that is the VIA [Values In Action Institute] Classification of Character Strengths Virtues. The Classification identifies 24 strengths of character that are nested under six higher order categories called virtues...".[216])

Let's look at level 6 of the model and consider the following qualities of character: Principles, Traits and Habits and Qualities per se.

Figure Six	Model 5

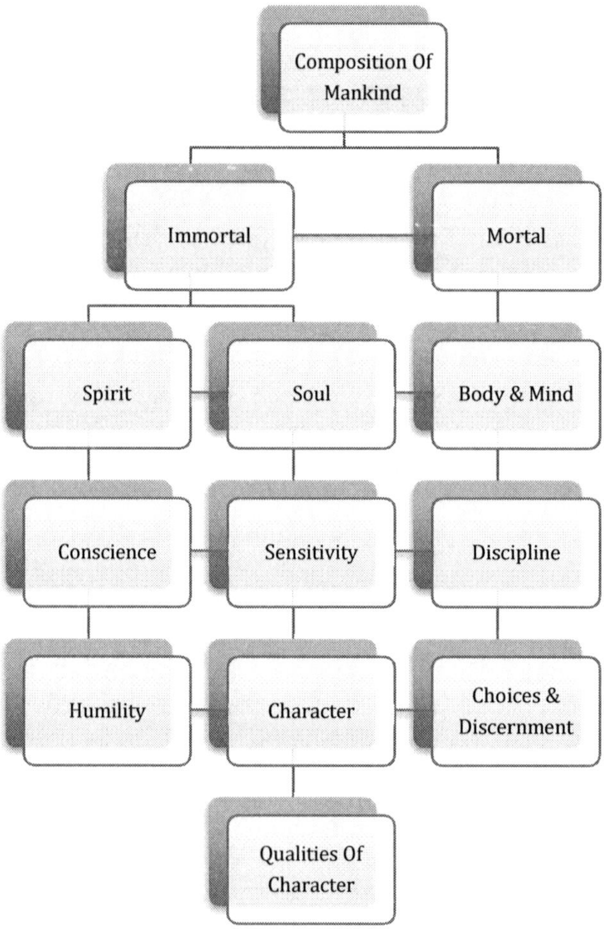

[216] Shannon Polly & Kathryn Britton; Character Strengths Matter; Pg 3; Positive Psychology News LLC; 2015

6.2 Principles Vis Á Vis Rules

One author has said "...Principles are guidelines for human conduct that are proven to have enduring, permanent value. They're fundamental...".[217] Another author has written "...Principles, of course are different from rules, customs or laws. Principles, we might say, are the abstract, generalizable guidelines and tests by which particular actions, laws or social policies may be made or evaluated...". [218] It has been said elsewhere that "...Principles are like lighthouses. They are natural laws that cannot be broken..."[219] and somewhere else it has been said "...These principles are part of most every major enduring religion, as well as enduring social philosophies and ethical systems. They are self-evident and can easily be validated by any individual. It's almost as if these principles or natural laws are part of the human condition, part of the human consciousness, part of the human conscience. They seem to exist in all human beings, regardless of social conditioning and loyalty to them, even though they might be submerged or numbed by such conditions or disloyalty...".[220] It seems that "...without a positive attitude you can't activate the other principles. Your success in life begins and ends with your attitude...". [221]

While Holy Scripture contains much helpful advice and guidance for living the Christian way, it does not (unsurprisingly) attempt to describe every possible scenario that we might encounter in our lives. There are some specific instructions but because the permutations in life are so many and so varied, the Bible contains many foundational principles and guidance as opposed to particular approaches to particular situations in all cases. One observer has remarked "...I expected to find in the New Testament dogma and doctrine on every page and unjustified dictats as to what I 'ought' to believe...".[222] Scripture is not a rulebook per se. Instead, Scripture provides us with what we might describe as 'principles' – to guide us in how we might choose to act in various types of circumstances. That said, there are many helpful verses in Scripture

---

[217] Stephen Covey; The Seven Habits Of Highly Effective People; Pg 43; Simon & Schuster; 1989;

[218] James W Fowler; Stages Of Faith; Pg 83; Harper One; 1981

[219] Stephen Covey; The Seven Habits Of Highly Effective People; Pg 41; Simon & Schuster; 1989

[220] Stephen Covey; The Seven Habits Of Highly Effective People; Pg 42; Simon & Schuster; 1989

[221] Jeff Keller; Attitude Is Everything; Pg 16; Attitude Is Everything Inc; 2012

[222] Peter May; The Search For God & The Path To Persuasion; Pg 179; Malcolm Down Publishing; 2016

about which we should be aware because they are specific instructions. There are too many to list in the text one by one but some examples have been provided in Appendix Three. Principles are foundational to attitude – and as we have seen, attitude determines action. Accordingly, principles are significant.

With respect to rules – it is frequently asserted that being a Christian infers that one has to satisfy a plethora of them. While tradition points to 613 commandments, "...There is no single definitive list that explicates the 613 commandments...".[223] In fact, more people are likely to be aware of the Ten Commandments than are likely to be aware of the 613 commandments. In writing about the Ten Commandments, Dallas Willard suggests that they "...really aren't very popular anywhere. This is so in spite of the fact that even a fairly general practice of them would lead to a solution of nearly every problem of meaning and order now facing Western societies. They are God's best information on how to lead a basically decent human existence...".[224] It is interesting that God has chosen not to set out a plethora of rules – presumably because we might be misled into thinking that adherence to such rules would guarantee us a place in His kingdom. This seems to be the sort of theology practised by the Pharisees that we read about in the New Testament. God does not want that sort of response – rather He says "...I will put my law in their minds and write it on their hearts...".[225] John Ortberg says "...my spiritual maturity is not measured by following rules...".[226] Once the Christian's heart dictates his/her attitude, the less the need for rules – because at that stage – the Christian is living in accordance with God's plan as that is what is natural to him/her. Like a road map, Principles help us by providing general guidance on the terrain – but they do not identify every small detail that makes up the landscape. Consider the following 3 Principles: Standards, Values and Virtues.

6.2.1 Standards

The English Oxford Living Dictionaries define 'standards' as "...principles of conduct informed by notions of honour and decency...". The definition complements the previous discussion in demonstrating the link between principles and conduct. Clearly principles inform conduct – which in turn

[223] 613 Commandments; Wikipedia
[224] Dallas Willard; The Divine Conspiracy; Pg 66; William Collins; 2014
[225] Jeremiah 31:33
[226] John Ortberg; The Me I Want To Be; Pg 20; Zondervan; 2010

demonstrates the link between principles and character. Where principles are informed by traits such as honour and decency, the value of standards in the formation of character will be optimised.

6.2.2 Values

In this case, the English Oxford Living Dictionaries define 'values' as "...principles or standards of behaviour; one's judgement of what is important in life...". Once again, there is a good fit between this definition and the previous discussion on the centrality of principles within behaviour – a product of conscience. One author believes that "...The grounding of ultimate values lies in the eternal nature and character of God Himself. It is God who is good, just, merciful, faithful, compassionate and kind...".[227] Later on (in chapter 8), the text comments on the nature and character of God.

6.2.3 Virtues

Stated simplistically, virtue might be considered as doing the right thing and avoiding doing the wrong thing. The Cambridge English Dictionary defines virtue as "...a good moral quality in a person, or the general quality of being morally good..." while the English Oxford Dictionaries define it as "...behaviour showing high moral standards...". One writer clarifies that "...right actions done for the wrong reasons do not help to build the internal quality or character called a 'virtue', and it is this quality or character that really matters...".[228] Someone else has said "...a virtue when it is acquired, becomes a relatively stable feature for our characters and leads to relevant motivation and behaviour over an extended period of time...".[229]

Stassen and Gushie have said that "...Many are urging Christian ethics to shift its focus much more toward virtues and the formation of character, and away from rules and principles. They argue that it is not enough to teach rules and principles about right and wrong; we need to nurture the kind of character and virtues that lead people actually to do the right thing and avoid the wrong. Deeds are right or wrong; persons are virtuous or not virtuous. Virtues are defined as qualities of a person that make that person a good person in

---

[227] Peter May; The Search For God & The Path To Persuasion; Pg 22; Malcolm Down Publishing; 2016;

[228] C S Lewis; Mere Christianity: Pg 80; HarperCollins; 1952

[229] Christian B Miller; The Character Gap; Pg 13; Oxford University Press; 2018

community, and that contribute to the good of the community, or to the good that humans are designed for. They are qualities of character – or the qualities that lead to making someone a good person. For example, a good person has integrity and seeks justice…". [230]

6.3 Traits and Habits

The Cambridge Dictionary says that a trait is a particular characteristic that can produce a particular type of behaviour. Traits may distinguish us from other people – and they can be positive or negative.

Although it is only part of this bigger matter we are considering, as Christians we should not underestimate the significance of the actions that we take most often – frequently referred to as 'habits'. In this respect, John Ortberg says "…Our only hope is not for more willpower; it is for a new set of habits…". [231] One such habit is prayer.

Habits are significant because by definition, they are actions that we take regularly. If our habits are inappropriate, our character will be affected. "…Our character, basically, is a composite of our habits…". [232] Earlier (Para 3.5), we considered a quote that said "…So, if everything is working right, if you are as God created you to be, then… My habits would line up with my values…" If we can exercise adequate control over those actions that are repeated most often, then our attitude will be reflected by a good character.

6.3.1 A Positive Disposition

A positive disposition is an extremely effective backdrop to living a life that has principles at its fulcrum. One author has said "…Without a positive attitude, you can't activate the other principles. Your success in life begins and ends with your attitude…". [233]

Another author has summed up well what sort of difference a positive disposition can make when he said "…There is very little difference in people –

---

[230] Glen H Stassen and David P Gushie; Kingdom Ethics: Following Jesus in Contemporary Context; Pg 32; Downers Grove, IL: InterVarsity Press; 2003 – as quoted in C Marvin Pate; From Plato to Jesus; Pg 276; Kregel Publications; 2011

[231] John Ortberg; Soul Keeping; Pg 150; Zondervan; 2014

[232] Stephen Covey; The Seven Habits Of Highly Effective People; Pg 54; Simon & Schuster; 2013

[233] Jeff Keller; Attitude Is Everything; Pg 16: Attitude Is Everything Inc; 2012

but that little difference makes a big difference. The little difference is attitude – the big difference is whether it is positive or negative…”.[234] One of the implications in adopting a negative approach is that it is cumulative. Soon, we risk seeing everything with a jaundiced eye – and as if that is not bad enough, frequently we fail to realise our approach until someone points it out – that is if someone points it out. In such circumstances, our reaction is likely to be adverse. We do not like being called to account – and most people avoid pointing out anything negative to anyone else – irrespective of the length or depth of their friendship – in case they are met with hostility leading to a lost friendship. We have such high opinions of ourselves and take ourselves so seriously that we cannot easily contemplate getting anything wrong. Hardly a humble approach. Growth is not possible in a life devoid of principles.

It seems that we might benefit from conducting some objective self-appraisal on a regular basis. As noted elsewhere, there are relatively few large decisions to be made in life – but there are lots of more minor decisions that need to be made on a daily basis – and it is the cumulative effect of these that should not be underestimated. Aristotle is attributed with the words – “…We are what we repeatedly do. Excellence then is not an act but a habit…”. The repetitive element in habits is what makes them so influential.

In this respect, Scripture reminds us that “…The good man brings good things out of the good stored up in him, and the evil man brings evil things out of the evil stored up in him. But I tell you that men will have to give account on the day of judgement for every careless word they have spoken. For by your words you will be acquitted, and by your words you will be condemned…”.[235] Sometimes, it may be necessary to risk a friendship by asking people to consider their own lives and assessing whether and to what extent those lives continue to reflect the Christian way. The stakes are high. This is no light matter and should be approached with great care and sensitivity.

6.4 Qualities

The Free Dictionary defines a quality as an inherent or distinguishing characteristic; a property. Consider the importance of the qualities described below:

---

[234] Quoted by S Daniels in an article “The Nature Of Work Is Changing”; Banking Ireland; Volume 100; No 2; Summer 1998

[235] Matthew 12:35-37

6.4.1 Integrity

It is important to understand the meaning of each of the qualities we are dealing with – and integrity is no different in this respect. Like so many personal attributes, integrity is not easy to define – but it has much to do with morality and is a pillar of character. The writer of Chronicles says "…I know my God, that You test the heart and are pleased with integrity…".[236] A concise short working definition is that integrity means doing the right thing. Character is at its finest when to act with integrity is not to a person's advantage and yet that person does the right thing. The word integrity is frequently used to describe behaviour – as in "…she is a person of complete integrity…". We mean by this that the person being described can be relied upon to do what she has committed to do, to act fairly and reasonably – and in accordance with high moral standards – in a true and honest way. Doing the 'right thing' is clearly important – but how do we know what the right thing is in a particular set of circumstances? Stealing is not right but not all actions are as clear-cut as stealing. How do we know what to do when there is more than one option – and none might be described as "bad"? There is no easy answer – but our conscience and sensitivity have capacity to influence our decision – which means that to be at their most effective, neither our conscience nor our ability to be sensitive must be allowed to become dulled through insufficient use. Notice the inter-play between conscience, character, behaviour, decisions and principles. They all interface with each other – they are complementary.

A person who behaves with integrity conducts him/herself in accordance with the same self-imposed standards – whether anyone else is aware or not. It doesn't matter whether anyone else is there – or that no one will ever find out or become aware of our behaviour. The acid test is whether we would feel in any way embarrassed if the whole matter was described in detail on the front page of a newspaper. Doing the right thing (as the definition suggests) requires much more than simply doing the easiest thing – in fact doing the right thing often means the thing that is not easiest – which infers a personal cost. Integrity and discipline go hand in hand. It takes discipline to behave 'properly' – at all times. Consider the case of Job "…Then the Lord said to Satan, 'Have you considered my servant job? There is no one on earth like him; he is blameless and upright, a man who fears God and shuns evil. And he still maintains his integrity, though

[236] 1 Chronicles 29:17

you incited me against him to ruin him without any reason.'..."[237] Integrity says much about who we are – for example – integrity means that when talking in a group scenario, we avoid saying negative things about people not present. One author has said "...One of the most important ways to manifest integrity is to be loyal to those who are not present...".[238]

When we consider how many of all the people we know could be described as people of integrity, I wouldn't be surprised that there are not so many. It sometimes seems that there are fewer people who behave with integrity today than at any other time in history. "...Integrity is much bigger than simply avoiding breaking the rules. It is becoming the kind of person who does the right thing. Integrity does not mean that I get really good at not doing the things I really want to do. It is not using lots of willpower to override my desires. It means I become the kind of person who actually wants to do what is right...".[239] However, I suspect the perception that there are fewer people who behave with integrity today is exacerbated because we are accustomed to hearing regularly about so many people in all walks of life who have demonstrated a lack of integrity. We are pummelled with all sorts of stories – involving scandals that include politicians; cyclists; footballers; entrepreneurs; entertainers – and sometimes, entire countries that have demonstrated lack of integrity. Why should this be? There are probably many reasons – but here are just two for consideration: (1) as human beings, our very nature is sinful and (2) we are totally undisciplined – and very prone to take the easy way out – often through lying. Faced with two choices, we will inevitably choose the easier option – or the option that is least detrimental to ourselves. This type of approach has led to a very sad state of world affairs – and this trend is progressively worsening. There are huge implications. For example – I wonder whether the 2008 global financial crisis (see Para 6.4.2 below) would have happened – or would have continued as long as it did – if everyone involved had behaved with integrity? "...The greatness of a man is not in how much wealth he acquires, but in his integrity and his ability to affect those around him positively...".[240]

Christians must behave with integrity if their attitude is to be appropriate.

---

[237] Job 2:3

[238] Stephen Covey; The 7 Habits Of Highly Effective People; Pg 206; Simon & Schuster; 1989

[239] John Ortberg; When The Game Is Over It All Goes Back In The Box; Pg 119; Zondervan; 2007

[240] Bob Marley (no other source information available)

6.4.2 Honesty

One author has made a startling observation in saying that "…one thing does seem to be consistently missing from most of us – the virtue of honesty…".[241] Meanwhile, another author has suggested "…human beings are, by and large, more moral than standard economic theory predicts…".[242] Everyone knows that honesty means telling the truth – but is that all there is to it? There is an argument to be made that honesty means much more – for example "…dishonesty is a prime example of our irrational tendencies. It's pervasive; we don't instinctively understand how it works its magic on us; and, most important, we don't see it in ourselves…".[243] Attitude beware!

It's not so difficult to mislead somebody else if one chooses not to tell the whole truth – and sometimes not being totally honest creates certain advantages at the time – and in this sort of scenario a huge moral dilemma might arise – so being honest includes not misleading people. Further at times, we might try to convince ourselves that the situation in which we are is not a life or death situation so a 'little white lie' or a 'fib' isn't serious and therefore is not really dishonesty. "…I believe that all of us continuously try to identify the line where we can benefit from dishonesty without damaging our own self-image…".[244] This is where conscience and character come into play – reminding us that whatever form it takes, cheating constitutes dishonesty.

Cheating is the opposite of honesty – whether in the form of a lie, a fabrication, a denial, opacity, or a fib. Violations of honesty include: fraud; corruption; breaches of the law such as tax evasion or breaching the conditions of a licence (e.g. failure to pay a licence fee to watch television). Honesty and integrity go hand in hand. Behaving honestly means acting transparently – not deceiving other people directly (for example by telling a lie) or indirectly (for example by telling the truth – but not the whole truth). Honesty is what prevents people from claiming more expenses than they are due – or from pretending to be sick if they merely don't feel like going to work. Honesty means telling someone that they have given you too much change. It means not dodging the fare on public transport and conducting one's income tax affairs with probity and candour. There are doubtless many other examples of what it means to be honest

---

[241] Christian B Miller; The Character Gap; Oxford University Press; Pg 114; 2018
[242] Dan Ariely; The (Honest) Truth About Dishonesty; Pg 238; Harper; 2012
[243] Dan Ariely; The (Honest) Truth About Dishonesty; Pg 254; Harper; 2012
[244] Dan Ariely; The (Honest) Truth About Dishonesty; Pg 28; Harper; 2012

– but these few will give a flavour of what we are talking about – and which have an effect on daily life. That said, these examples are hardly necessary – we all have a really good idea what honesty means. The problem is not misunderstanding, it is the application.

Sometimes, to be honest might mean causing someone else hurt. This might be described as being 'brutally honest' (and should be avoided if possible). For example – when explaining what we think, we need to couch what we say sensitively in order to be true to our personal credo but simultaneously avoiding causing offence whenever possible. Note that this is not the same as lying about what we believe – it's using empathy in speaking about what we believe. Christians must be honest.

If honesty has implications for us as individuals – it has even more impact on communities as a whole. One person acting dishonestly is bad enough but the implications are compounded when groups of people or whole communities do so in concert. This is often difficult to 'police' – but in some matters, society requires governments to create organisations to ensure that service providers are held responsible for their conduct (and that of their employees) – by acting in accordance with their mandate. Take financial services companies as examples. All other things being equal, organisations that accept money from the public – and use it until repayment is requested by the owner – are only able to conduct such business if they have an appropriate licence. Their mandate requires them to act in accordance with the conditions attached to that licence. Governments establish regulatory authorities to 'police' the activities of licensees and to ensure they do not breach the rules. The whole point is that the authorities set certain standards and impose certain safeguards to ensure – so far as it is possible – that when repayment is requested – the money is available to hand back to whomever owns it. Although money is not the key issue with other licensed organisations, some of the same principles apply – for example – hospitals, airlines, police forces and other organisations serving the public. That is to say, the greater the 'duty of care' to the public, the greater the need to have controls in place to protect the public. The public has little option than to trust the provider of these types of services to perform their role diligently – exercising care to protect those relying upon them – so there is a need to enforce the rules to ensure that protection is not impaired by breaches or by deliberate manipulation. Naturally, deficiencies in the standard of care provided can arise from human error – but it can also arise from dishonesty and malpractice.

The 2008 financial crisis is a case in point. As it turned out, 'human issues' were material factors in the crisis as it unravelled. Questions arose concerning the extent to which the attitude and management style of some senior bankers contributed to the crisis and as more information came to light, it seems that greed, mismanagement and failure to adhere to the principles of both personal and corporate governance played a material part in the crisis. The connectivity and overlapping of technical factors coupled with the complexity of the human dimension – interwoven with matters of morality and trust gave rise to serious systemic challenges that regulatory oversight was unable to remedy. People did not behave honestly. Still on financial matters, in an article about financial crime in The Economist in 2015, the text said "...On May 20th a consortium of American and British government agencies announced settlements with six international banks regarding claims that they had manipulated currency markets...As one of them [the employees involved] wrote in a chat session '...If you ain't [sic] cheating, you ain't trying...'...Admitting to criminal behaviour in America was once a guarantee of bankruptcy...another multinational bank, admitted to charges related to its clients' tax evasion last year, but received waivers from various regulators that allowed it to stay in business...".[245] Such reports make it seem that dishonesty is less significant but no less prevalent than it used to be.

Note that the need for honesty applies not only to individuals or to those who owe a duty of care to members of the public. Honesty also applies to wider social behaviour – sport for example. We are all too aware of controversy after controversy arising where athletes from a range of disciplines (including cycling, gymnastics, swimming and tennis) have been accused of enhancing their performance through the use of banned substances. "...On March 5th [2018], a parliamentary committee published a report on doping which found 'acute failures in several different organisations in athletics and cycling'...".[246] Even more recently – "...Michel Platini, the former UEFA president, has been arrested over the controversial vote which handed the 2022 World Cup to Qatar. The former France captain, who was part of the FIFA tournament organising

---

[245] Financial Crime – Unsettling Settlements; The Economist; Pg 65; 23 May 2015
[246] "Faster, Stronger...Higher?"; The Economist; Pg 31; 10 March 2018

committee, was taken into custody by French officers as part of an investigation by the Anti-Corruption Office of the Judicial Police (OCLCIFF)…" [247]

"…Not so for all sportsmen and women. Take the (2009) case of Rebecca Adlington (who won 2 gold swimming medals in Beijing in 2008). The headline in a Times article read 'Fair Play To Rebecca Adlington, A Champion Of Honesty'. The article said she was 'the voice of reason' – describing her decision not to wear a performance enhancing swimsuit…because she thinks it is cheating – even though it's legal and will help her go faster…and in doing so, has broken the modern sporting code, by which athletes cheat, lie and con their way to the top…The truth is cheating is an intrinsic part of sport…".[248] Regrettably, the era when a man or a woman's word was their bond has long since gone. Why have we lost sight of the old values of probity, candour, honesty and integrity – it's not because they don't work – it's because we are insufficiently disciplined to make them work.

6.4.3 Trust

Trust can be considered as confidence that another person will do what (s)he says or as the Merriam Webster dictionary says, trust is "…assured reliance on the character, ability, strength, or truth of someone or something…".

Sadly, most of us are more used to people not following through on their promises and/or commitments. In order to protect ourselves from disappointment, we just assume that the other person will not deliver as promised – and often we come to this conclusion on the basis of that person's past performance.

As Christians, we have huge responsibilities in this area. One author believes that "…Central among the qualities that make and keep humans is our capacity for trust and fidelity…".[249] We must mean what we say and also say what we mean. We should never give our word lightly (especially to a child) – because to do so breaches the trust that the other person has in us – and this is particularly offensive when we disappoint a child. Our word must be our bond. The rule of thumb is if you can't be sure – don't promise. We often hear in American movies

---

[247] "Former UEFA president Michel Platini detained by police over awarding of 2022 World Cup to Qatar"; Tom Morgan and Henry Samuel; The Telegraph; 18 June 2019

[248] "Fair Play To Rebecca Adlington, A Champion Of Honesty"; Timesonline; 21 July 2009

[249] James W Fowler; Stages Of Faith; Pg 292; Harper One; 1981

one actor telling another that everything will be all right – adding gratuitously "I promise". We cannot make promises that we have no idea whether we will be able to keep or not – it is irresponsible and foolish to do so. The trouble is "...dramatic commitments receive most of our attention, but the routine and unspoken commitments are the ones that drive our lives...".[250]

Trust is a fundamental factor in the Christian experience. Scripture says "...faith is being sure of what we hope for and certain of what we do not see...".[251] Christians trust in their Saviour – by faith. The difference between a Christian's trust and that applicable amongst human beings is that with Christ, there is no chance whatsoever that our trust has been misplaced or that we are in jeopardy or at risk that we will be disappointed or let down. Jesus Christ epitomises trust.

I want to be known and remembered as trustworthy – trusted not to break a confidence, trusted to do what I have committed to do, trusted to do to the best that my ability allows – in whatever I undertake to do, trusted not to lie, trusted that I am worthy of the confidence that people choose to place in me. I still have some way to go to achieve all this – but I have started – what about you?

6.4.4 Gratitude

By way of definition, "...gratitude is the return justly required from the objects of His (God's) beneficence; yet it is often withheld from our great Benefactor simply because His goodness is so constant and so abundant...".[252] "...We feel better when we are grateful because the fundamental mind-set of the life of the soul is gratitude..."[253] Gratitude is an outward expression of humility. It is not possible to express gratitude in the absence of humility – and that may explain why it is so difficult for many people to be grateful.

Someone (unattributed) – but very wise – has observed that "Yesterday is history, tomorrow is a mystery, today is a gift of God, which is why we call it the present." Why are we not grateful for today – for everyone and everything in it – for the blessing of life and for all that Almighty God has done for us and is doing at this very moment? Scripture enjoins us to "...consider what great things

---

250 John Ortberg; When The Game Is Over It All Goes Back In The Box; Pg 101; Zondervan; 2007

251 Hebrews 11:1

252 A W Pink; The Attributes of God; Loc 1122; Chapel Library Resources; 1993

253 John Ortberg; Soul Keeping; Pg 170; Zondervan; 2014

He has done for you…”.[254] According to one author, “…The truth is, all of us get so caught up in ourselves that we too often don’t take the time to be grateful – to God and to others…”.[255]

Perhaps one of the most moving stories in the New Testament is the parable of the ten men who were suffering from leprosy. These men were in a terrible plight – ostracised and alone with no one to look after them or to attend to even their smallest needs. They were forced to leave their homes and villages and they were required to shout out when they saw other people – to warn them to keep away in case they also contracted the disease. They were without hope and without help. How terrible was their existence! Then one day, completely out of the blue (as far as they were concerned), Jesus came across them. He didn’t flinch or walk away or pretend He hadn’t noticed them. Instead He approached them and spoke to them – and miraculously cured all ten of them. What a miracle! Note what happened next. Only one of the ten men came back to say thank you. Luke tells us that “… Jesus asked, ‘Were not all ten cleansed? Where are the other nine? Was no one found to return and give praise to God except this foreigner…?’”[256] In Luke’s words, you can almost feel Christ’s disappointment at the ingratitude of the nine. This parable indicates the importance that Christ attaches to expressing gratitude. We are told to “…be thankful…”[257] and to “…Give thanks to the God of heaven…”.[258]

We all have so much for which we ought to be thankful – but for Christians in particular, “…as you received Christ Jesus as Lord, continue to live in Him, rooted and built up in Him, strengthened in the faith as you were taught, and overflowing with thankfulness…”[259] <u>Each day should begin with thanking God for all that He has done for us and each day should end with a similar expression of gratitude.</u> Throughout each day, we should take a moment to say thank you Lord for all You have done and all that You are doing – and all that You will do for me. <u>Take every opportunity to thank those around us for all they do for us – even if it is just opening the door.</u> When was the last time you thanked someone for preparing a meal for you – or for laying food down on a table in front of you – or for washing and/or pressing your clothes? It doesn’t take a great deal of

---

[254] 1 Samuel 12:24
[255] John Ortberg; Soul Keeping; Pg 170; Zondervan; 2014
[256] Luke 17:18
[257] Colossians 3:15
[258] Psalm 136:26
[259] Colossians 2:6

effort to show gratitude or to encourage people – provided you are sufficiently sensitive. "...We pray for the big things and forget to give thanks for the ordinary, small (and yet really not small) gifts. How can God entrust great things to one who will not thankfully receive from Him the little things?..."[260] One writer has said "...Gratitude is the gift that God gives us that enables us to be blessed by all His other gifts, the way our taste buds enable us to enjoy the gift of food. Without gratitude, our lives degenerate into envy, dissatisfaction, and complaints, taking what we have for granted and always wanting more...".[261]

We all like to be appreciated – every last one of us. "...Let the Word of Christ dwell in you richly as you teach and admonish one another with all wisdom, and as you sing psalms, hymns and spiritual songs with gratitude in your hearts to God..."[262] <u>Let's try to cultivate an attitude of gratitude in worship of our loving Saviour and in service of our fellow men and women.</u> "...Praise the Lord, O my soul, and forget not all His benefits..."[263] and "...Be joyful always; pray continually; give thanks in all circumstances, for this is God's will for you in Christ Jesus...".[264]

"...The great secret joy in life – the prize that we think getting richer will bring us – is the ecstasy of gratitude. Gratitude is how those rich toward God – rich in *being*, not just *having* – play the game...".[265]

6.5 Summary

I suspect that some readers might think this is all just pie in the sky – that it would be nice if it was feasible – but in fact, all this is little more than fantasy and that all the words we distinguished mean roughly the same thing. It might be argued that it is just not possible for people to adopt all the principles, traits and characteristics described above as part of daily living. If this is what you believe, please allow me to differ.

---

[260]20 Influential Quotes by Dietrich Bonhoeffer; Emily Maust WoodCrosswalk.com

[261] John Ortberg; When The Game Is Over It All Goes Back In The Box; Pg 149; Zondervan; 2007

[262] Colossians 3:16

[263] Psalm 103:2

[264] 1 Thessalonians 5:16-18

[265] John Ortberg; When The Game Is Over It All Goes Back In The Box; Pg 74; Zondervan; 2007

By way of (indirect) example of how human behaviour changes, remember that not all that long ago, many people believed that it would be impossible to convince everyone to wear seat belts. It was anticipated that despite this being for their own good, people would just not conform – even if legislation required it! It was a good idea some thought – but totally unenforceable so it was no more than 'pie in the sky'. Consider what happened next. It is virtually inconceivable today for anyone getting into a car not to 'buckle up'. In fact, this is the first thing we do when we get into a car – it's an automatic action. So – human behaviour can be changed – if there is a willingness to change it. Take another example. More recently, it was suggested that it would be well-nigh impossible to stop people smoking in pubs and other public places. People would just not stand for it we were told. It would be completely unworkable. This was tradition for some people – the habit of a lifetime. Consider what happened next. Today, there is a general prohibition with respect to smoking in pubs and public places. Smoking in public places is no longer acceptable behaviour – forcing many office workers to go outside their building if they want to smoke. In addition, in some cases, they may not smoke within a certain distance of the building. This is another example of the potential that exists to change human behaviour. The fundamental criterion for success is that there must be willingness to change – because nothing changes if nothing changes.

Accordingly, I don't believe that encouraging people to live differently from how they live currently is a waste of effort. Why should it be any less successful than encouraging people to wear seat-belts or stop smoking in public places? Here is the difficulty – if I want things to change – that change process must begin with me – and you – in our respective environment! Are you willing to accept this challenge and live your life according to the types of principles and traits and qualities described above? If so, I think this might just catch on – maybe one person at a time. This type of behaviour might be infectious. When people see the changes brought about by someone living a life with principles at its centre, I think they will want some of the same. "...Nothing can stop the man with the right mental attitude from achieving his goal. Nothing on earth can help the man with the wrong attitude...". [266]

This chapter has looked deeply into 'Character'. In doing so, we have thought about types of principles and traits and qualities (howsoever one may care to

[266] Thomas Jefferson as quoted by Jeff Keller; Attitude Is Everything; Pg 1; Attitude Is Everything Inc; 2012

define them or to categorise them). These are transformational catalysts in adopting attitudes that will change individuals and societies – not only locally but globally as well. They can be applied cross culturally and do not depend upon race or religion. They are however difficult aspirations – and like everything else worth doing – they are demanding. The good thing is that the types of approaches described require only willingness. Successful adoption of principles, traits and qualities is an important step in adopting the right attitude. It is important to remember that perfection is not the goal – the goal is continuous improvement. The principles, traits and qualities described are not unattainable for those who consider that the cost is worth the benefit. Accordingly, this all boils down to one question – are you willing to review your attitude and assess it with reference to the principles, traits and qualities that this chapter has been considering? The next chapter (7) continues with character at its centre and concludes this part of the discussion with a brief overview of other influences.

Chapter Seven
Other Influences

7.1 Introduction

The text began with a sober reminder of the immortal and the mortal dimensions of humankind. We noted the two immortal elements of our being – spirit and soul – and also the mortal component – body and mind. This is where the attitude formation process begins. If at this stage we recognise the eternal significance of spirit and soul, the effect on the attitudes we accept thereafter will be to move us in the direction in which our life's contribution sits comfortably with God's plans. If, however, the significance eludes us for whatever reason, we will never achieve the potential for great things that Almighty God has given to us.

After that, we considered a number of components that influence our attitudes – including conscience, sensitivity and discipline. Then, we introduced character – a central component in the maturing of our attitudes – and we considered 3 qualities of character (principles, traits and habits and lastly qualities.) In turn 'principles' comprise standards, values and virtues while 'qualities' include integrity, honesty, trust and gratitude). It is important to note that all these components might be defined or categorised in ways that are different from the way they are treated in this text. The most important point is that their definition and categorisation is not so important as is appreciation of their significance. It's a matter of substance over form.

We considered humility as a particularly potent source of influence on our character – and we noted how the processes we adopt in making decisions in our body/mind are affected by all the components discussed thus far.

Consider the model below – expanded to include the final level (7) – in anticipation of reading this chapter. Chapter 7 looks at five other influences on attitude: (1) Experience; (2) Environment; (3) Expectations; (4) Perceptions and (5) Other Stimuli or Trigger Events.

Figure Seven	Model 6

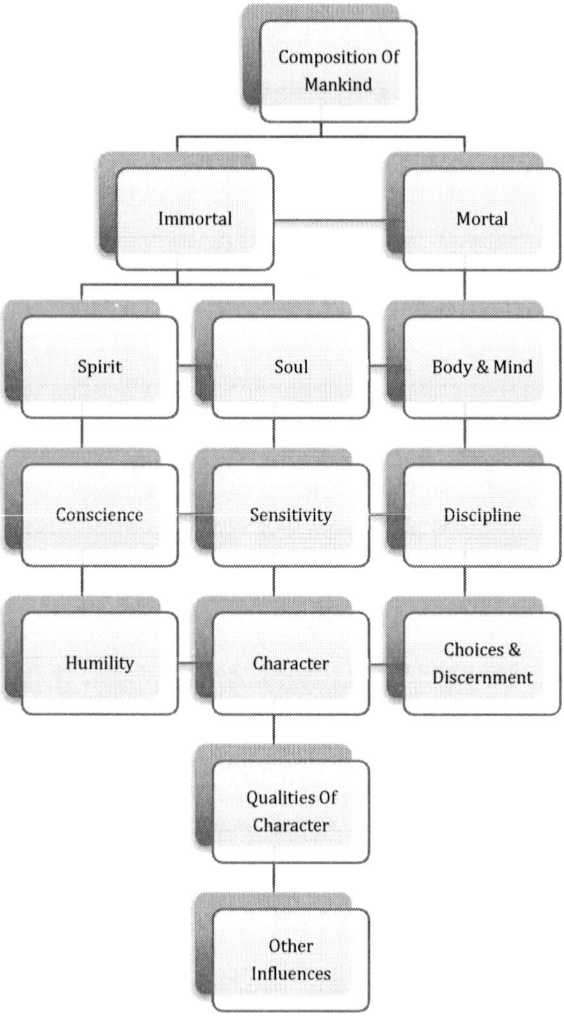

7.2 Experience

Our experiences in life have a profound effect on how we perceive everything. Accordingly, experience is very meaningful. "…Think of your attitude as the mental filter through which you experience the world…your attitude affects the way you see everything in your life…". [267] The narrower our experiences in life, the smaller our frame of reference in interpreting events as they unfold around us. It follows that if our experiences are wider, then the

[267] Jeff Keller; Attitude Is Everything; Pgs 12 and 14; Attitude Is Everything Inc; 2012

greater the likelihood that we will be more 'grounded' and that we will reach conclusions by reference to a more meaningful set of criteria. Accordingly, opportunities to broaden experience should be welcomed.

For example, living and working somewhere other than where we were born can be a potent factor in enhancing our experiences in the process of maturing. Such experiences are likely to expose us to different approaches to life within a cultural environment that is not the one into which we were born. In addition, ethnicity and culture may be strong drivers in forming attitudes. For example, we don't all live in the same climatic conditions – and this affects many aspects of living – including what we wear and when we wear it; what we eat (and don't eat); the language(s) we speak – and how we communicate. Some of us live in more hostile economic environments than others – and how we manage our economic resources – whatever the quantum – may be a material influence in forming our perspectives. In addition, social norms are not standardised globally – for example a friendly gesture in one country might have a completely different meaning in another country. Accordingly, mixing with people who hold different views or whose work and background are different from ours, provides very valuable opportunities to broaden our perspectives – and all the more so if we are exposed to such experiences somewhere other than where we were born.

This means that when we develop a view, we should remember that our perception is based (inter alia) on our experiences – and these are peculiar to each of us as individuals. This infers that <u>a degree of tolerance is required in being open to explore the views of others – based on their respective background and circumstances.</u> We should respect those experiences – and not jump to conclusions about who is right and who is wrong – because often right and wrong have more than one dimension. Some maturity is required to be able to ask oneself whether our attitude to what we consider to be a problem is in fact contributing to a failure to resolve it. Mark Twain said "...when I was a boy of fourteen, my father was so ignorant, I could hardly stand to have the old man around. But when I got to be twenty-one, I was astonished at how much he had learned in seven years...". Experience is invaluable to our development and maturity – but <u>our mind must be sufficiently receptive to allow experience to affect our attitude.</u>

While it is not the norm for everyone to go and live somewhere other than where they were born, there is more than one way to enhance experience. One such is to <u>speak less and to listen more.</u> Someone very clever has suggested that there is a reason we have two ears and only one mouth. We discussed above how frenetic life has become. One of the implications is that communication has sped up – leaving less time for meaningful conversation. This is a great shame because there is much to be learned from listening to others – and thereby increasing our experience and knowledge. That said, listening is a skill in itself. It has to be learned – and the process can be difficult – especially for those of us who are more loquacious or less patient than the rest of us. We should not underestimate the value in being a good listener. Sometimes, people crave to have someone just listen to what they have to say – to listen patiently and intently – without interruption. I can't say whether this is something you need to absorb – but I can say that I need to improve my listening skills.

In addition to enhancing our own experience (and the experience of others) in this way, we have virtually unlimited opportunities to read all sorts of literature. For the Christian, reading Holy Scripture should be an imperative – and if we do so in the right attitude, we are likely to learn a lot. We should want to know and understand what Scripture says – we should not feel coerced to do so. The King James version of the Bible tells us "…Study to shew thyself approved unto God, a workman that needeth not to be ashamed, rightly dividing the word of truth…".[268] One of the ways that God speaks to His people is through His Word – and that is why Scripture is quoted extensively in this text – so that readers have an opportunity to remind themselves (or perhaps realise for the first time) what God's truth has to say about the matters we are considering. "…The unfolding of your words gives light; it gives understanding to the simple…".[269] J I Packer says "…Jesus' way of speaking to us now is not by uttering fresh words, but rather by applying to our consciences those words of His that are recorded in the gospels, together with the rest of the biblical testimony to Himself…".[270] These are valuable words indeed.

It is a great shame that despite having such easy access to the Bible, so few of us use that privilege to the fullest extent – or even refer to it or pay adequate attention to it. Would you be embarrassed if a non-Christian asked you (as a Christian) how familiar you were with the Bible – whether you had ever read the Bible – and if so, how often? When God commissioned Joshua after the death of Moses, God told Joshua "…Do not let this Book of the Law depart from your

---

[268] 2 Timothy 2:15
[269] Psalm 119:130
[270] JI Packer; Knowing God; Pg 41; Hodder & Stoughton; 2013

mouth; meditate on it day and night, so that you may be careful to do everything written in it. Then you will be prosperous and successful…".[271] We Christians need to absorb Scripture – otherwise we will not be able to benefit from its teaching or instruction – and we will certainly not be able to share it with anyone else. Remember "…All Scripture is God-breathed and is useful for teaching, rebuking, correcting and training in righteousness, so that the man of God may be thoroughly equipped for every good work…".[272] We sometimes hear it said that Scripture is not attuned to the norms of the society in which we live. In light of the discussion on principles in previous chapters, we might consider whether it's not more the case that the principles set out in the Bible remain valid and that it is the norms of our society that are warped. Sacrifices beyond the imagination or knowledge of most of us have been made to enable us to have our own copy of the Bible in our own language and to be able to read it freely and without hindrance. The frequency and intensity of our use of Holy Scripture will deepen and broaden our experience and Christian maturity – if we are prepared to devote the time and effort to it. Our attitudes cannot be Christ-like by accident. The tenets of Scripture should be part of our DNA if we want our attitude to be attuned to Christ's teaching. To complement Holy Scripture, there are a plethora of good books available to anyone who wants to broaden their experience. Naturally, we need to select from the literature available with care. (The authors quoted in this text are a small sample of many whose work is worth reading.) For people who do not enjoy reading, there are many audio books available – requiring us only to listen. If you choose not to broaden your knowledge of Scripture then you will remain unaware of so many things that the Bible teaches.

The factors mentioned above are not the only ones that stimulate our experience – and thereby our attitude. Attitude may also be influenced by art, film, nature, dance and music – and the experiential effects of these media are not to be underestimated. Sometimes, representations via these media convey much more to some people than words could ever express to them. The point is that we should never lose our capacity to learn and absorb and to review – because when we stop to consider all that our God has given to us and has made available to us, we are at a loss to describe His unending love, mercies and provision. How great is the God we adore! Albert Einstein made at least two important statements in this respect. Firstly, "…Learn from yesterday, live for

[271] Joshua 1:8
[272] 2 Timothy 3:16-17

today, hope for tomorrow. The important thing is not to stop questioning…" and secondly, "…The only source of knowledge is experience…". It has been said for example "…The artist strains for what cannot be said, cannot be expressed, cannot be contained in conventional forms. It cannot be contained, because it's from God; and God cannot be contained, or fathomed, or comprehended…Art is where we imitate the nature of God, in the excess of energy that created the universe, the exquisite miniature that constituted the incarnation, the harrowing agony that underwent the cross, the restorative joy that burst out in the resurrection and the dance of delight that caught fire at Pentecost. Because God is the great artist, and each human life is an event of recognition, interpretation and improvisation on the wondrous imagination of God…". [273] Stop and ask yourself – if God was speaking to me through (say) art, film, nature, dance or music, would I be sufficiently sensitive to realise that?

We all have experiences – and each set is unique. Whether we realise it or not, these experiences have had – and will continue to have – an effect on our attitudes and therefore upon our actions. <u>You might find considering your personal experiences is a valuable exercise</u> – that is those that are unique to you – and then ponder what they have taught you about your attitude to living. It has been said that "…all of us have a concept of ourselves made of things we believe, or want to believe about ourselves…three aspects of our self-concept are of special importance in determining how well we regard ourselves – self-esteem, self-respect and self-confidence…". [274] This might form a useful model to employ in considering personal experiences.

7.3 Environment

It has been said that "…we are actually powerfully influenced by our surroundings, our immediate context, and the personalities of those around us…".[275] Another author has said that "…one's identity is founded in important ways by one's identification with family, groups and a social-institutional order that protects them…".[276]

---

[273] Samuel Wells; Learning To Dream Again; Loc 1393; Canterbury Press; 2013

[274] David Keirsey; Please Understand Me II; Pg 136; Prometheus Nemesis Book Company; 1998

[275] Malcolm Gladwell; The Tipping Point; Pg 259; Abacus; 2001

[276] James W Fowler; Stages Of Faith; Pg 78; Harper One; 1981

As you read this, you may be reminded of a particular environment that has had an effect on you – maybe a national park or a mountain range or an angry sea. It may be a river, it may be a quaint cottage in the country. We are all affected differently by what we experience around us. At first glance, the word 'environment', might infer geographic location exclusively – but it would be more accurate to think of ourselves within a number of environments. For example, many of us work in 'office environments' or a 'factory environment'. Many of us identify with a 'home environment' – or live in a 'foreign environment'. In any event, we are all affected by the variables in the geographic environment where we live and spend our time – whether this is in a large modern city or a village – or in a first or third world country – or where it is very cold or where it is very warm. All these factors within the physical and geographic environments have the potential to affect our attitude.

Then there is the natural environment. Some people are deeply affected by nature. It has been said "...Nature is man's teacher. She unfolds her treasures to his search, unseals his eye, illumes his mind, and purifies his heart; an influence breathes from all the sights and sounds of her existence...".[277] Many of us are moved when we see high mountains, fast flowing rivers, weather in action, snow, ice, sand dunes – not to mention animals and birds and fish in their natural environments. "...God's revelation in nature, as in Scripture, is clear, if subtle...The evidence from nature has a similar ambiguity. We can superficially say, 'How awesome!' but fail to see its implications...".[278] Sensitivity once again.

Environment was important to Jesus. For example, with respect to prayer, Scripture tells us that "...Very early in the morning, while it was still dark, Jesus got up, left the house and went off to a solitary place, where He prayed...". [279] Clearly, Jesus found quietness and solitude conducive to concentration that enabled Him to pray in a focused manner to Almighty God. Jesus prayed at a particular time of day – morning – a special time of day for some people. This is a time when our heads are clear and when the issues of the day have not yet had opportunity to suffocate the calmness and serenity associated with mornings that may be somewhat surreal. Note also that Jesus chose a solitary place – where

---

[277] Alfred Billings Street; As Quoted By Stephen R Covey; A Roger Merrill and Dewitt Jones; The Nature Of Leadership; Pg 19; Franklin Covey Co; 1998

[278] Peter May; The Search For God & The Path To Persuasion; Pg 104; Malcolm Down Publishing; 2016

[279] Mark 1:35

there were no distractions that could impinge upon His communion with His Father. Maybe we would like that sort of experience but it's just not physically possible. In this case, create the next best thing for you. This might require imagining what we cannot experience physically – or leafing through old photographs that display the enormity of the natural environment. It might mean walking through a forest kicking the leaves or walking through sand in your bare feet. It might mean sitting on a park bench or on some grass enjoying the solitude that doing so brings. It might just mean going to a room where you can be alone. It might mean sitting on a chair in an outdoor café. The point is that there are many permutations – just consider what in your environment is available and that enhances your relationship with God – and use that to draw close to Him.

So, the geographic environment and the natural environment can be important influences upon who we are – but as indicated above, 'environment' might not only embrace geography and nature – but might include also the people who are at a particular location and the reason they are present. As human beings, most of us spend a great deal of time mixing with others – and the people with whom we mix – all have potential to influence our attitude. (We should be very grateful to have friends and other people with whom we can mix but we should not lose sight of those older people [with whom perhaps we socialised at one time] who are often very lonely and who have no one to speak with. We should be sensitive to the needs of such people.) The permutations are innumerable – ranging from those whose influence on us is nil or negligible – to those whose influence is very great – and in between there are those who exercise influence about which we may or may not be aware. The way we perceive the influence of others has substantial potential to affect our attitude. Consider for example a performance review. If my superior gives me a poor review, it will have little effect if I do not respect her/him – especially if the discussion is just between her/him and me. However, if I respect my superior and trust her/his judgement, the effect is likely to be much greater – and especially so if others are present at the time or are likely to come to know about the results later. None of us like to be embarrassed or to appear less than 'good enough'. John Ortberg points out that "…we are not the passive victim of others' opinions. Their opinions are powerless until we validate them. No one's approval will affect us until we grant it credibility and status. The same holds good for disapproval…". [280]

---

[280] John Ortberg; The Life You Have Always Wanted; Pg 163; Zondervan; 2002

Perversely, individuals might or might not adopt the same attitude in similar circumstances if they were to recur – and the presence of others (whether as observers or controllers in particular situations) may also be influential. For example, someone not normally assertive or impatient might become so in a dangerous situation (such as a fire) that (s)he perceives to require immediate, decisive action where (s)he sees no one else taking action. However, that person may be less likely to act if (s)he sees someone else providing appropriate leadership. Further, if my perception is that the fire is likely to become very much worse very quickly, my attitude concerning how to remedy the situation will be different to what it would be if I reasoned that there was no major cause for alarm. In his book 'The Character Gap',[281] quoted elsewhere in this text, the author describes many research studies regarding the behaviour of individuals in a variety of situations. The results are very informative – and often in ways that are surprising.

It has been said that "...our first impressions are generated by our experiences and our environment, which means that we can change our first impressions – we can alter the way we thin slice – by changing the experiences that comprise those impressions...".[282]

There are many lessons to be learned here – but fundamentally – as human beings, we are all vulnerable. Some of us may be able to hide behind a façade, but underneath, our environments (in the widest sense of that word) affect how we think and how we behave – attitude in action. Accordingly, we need to be aware of this and to be careful about the environments in which we spend our lives – we need to recognise their potential to influence us. We all can exercise choice concerning which environments are conducive for us. Remember that to make no decision in this respect is to decide to adopt the status quo. This may not have been what we intended. Sometimes, we need to sacrifice the good for the very best.

We should not forget the social environment. One author has said that "...We are born into a social field and we live out our lives in that field, never, for long, stepping outside of it into some no-man's land disconnected from social reality. Of course, we can be disoriented for short periods of time, owing to a surprise, a danger, or a shock. But we soon reorient ourselves and return to our ordinary waking social frame of reference. Indeed, we are the most social of all the

---

[281] Christian B Miller; The Character Gap; Oxford University Press; 2018

[282] Malcolm Gladwell; Blink; Pg 97; Penguin Books; 2005

animals, with our choice of social membership groups creating our life long framework, and with our sociability ending in massive and complex societies…".[283] This quote suggests that the massively complex societies in which we choose to live are likely to have marked and long-lasting influence upon our lives – and if this is so – then also upon our attitudes. The same author believes that "…each act and attitude is shaped and governed by a prevailing outlook or perspective determined by our social matrix…".[284] Accordingly, society is one of the stimuli mentioned at the outset – and importantly, this societal influence is likely to pass from one generation to the next. "…The ultimate test of a moral society is the kind of world that it leaves to its children…".[285] We might be forgiven for thinking that as individuals, we have no power to influence the society in which we live. This is incorrect. In the same way that the longest journey begins with the first step (Lao Tzu), every change process begins with the person sufficiently motivated to initiate that change. Have you ever stopped to consider what form society might take if it operated upon the basis that Christ promoted? The difference would be transformational – but transformation requires the first step (and then the rest) to be taken.

7.4 Expectations

The characteristics and traits of the people involved in any situation derive from many stimuli – such as past experiences (e.g. whether someone has been in this type of scenario previously), environment (e.g. does the existing environment make the scenario more or less advantageous), perceptions (e.g. our view as to how this scenario might conclude). All this suggests that what we expect from a current, particular event or scenario or exchange may well differ between individuals – because as individuals our experiences, environments and perceptions are uniquely relevant to each of us. What one person considers as dangerous, funny, insulting or acceptable for example – need not be considered as such by someone else. This infers that a degree of maturity and sensitivity is required if we are to avoid causing offence to other people – not only by what we say and do – but by how we say and do it. <u>The perceptions of what other</u>

[283] David Keirsey; Please Understand Me II; Pg 132; Prometheus Nemesis Book Company; 1998

[284] David Keirsey; Please Understand Me II; Pg 89; Prometheus Nemesis Book Company; 1998

[285]20 Influential Quotes by Dietrich Bonhoeffer; Emily Maust WoodCrosswalk.com

people may find acceptable should not be taken for granted. Humour is no exception. Sometimes, it is only after an exchange has ended in an argument or offence being taken that people realise that they just didn't think before they spoke. It has been said that "...you are not what you think you are. But what you think you are...We become what we think about (the Law of Dominant Thought)...". [286] The part that sensitivity plays in our lives is significant.

Expectation and frustration go hand in hand. Frustration means unmet expectations. Frustrations give rise to attitudes such as disappointment and impatience. It would be useful if we had the presence of mind to test our own expectations – just to make sure that they are reasonable in the circumstances – because sometimes those frustrations are not reasonable. More often than not, we have neither the presence of mind – nor the sensitivity – nor the maturity – nor the magnanimity – that would make a situation more likely to end positively rather than negatively. Regrettably, we are more inclined to expect other people to behave in a way that we expect – and fail to think what the other person might expect of us. We often fail to ask ourselves why we believe what we believe? If we are right in what we believe then we don't need to talk down to the other person – and if we are wrong – we have no right to do so. Could it be simply that once adopted, our conclusions become the norm for us and we no longer think we could be wrong and therefore we have a right to be dogmatic in how we express our views? How often do we ask ourselves whether there might be a better – approach in the circumstances – one that will simultaneously protect the integrity of what we believe and the integrity of the other person's personality? Could our expectations reflect our own prejudices? Before assuming that our way is the right way, we would do well to re-examine our approach from time to time to make sure. Why is it always easier to see faults and weaknesses in other people than to see any weakness in ourselves? Could it be because we are using the wrong lens? Matthew drew attention to this foible in human nature when he wrote "...Why do you look at the speck of sawdust in your brother's eye and pay no attention to the plank in your own eye...?"[287]

Then there is the question of ego. It is sometimes difficult to concede that we are wrong – even when we realise the other person is right. To concede that we are wrong is often thought to be a sign of weakness – whereas in actual fact, it is often a sign of strength. Many of us realise this but despite that, it is often too

---

[286] Jeff Keller; Attitude Is Everything; Pgs 3 and 19; Attitude Is Everything Inc; 2012

[287] Matthew 7:3

difficult for us to concede. On the other hand, how can it be rational to continue pursuing a point of view that we know to be wrong? The answer is often that it is not rational – but instead it is pride trying to overwhelm our integrity.

7.5 Perceptions

Perceptions influence attitude. It follows that if we want to change our attitude, we need to work on changing our perceptions first. How we perceive things is determined by the way we think – which in turn – determines our response – and ultimately our actions (see below). Consequently, the question arises – what influences our perception?

Our perception of how things are or should be – is a product of our experiences – such as family, friends, environment, religious convictions, work, study, location and so on. Once we have reached certain conclusions, we do not often question whether our perceptions remain valid. So, once we come to a point of view, we adhere to that view – sometimes rigorously and sometimes very defensively. We need to remember that two people can react entirely differently to the same scenario – and both can be right simultaneously. Often, "…We simply assume that the way we see things is the way they really are or the way they should be. And our attitude and behaviours grow out of those assumptions. The way we see things is the source of the way we think and the way we act…".[288] So, we must teach ourselves to distinguish between how things are and how we expect things should be. We must be careful also not to lose our objectivity. It has been suggested that "…if you are surrounded long enough by people who think like you think, you will become more and more certain that's the best way to think…".[289]

More particularly, our perception of ourselves is a fundamental determinant of attitude. "…Perception is a choice…".[290] Some of us like to think that we are bigger, better and more beautiful than others. Simultaneously, some of us do not think highly enough of ourselves. Eleanor Roosevelt once observed "…No one can make you feel inferior without your consent…". [291] Some of us believe that our condition is such that it cannot be improved. In this respect it has been said

---

288 Stephen Covey; The Seven Habits Of Highly Effective People; Pg 32; Simon & Schuster Ltd; 1992

289 Andy Stanley, Reggie Joiner & Lane Jones; Seven Practices Of Effective Ministry; Pg 140; Multnomah Books; 2004

290 Robert Holden; Shift Happens; Pg 235; Hodder & Stoughton; 2000

291 This Is My Story; Eleanor Roosevelt; 1937; Harper Torch

"...The greatest discovery of my age is that men can change their circumstances by changing the attitude of their mind...".[292]

The lesson is to keep challenging our own perceptions – and to listen to the opinions of other people – and concede within ourselves that even though we know another opinion differs from our own – there is value in trying to understand it. This is another opportunity to learn from experience – but this time it is the experience of others that may be relevant – if we have enough maturity to consider that experience objectively.

7.6 Other Stimuli (or Trigger Events)

A 'Stimulus or Trigger' may be thought of as an event that gives rise to the attitude manifested in a particular circumstance. Attitudes are adopted as reactions to a stimulus. This brings us back to the discussion in chapter 1 – represented by the diagram introduced earlier:

Figure Eight	Stimulus/Attitude/Response

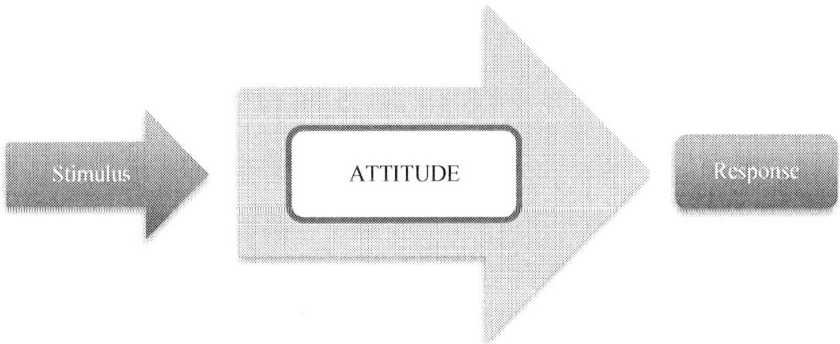

The 'stimulus' could be almost anything – for example: mood, well-being, grief, ill health, disbelief, danger, cynicism, the tone of an email received, a telephone conversation. It might be a missed deadline, an error or a deal that has collapsed – or it might be a response to witnessing something that has affected the observer deeply. The stimulus might also be an event such as a car accident, a breakage, the loss of a job, theft, redundancy – or simply being ignored or insulted. The list is virtually endless. In the absence of knowledge as to why another person's attitude differs from mine (and often in everyday living, we are

[292] William James

not privy to such knowledge), I need to exercise care to avoid jumping to the wrong conclusions. This is another reason why sensitivity is so important for Christians (see Para 4.3). Ordinarily, we will not know all the things that are happening in the lives of others around us. That being so, we will not always be able to understand why others adopt the attitudes they do. When Christians 'get alongside' others, there is a much greater likelihood that sensitivity will be greater as trust between individuals grows to the extent that people are comfortable about sharing with others the things that are happening in their lives. It is simply the case, that most of us are probably somewhat unaware about what is happening in the lives of family members and people with whom we are friendly – but it is also the case that we are totally unaware about what is happening in the lives of people outside our immediate circle of friends.

As inferred above, the tone and style of behaviour adopted by one person is very likely to affect how others involved react to that tone or behaviour. For example, failure to accept reasons for actions/reactions or to offer empathy often incites frustration at best and at worst anger or aggression in someone else. Strength of character is required to demonstrate a positive reaction (or at least a reaction that is not negative) to a negative tone and/or negative behaviour adopted by someone else. This is so difficult for most people and requires more than an exceptional amount of grace. In reacting, it is often useful to remember to exercise care in using a sentence that includes the words 'you are' – because the next word is critical. Here are some examples of what the next word could be: you are always moaning; you are never satisfied; you are very negative; you are a real pain and you are always criticising me. On the other hand, think of the effect of the following types of statement: you are a true friend; you are very thoughtful; you are a good person; you are a good worker and you are fun to be around. Which type of 'you are' statement are you more likely to use?

7.7 Behavioural Implications

One of the reasons why attitude is so significant is because of the intrinsic link between attitude and behaviour. Our emotional maturity, personal discipline, courage, the extent to which our ego prevails in our personality – with all the implications for selfishness, jealousy, pride, and so on – all affect our attitude. For example, an optimistic or a pessimistic outlook has a great deal to do with outcomes. Our attitude towards money is a case in point because it determines whether we spend it – and also how we spend it, how quickly and how prudently. As noted elsewhere, sensitivity is very significant. In fact, it is another driver of behaviour – a sensitive person is less likely to behave in a manner that will lead to negative implications for someone else. It has been said that "...even the smallest and subtlest and most unexpected of factors can affect the way we act...".[293] This is significant not only for Christians themselves – but also with respect to how they are perceived by others – "...more will be affected by what they see than will be affected by what they hear...". [294] From another perspective, it's good to remember that "...we are far more affected by the impact of people on our lives than most of us realise. We are always – always! – being energised or drained by every interaction...".[295] It might be helpful to ask ourselves to consider objectively and honestly whether we are an 'energiser' or a 'drainer'?

The opposite holds true also – one writer believes that "...people who cannot feel – punish those who do ...". [296] Neuro-Linguistic Programming explores the interaction of thoughts, verbal and non-verbal communication and patterns of behaviour and emotional responses. It is really important to understand that "...as human beings, we are responsible for our own lives. Our behaviour is a function of our decisions, not our conditions. We can subordinate feelings to values. We have the initiative and the responsibility to make things happen...".[297] This means that we cannot excuse our own or another's behaviour by saying – that is just the way I am or – you must take me as I am. We choose who we are – and we must accept responsibility for that if we are to behave as mature, grounded people.

7.8 Social Roles and Maturation

It has been said that "...It is impossible not to play a role in all of our social transactions, and there are two kinds of social roles, those that are allotted to us by virtue of our position in our social milieu, and those that we reach out and take for ourselves. We perforce play offspring to our parents, siblings to our brothers and sisters, and relatives to our extended family members. On the other hand, we choose to play mate to our spouse, parent to our offspring, superior to

[293] Malcolm Gladwell; The Tipping Point; Pg 27; Abacus; 2001
[294] Philip Yancey; Vanishing Grace; Hodder & Stoughton; 2014
[295] John Ortberg; The Me I Want To Be; Pg 204; Zondervan; 2010
[296] Eleanor May Sarton
[297] Stephen Covey; The Seven Habits of Highly Effective People; Pg 78; Simon & Schuster; 1989

our subordinate, subordinate to our superior, friend to friend, and so on. Allotted or embraced, we have no choice but to enact our roles, since to interact with others can never be role free…".[298] If this statement is correct in saying we have no choice but to enact our roles, we should remember that in doing so, we have a choice what attitude to adopt.

There are not only roles that apply to each of us and about which we have no choice, there are also different stages in life – which are also affected by attitude. Daniel Levinson's 'Eras Of The Life Cycle' provides a useful synopsis of a human life cycle. He identifies four 'transitions' as follows: (1) Early Childhood; (2) Early Adult; (3) Mid-Life and (4) Late Adult. These correspond to four 'eras': (1) Childhood and Adolescence; (2) Early Adulthood; (3) Middle Adulthood and (4) Late Adulthood.[299] Using this framework for the purposes of considering how attitudinal changes occur with age produces much informative food for thought.

For example, many readers will have personal experience in dealing with uncooperative children and young people. As we all know, young children can demonstrate attitudes vigorously and transparently. I am reminded of a recent flight during which a toddler cried for most of the first two hours flying time – eventually putting himself to sleep with exhaustion. I have to admit I didn't feel too lively either – but my choice was either to give the child the benefit of the doubt (because he was tired and restless) or kick up a fuss because his parents were not able to placate him. Which course would you have chosen? Parents and 'observers' are often prepared to tolerate a degree of misbehaviour in a child – but as that child becomes a (young) teenager – less tolerance is on offer. After that – misbehaviour (however that may be defined) is (or should be) frequently met with zero tolerance – regrettably some in our society never progress beyond the I, me, mine and 'no' responses that identify toddlers. The difficulty is that if by early adulthood, young people remain unaware about what are acceptable manifestations of attitude and what are unacceptable, it will be much more difficult to exert positive influence on them as they enter the middle and late adulthood categories. By these stages, attitudes are frequently entrenched through years and years of not realising the potential benefits that change could

---

[298] David Keirsey; Please Understand Me II; Pg 193; Prometheus Nemesis Book Company; 1998

[299] Daniel J Levinson et al; Seasons Of A Man's Life; as quoted by James W Fowler; Stages Of Faith; Pg 111; Harper One; 1981

generate – if only given the opportunity. There are a lot of children out there in adult bodies.

The gravity of at least some of the implications of the last paragraph is demonstrated in research conducted by Dr Ana-Maria Rizzuto. This research concluded "...despite our secularization and religious fragmentation, religious symbols and language are so widely present in this society that virtually no child reaches school age without having constructed – with or without religious instruction an image or images of God...".[300] On the one hand this is positive if our children are nurtured and educated by people who approach their work with the right attitude – but on the other hand – consider the potential for harm if our children come under the tutelage of people whose attitude is not appropriate.

7.9 Summary

At this stage, we have considered humankind's 'infra-structure' – under the headings spirit, soul and body. We have examined the role that each plays in creating 'mechanisms' that will contribute to the formation of attitude. Our spirit embraces our conscience – and that leads to patterns of behaviour and underscores the extent to which we are humble. Our soul uses our sensitised conscience to formulate character. And our mind exercises discipline to discern good from evil in making good choices.

It is our humility and character that influence the choices we make and that lead to qualities of character that create our patterns of behaviour and the creation of a personal credo that will form the basis of the attitude that we will adopt in everyday living. We have examined a number of qualities of character including principles, traits and habits and qualities per se. In this chapter, we have considered some of the external influences (such as environment, expectations, perceptions and other stimuli) that have a bearing on the attitudes we adopt and the behavioural implications. The model is now complete and is reproduced below in its final format.

The original working definition suggested that 'attitude' might be described as a pattern of thought that stimulates an individual in a particular environment to think, act or to react in a particular way. In light of subsequent discussion in the text, the definition might now be refined as follows:

---

[300] The Birth Of The Living God; Dr Ana-Maria Rizzuto; as quoted by James W Fowler; Stages Of Faith; Pg 129; Harper One; 1981

Figure Nine	Definition Of Attitude

Attitude is a pattern of thought that arises through the interaction of spirit, soul and body. It involves the operation of conscience, character and principles – combining to persuade an individual in a particular environment to think, behave or to react in a particular way.

It is clear then that attitude does not just happen. It is neither haphazard nor independent. On the contrary, it is affected by past experiences and by relationships – and by all those things in our lives (stimuli) about which we are sensitive. Attitude is the application – on a daily basis – of the principles that we have internalised. In turn, this affects our behaviour – promoting action that reflects our conscience.

Therefore, our attitude cannot be right before God, unless our conscience, character and the principles by which we live are all attuned to the way that Scripture prescribes. There must be equilibrium. If any one of these three factors is not completely synchronised with the others, disequilibrium occurs. In this case, our attitude cannot be in accordance with the Christian way.

We should be aware that even when our attitude conforms to the way God intended it to be, adhering to the values and standards in accordance with our conscience and living in conformity to our character and our principles – to produce acceptable behaviour (both verbal and in action) is a continuous challenge. This is because Satan is continually attempting to bring us down.[301] We should not be confused. 'Success' in this respect is not a one point in time achievement – it is a process – and as Aristotle has said, "We are what we repeatedly do. Excellence, then, is not an act, but a habit…"

It should be noted that often things are never as simple as they seem – and this model is no exception. Life is not like that! In life, it is not possible to place everything in neat little boxes. The purpose of the diagram is merely to present a pictorial representation that points to the complexities of attitude. The text thus far indicates the sorts of overlaps there are everywhere within the model – and the extraordinary number of permutations that arise. The core point to be made is valuable for each of us – and that is – attitude does not just happen – it arises as the result of complex interactions between all the variables described in the

[301] 1 Peter 5:8

preceding text – producing innumerable variations in the patterns of behaviour we exhibit as human beings. The lesson is to avoid approaching attitude superficially – which we are all inclined to do. The value of not doing so is to exercise a degree of discipline over all the matters described earlier. To do so might just help us to become better people – and if we manage to become more like Christ – we will be making a greater contribution to turning this world into a better place by helping to repair some of the broken bits.

This marks the end of section 2. The model has served its purpose and the focus of the text now changes. Section 3 is about relationships.

Figure Ten	Model 7

Section Three
God's Attitude Towards Humanity

Chapter Eight
God's Person and Plan

8.1 Introduction

In Sections 1 and 2 we considered what attitude is all about – what it means and where it comes from – and the extent to which it influences our daily lives. We saw that these matters are not one-dimensional. On the contrary, we have shown that there are many inter-relationships amongst the variables we considered. Now we want to take stock and to place these matters in their wider context – that is to say that so far we have considered only the attitudes of the created – but now we will turn our attention to the attitude of the Creator.

Accordingly, in section 3, we will consider firstly God as Creator, who He is – and His awesome holiness and purity in chapter 8 – and then in chapter 9, we will contrast the majesty of God with the degradation of humankind. The section will conclude with chapter 10 – which includes some thoughts on humankind's generic negative attitude to living with other members of the human race.

We start Section 3 by considering who God is (chapter 8) and what His plan is for each of us. (I should clarify that when I make reference to God's plan for each of us, I do not presume to be privy to God's plans for any other individual. Instead, I mean to present a general outline of the type of life that I believe Holy Scripture teaches we should be living as Christians – what has been referred to as 'the Christian way' in earlier chapters.) While Almighty God has indicated how He would like us to conduct ourselves in the life He has given us, He does not force us to conform. On the contrary, our Creator has allowed us great latitude in deciding how we should live our lives – but this latitude should not ignore the existence of certain fundamental principles – including accountability and consequences. This means that our individual attitude to these principles is a matter of great importance.

Weighty tomes have been written about God's Person and Plan – so one chapter in this text is very unlikely to add anything new. However, that is not the objective. Rather, the aim of this chapter – as we rehearse some of these principles together – is to provide a context to our humanity and to see – perhaps for the first time – or to remind ourselves as the case may be – that it is to Almighty God and to the Holy Spirit and to Jesus Christ that we should be looking for guidance, grace and direction in adopting and acting upon appropriate attitudes – "...what is man that You are mindful of him, the son of man that You care for them...?"[302]

8.2 Who Is God and Who Is The Lord Jesus Christ?

If someone asked you: "Who is God?" – how do you think you might answer? You might refer to God's own description of Himself: "...I AM WHO I AM..." [303] or you might refer to a definition that someone else has written. I imagine that most of us would not be able to answer this question as eloquently or as reverently as Adam Clarke – who many years ago said that God is "...the eternal, independent and self-existent Being: the Being whose purposes and actions spring from Himself, without foreign motive or influence; He who is absolute in dominion; the most pure, the most simple, the most spiritual of all essences; infinitely perfect; and eternally self-sufficient, needing nothing that He has made; illimitable in His immensity, inconceivable in His mode of existence and indescribable in His essence; known fully only by Himself, because an infinite mind can only be fully comprehended by itself. In a word, a Being who, from His infinite wisdom, cannot err or be deceived, and from His infinite goodness, can do nothing but what is eternally just, and right and kind...".[304] What an eloquent and profound description – and one that humbles me each time I read it. How great is the God we adore! We really need to know who our God is if we are to understand who we are and what we need to be. The process begins in reading Scripture. Of course, there is more to knowing God than simply understanding an eloquent description of Him – in its fullest sense, 'knowing

[302] Psalm 8:4
[303] Exodus 3:14
[304] John M'Clintock and James Strong, eds, Cyclopaedia of Biblical, Theological and Ecclesiastical Literature, vol 3 (New York: Harper & Brothers, 1894). Pp.903-904 – as quoted by Dallas Willard; The Divine Conspiracy; Pg 76; William Collins; 2014

God' is a life-long exercise – focused on learning what God's love means for humankind.

From the very beginning of the Bible, we start to learn about God's attributes – His absolute power in creation, His love for Adam and Eve, His desire to communicate with humankind, His love and His justice. The story continues in the Old Testament – for example "...The Lord, the Lord, the compassionate and gracious God, slow to anger, abounding in love and faithfulness, maintaining love to thousands, and forgiving wickedness, rebellion and sin...".[305] God's patience and perseverance are seen throughout Scripture. Consider when He brought His people out of Egypt through the Red Sea (and was faced with continuous complaints and grumbling) after which His people disobeyed Him again and again – ignoring His direct instructions. The story continues in the New Testament – for example, we read that Jesus "...committed no sin, and no deceit was found in His mouth. When they hurled their insults at Him, He did not retaliate; when He suffered, He made no threats...".[306] "...He is absolute purity...".[307] In fact, Jesus said when He was being killed mercilessly "...Father, forgive them, for they do not know what they are doing...".[308] <u>Jesus' trust in God was absolute.</u> He knew from the beginning of time what it would take to redeem the world – and the cost was supreme – to the extent that Jesus prayed "...Father, if you are willing, take this cup from Me; yet not My will, but Yours be done...".[309] <u>Jesus was in continuous communication with his Father – to whom He humbly and unendingly remained faithful.</u> Scripture is replete with information that describes who God is, His character, His plan for humankind and His endless love and mercy.

For example, Scripture tells us that "...The Lord is gracious and compassionate, slow to anger and rich in love. The Lord is good to all, He has compassion on all He has made...".[310] Elsewhere, we are told that God's work "...is perfect, and all His ways are just. A faithful God who does no wrong, upright and just is He...".[311] According to Scripture, this has universal application – Jesus loves the 'whosoever' – which means everyone.

---

[305] Exodus 34:6-7
[306] 1 Peter 2:22-23
[307] A W Pink; The Attributes Of God; Loc 723; Chapel Library Resources; 1993
[308] Luke 23:34
[309] Luke 22:42
[310] Psalm 145:8-9
[311] Deuteronomy 32:4

In a recent chapter of this text, we noted how often Scripture reminds us of the compassion of our Saviour – for example "...When He saw the crowds, He had compassion on them..."[312] – and He felt such sorrow at the death of Lazarus to the extent He wept (John 11:35).

Scripture also tells us that there can be no forgiveness without the shedding of blood (Hebrews 9:22). The word 'blood' infers life (see Leviticus 17:11). Accordingly, humankind would have been lost – that is to say would have been forced to continue as perpetual slaves to the consequences of its own collective sins – were it not for the substitution of Christ at Calvary. It was here that Christ sacrificed His life on our behalf to liberate us from this slavery – for "...God so loved the world that He gave His one and only Son, that whoever believes in Him shall not perish but have eternal life...".[313] At Calvary, Christ died once – for all mankind.[314] "...For the joy set before Him endured the cross, scorning its shame...".[315] What more could He give – what more could we ask Him to give? What more is there to give?

Jesus has done all that is necessary to save us from the punishment rightly due to us. For our sake "...God made Him who had no sin to be sin for us, so that in Him we might become the righteousness of God...".[316] Elsewhere, Scripture tells us that "...when we were still powerless, Christ died for the ungodly...".[317] Although humanity was created perfect, sin was created through the actions of Adam and Eve – and through them it was passed on to the rest of humankind. "...Therefore, just as sin entered the world through one man, and death through sin, and in this way, death came to all men, because all sinned...".[318] In fact, "...God demonstrates His own love for us in this: While we were still sinners, Christ died for us...".[319]

Scripture tells us to "...live a life of love, just as Christ loved us and gave Himself up for us as a fragrant offering and sacrifice to God...".[320] The attitude of Christ towards humankind is demonstrated in His supreme sacrifice – "...This is how God showed His love among us: He sent His one and only Son into the

---

312 Matthew 9:36
313 John 3:16
314 1 Peter 3:18
315 Hebrews 12:2
316 2 Corinthians 5:21
317 Romans 5:6
318 Romans 5:12
319 Romans 5:8
320 Ephesians 5:2

world that we might live through Him...".[321] We should understand that "...Greater love has no one than this, that He lay down His life for his friends...".[322] Further, "...He was pierced for our transgressions, He was crushed for our iniquities; the punishment that brought us peace was upon Him, and by His wounds we are healed. We all, like sheep, have gone astray, each of us has turned to our own way; and the Lord has laid on Him the iniquity of us all...".[323] God loves each and every one of us with a love that is so pure that it is impossible to comprehend – never mind to describe in mere words – it defies description! Despite that, we can experience it – all day every day – even though we cannot earn it or deserve it. "...But seeing that He is clothed with omnipotence, no prayer is too hard for Him to answer, no need is too great for Him to supply, no passion too strong for Him to subdue, no temptation too powerful for Him to deliver from, no misery too deep for Him to relieve...".[324]

"...There is no one like You, O Lord, and there is no God but You...".[325]

8.3 The Attributes of God

In his book 'Knowing God',[326] J I Packer says that the reformed theologians used to categorise God's attributes as incommunicable attributes (that is to say characteristics of God alone which man is unable to share), or communicable attributes (these qualities were communicated to mankind when God created them and correspond to God's own qualities. "...In the first group, they put those qualities which highlight God's transcendence and show how vastly different a being He is from us, His creatures...". Incommunicable attributes include: God's independence, His immutability, His infinity and His simplicity. Communicable attributes include: God's spirituality, freedom and omnipotence, and all God's moral attributes – goodness, truth, holiness, righteousness, wisdom, etc.

What is God like? One writer has said "...For years I thought of the Sermon on the Mount (Matt. 5–7) as a blueprint for human behaviour[327], a standard no one could possibly meet. How could I have missed the true meaning? Jesus spoke these words not to encumber us, but to tell us what God is like. Why should we

[321] 1 John 4:9
[322] John 15:13
[323] Isaiah 53:5-6
[324] A W Pink; The Attributes Of God; Loc 928; Chapel Library Resources; 1993
[325] 1 Chronicles 17:20
[326] J I Packer; Knowing God; Pg 111; Hodder & Stoughton; 2013
[327] Philip Yancey; Safety Net; Our Daily Bread; 11 June 2016

love our enemies? Because our merciful Father causes His sun to rise on the evil and the good. Why store up treasures in heaven? Because the Father lives there and will lavishly reward us. Why live without fear and worry? Because the same God who clothes the lilies and the grass of the field has promised to take care of us. Why pray? If an earthly father gives his son bread or fish, how much more will the Father in heaven give good gifts to those who ask? Jesus preached the Sermon on the Mount (Matt. 5–7) not only to explain God's ideal toward which we should never stop striving but also to show that in this life none of us will ever reach that ideal. Before God, we all stand on level ground: murderers and tantrum-throwers, adulterers and lusters, thieves and coveters. We are all desperate, and that is the only state appropriate to a human being who wants to know God. Having fallen from the absolute ideal, we have nowhere to land but in the safety net of absolute grace…". Truly, "…the Lord is full of compassion and mercy…"[328] – even our tears are significant to Him.[329]

Some of the attributes of our God are described in the paragraphs below.

8.4 Holiness

Of all the attributes of Almighty God – whether metaphysical[330] (for example – His omniscience, His omnipotence and omnipresence) or moral (His holiness, love, justice and truthfulness), His holiness is so significant that it must be given appropriate attention. Regrettably, many amongst us seem not to understand its significance – but Isaiah reminds us that there are many who hear but don't understand and many who see but never perceive.[331] Thus it was when our Lord preached salvation on this earth – and so it remains today. In an epoch of time when so many are unaware of their eternal status before Almighty God, it behoves we Christians to sharpen our focus on our Creator and Lord – and <u>holiness involves understanding who our God is and who and what we are as we stand before Him.</u>

Holiness is not easily defined – but as Christians we know that it is very significant because God told His own people "…I am the Lord who brought you up out of Egypt to be your God; therefore, be holy, because I am holy…".[332] In

---

[328] James 5:11
[329] Psalm 56:8
[330] J I Packer; Knowing God; Pg 66; Hodder & Stoughton; 2013
[331] Isaiah 6:9
[332] Leviticus 11:45

obedience to God's instruction, we need firstly to understand what holiness means. One verse provides some background – "...Since we have these promises, dear friends, let us purify ourselves from everything that contaminates body and spirit, perfecting holiness out of reverence for God...".[333] This infers that holiness includes giving God the respect and awe that are rightly His – and our separation from anything that might contaminate either body or spirit. This requires an attitude of mind. There appear to be two dimensions to holiness – firstly, that of God and secondly holiness with respect to humankind.

8.4.1 God Is Holy

Scripture says "...There is no one like you, O Lord, and there is no God but you...".[334] Further "...Who will not fear You, O Lord, and bring glory to Your name? For You alone are holy. All nations will come and worship before You, for Your righteous acts have been revealed...".[335] In considering God's holiness further, it may be useful to do so in terms of His attributes. For example, our God is majestic. "...Now, 'majesty' is a word which the Bible uses to express the thought of greatness of God, our Maker and our Lord... 'the Lord reigns, He is robed in majesty...Your throne was established long ago' (Ps. 93:1f.). 'They will speak of the glorious splendour of Your majesty, and I will meditate on Your wonderful works' (Ps 145:5). Peter, recalling his vision of Christ's royal glory at the Transfiguration, says, '...we were eyewitnesses of His majesty...' (2 Pet 1:16)...".[336] Isaiah saw God "...seated on a throne, high and exalted..."[337] – and "...Who among the gods is like You, O Lord? Who is like You – majestic in holiness, awesome in glory, working wonders..."?[338]

God is unique "...There is no one holy like the Lord..."[339] – and as just noted, Scripture says "...Among the gods there is none like you, O Lord...For You are great and do marvellous deeds; You alone are God...".[340] JI Packer says "...There is not space enough here to gather up all that the book of Daniel tells us about the wisdom, might, and truth of the great God who rules history and

---

[333] 2 Corinthians 7:1
[334] 1 Chronicles 17:20
[335] Revelation 15:4
[336] J I Packer; Knowing God; Pg 91; Hodder & Stoughton; 2013
[337] Isaiah 6:1
[338] Exodus 15:11
[339] 1 Samuel 2:2
[340] Psalm 86:8 and 10

shows His sovereignty in acts of judgment and mercy towards individuals and nations according to His own pleasure. Suffice it to say that there is, perhaps no more vivid or sustained presentation of the many-sided reality of God's sovereignty in the whole Bible…These were the thoughts of God which filled Daniel's mind…". Praise be to the name of God forever and ever; wisdom and power are His. He changes times and seasons; He sets up kings and deposes them. He gives wisdom…He knows what lies in darkness, and light dwells with Him (2:20-22); "O Lord, the great and awesome God, who keeps His covenants of love with all who love Him and obey His commands…Lord You are righteous…the Lord our God is merciful and forgiving…the Lord our God is righteous in everything He does…(9:4,7,9,14) …".[341] God is holy because of His righteousness and He is exalted by His justice.[342] God requires His holiness to be respected. He told Moses to remove his sandals because he was standing on holy ground.[343] It should never cease to amaze those of us who love Him that in all His holiness, Almighty God deigns to stoop down to love us. He had to make the first move. In all our sinfulness, we could never have bridged the gap that exists between His purity and our sinfulness – it took Christ's sacrifice on Calvary to make a relationship possible between God and men. "…This is love: not that we loved God, but that He loved us and sent His Son as an atoning sacrifice for our sins…".[344] God is separate from us – He is so holy that sinful mankind cannot look at Him and live. "…No one has ever seen God, but God the one and Only, who is at the Father's side, has made Him known…".[345] Elsewhere, Scripture tells us "…the Lord said, 'I will cause all My goodness to pass in front of you, and I will proclaim My name, the Lord, in your presence. I will have mercy on whom I will have mercy, and I will have compassion on whom I will have compassion. But,' He said, 'You cannot see My face, for no one may see Me and live…'…"[346] Having given Moses the ten commandments, Scripture says "…When Moses came down from Mount Sinai with the two tablets of the Testimony in his hands, he was not aware that his face was radiant because he had spoken with the Lord. When Aaron and all the Israelites saw

---

[341] J I Packer; Knowing God; Pgs 29, 30, 31; Hodder & Stoughton; 2013
[342] Isaiah 5:16
[343] Exodus 3:5
[344] 1 John 4:10
[345] John 1:18
[346] Exodus 33:19-20

Moses, his face was radiant, and they were afraid to come near him…”.[347] Is this not a reminder of the awe in which we should approach our Lord and our God – just as the seraphs worshipped God – “…Holy, holy, holy is the Lord Almighty; the whole earth is full of His glory…”?[348] This is the same worship offered by the four living creatures we read about in Revelation – some 800 years after the same praise recorded in Isaiah “…Each of the four living creatures had six wings and was covered with eyes all around, even under its wings. Day and night they never stop saying: ‘Holy, holy, holy is the Lord God Almighty, who was, and is, and is to come…”.[349]

8.4.2 Holiness and Humankind

On the other hand, humankind is unholy – in fact – born in sin “…Surely, I was sinful at birth, sinful from the time my mother conceived me…”.[350] As one thinks about what this means in respect of how we live our lives, it just gets worse and worse. We are all aware from our individual experiences of the sinful nature of those around us – and those we hear about all over the world – in all sorts of circumstances. (We are all aware of our own shortcomings too – or at least those of them to which we admit – but it’s so much easier to identify sin in others than in ourselves.) Regrettably, we all have a tendency to compare ourselves with our fellow humans – and often when we do so, we consider that perhaps we are not so bad after all. This shows how utterly futile this exercise is. A much more important question is how do we compare with the God who created us – the epitome of love and purity? The only answer is that there is no comparison at all! We fall so far short of the example set by Jesus Christ that we should be prompted to take action. If we are unable to see this clearly, then either our view of God is too small or our view of ourselves is too big. Naturally, the process of becoming ‘holy’ cannot begin until we acknowledge God as saviour – because it is Christ’s atoning sacrifice on Calvary that enables God to initiate a close relationship with us as one of His people. Note that God will not force this issue – because He has allowed us free will.

We read of at least two men in the Bible who took stock of their own condition. The first was Isaiah. When he saw ‘the King, the Lord Almighty’ he

---

[347] Exodus 34:29-30
[348] Isaiah 6:3
[349] Revelation 4:8
[350] Psalm 51:5

quickly came to the conclusion "…Woe to me…I am ruined! For I am a man of unclean lips, and I live among a people of unclean lips…".[351] The conclusion of the second man – Paul – was similarly a call to be humble. He said "…Here is a trustworthy saying that deserves full acceptance: Christ Jesus came into the world to save sinners – of whom I am the worst…".[352] For the Christian, understanding the awesome purity and majesty of our Creator and the utter wretchedness of our own sinful state must be amongst the first steps in the process of becoming holy.

Note two things. Firstly, holiness is a process that continues throughout the lifetime of a Christian. It is not a once and for all time achievement. It involves experience and refinement as our knowledge of the Lord increases and as our relationship with Him is deepened. It involves the development of an understanding of Scripture in general and the Christian way in particular. It involves daily experience and exercise of the fruits of the spirit. Secondly, holiness does not mean strict religious observance – or abstention from vices – moral or otherwise. If this was the case, there are many people in the world who could claim to be holy. Instead, God wants His people to: acknowledge Him as Lord and to be loving, moral, upright and all things good – but these emanate from holiness – gradually and progressively after entering into a relationship with Jesus Christ. So, holiness must begin with a proper assessment of who God is and who we are – and this requires humility and a proper understanding of our status vis-à-vis our God. We must learn what reverence and awe are – and then all these fundamental components of the Christian way will contribute to the new person we are in Christ – because Scripture says "…if anyone is in Christ, he is a new creation; the old has gone, the new has come!…".[353] The implication is that as God's own people, we will be set apart – not because we are better than anyone else – but because our approach to God and to our fellow human beings is grounded in humility – and therefore, we are different from those who believe otherwise. As Christians, our perspective of God and of life will be different from many of the people with whom we come into contact – and the real test is whether others see that it is Christ in us that makes that difference?

Fundamentally, holiness depends upon attitude. Our attitudes – and consequently, our priorities and behaviour must change from what they were –

---

[351] Isaiah 6:5
[352] 1 Timothy 1:15
[353] 2 Corinthians 5:17

to reflect who we are now and what we are now. These changes must become subject to God's divine influence and control if we are to make progress in becoming holy. To repeat the often-quoted approach – we must be 'in' the world – but we cannot be 'of' the world. That is to say, we live alongside every other human being each day of our lives – but that does not mean that our attitudes must conform to those of the people with whom we rub shoulders. This is summed up by Peter as follows: "...As obedient children, do not conform to the evil desires you had when you lived in ignorance. But just as He who called you is holy, so be holy in all you do; for it is written: 'Be holy, because I am holy'...".[354]

"...Today, vast stress is laid on the thought that God is personal, but this truth is so stated as to leave the impression that God is a person of the same sort as we are – weak, inadequate, ineffective, a little pathetic. But this is not the God of the Bible! Our personal life is a finite thing: it is limited in every direction, in space, in time, in knowledge, in power. But God is not so limited. He is eternal, infinite and almighty. He has us in His hands but we never have Him in ours...".[355]

8.5 The Eternal Dimension

We must remember that although the Bible begins with an account of Creation (Genesis Chapters 1 and 2), Almighty God, the 'I AM' of Scripture is the God of Eternity – that is to say past, present and future. Accordingly, while eternity embraces today – it does not start at a point of time in the past and end at some point in the future. This means that the creation of humankind falls within the time-frame of eternity. God pre-dates the created earth. In his book, 'The Case For A Creator', Lee Strobel presents a very helpful analysis "...from the fields of cosmology, physics, astronomy, biochemistry, DNA research and the study of human consciousness...", [356] that provides the context in which Almighty God exists. We are in danger of losing sight of how humble we should be before our Creator – and this being so, it is a humbling experience to read Lee Strobel's book and then to contemplate our Creator afresh. The word 'awe' comes to mind – but neither this word nor any other(s) within the lexicon of our vocabulary is able to do justice to any description of our God. Nevertheless,

---

[354] 1 Peter 1:14-16
[355] J I Packer; Knowing God; Pg 92; Hodder & Stoughton; 2013
[356] Lee Strobel; The Case For A Creator; Flap; Zondervan; 2004

vocabulary is all that we have to create any description and despite its limitations in this respect, we can get something of the flavour of the greatness of our God and the redemption story when we consider words such as those that follow. This particular spiritual song celebrates the total splendour of nature in praising God:[357]

O Lord my God, When I in awesome wonder,
Consider all the worlds Thy Hands have made;
I see the stars, I hear the rolling thunder,
Thy power throughout the universe displayed.
Then sings my soul, My Saviour God, to Thee,
How great Thou art, How great Thou art.
Then sings my soul, My Saviour God, to Thee,
How great Thou art, How great Thou art!
When through the woods, and forest glades I wander,
And hear the birds sing sweetly in the trees.
When I look down, from lofty mountain grandeur
And see the brook, and feel the gentle breeze.
And when I think, that God, His Son not sparing;
Sent Him to die, I scarce can take it in;
That on the cross, my burden gladly bearing,
He bled and died to take away my sin.
When Christ shall come, with shout of acclamation,
And take me home – what joy shall fill my heart.
Then I shall bow, in humble adoration,
And then proclaim: “My God, how great Thou art!”

While I do not have the sensitivity of a poet that would enable me to write such clear descriptions of God’s handiwork – and while I don’t have the depth of feeling of a musician to blend such words as these with the music that glorifies them, I feel truly blessed by those who have such gifts and who use them in ways such as in this tribute to our Creator, King.

In short, the starting point in understanding the context to which I referred above is a perception of the absolute majesty and holiness of eternal God. Note

---

[357] How Great Thou Art; Based On A Swedish traditional melody and a poem written by Carl Gustav Boberg (1859–1940) in Mönsterås, Sweden in 1885

the word ‘perception’. This conveys something of the way these fundamental Scriptural facts are understood and interpreted – but it is merely an attempt to understand God’s holiness and absolute perfection. Neither our words nor our experiences enable us to adequately understand or describe these matters accurately. The King James Version of the Bible captures this in the verse “…For now we see through a glass, darkly; but then face to face: now I know in part; but then shall I know even as also I am known…”.[358] One day – when our Lord returns or when He calls us home – all will be revealed and we will understand all those things that we trust in faith for the time being.

8.6 Perfection

God is perfect – and when He created the heavens and the earth (Genesis 1:1) and the Garden of Eden – where He placed Adam and Eve (Genesis 2:8) – everything there was perfect also. That is to say, God created humankind in perfection and in the absence of sin – in fact sin had not even entered into the scheme of things. Accordingly, there was neither sickness nor death nor pain nor suffering; there was neither strife nor conflict – nor shortages of any kind – and the climate – well it was entirely agreeable – neither too hot nor too cold. There were no weeds in the garden – but there were trees that provided food (Genesis 2:9), and a river (Genesis 2:10). There were animals and birds (Genesis 2:19). The birds sang and contributed to this idyllic place. The animals wandered about but they didn’t need to tear each other apart for food – because there was no food chain. Total serenity and peace prevailed – there was nothing adverse or negative. It was perfect! God made it that way and He was pleased with what He had created (Genesis 1:31). It’s fascinating to consider all this – but this perfect creation existed and was made thus so that Adam and Eve could enjoy it completely. This is how much God loved His creation. This is very difficult for us to imagine – let alone to absorb – and once again, mere words cannot adequately convey pure perfection – but words are all we have got. Despite this limitation, we have some flavour – albeit limited – of what perfection might have meant. Not only do we not have the right words to describe God’s creation in its sublime beauty but also our perception limits us. This is because our intellect has been tainted by our experience of a fallen world – stained and bruised in every quarter by sin and by its consequences. We need to reflect on how the world once

---

[358] 1 Corinthians 13:12

was and how it is now – because the way it is now is not how God intended it to be! We need to make this comparison and understand that humankind is responsible for those adverse changes between then and now. "…If the glory of God is reflected in all of creation, if the effects of sin reach to all of creation, and if the goal of redemption is to restore all of creation, then what should you and I care about? EVERYTHING!…".[359] Attitude is all-encompassing – affecting every aspect of our being.

In the same way that God perfected Eden for Adam and Eve, He continues to want the best for His people. I wonder whether we really understand this? God wants our world to be perfect and He wants us all to be perfect too. Samuel reminded the Lord's people way back when that "…The Lord was pleased to make you His own…"[360] This is so difficult to reconcile with the world as we know it today – full of war, strife, inhumanity, poverty, inequality, perversion, corruption and every kind of evil – harder still to reconcile when we remember these adversities are the inevitable consequences of humankind turning from God to go its own way. This is not what God wanted – or what He had planned. The only hope we have begins with the realisation that it is God's wish that every human being should be in a right relationship with Him. God our Saviour wants "…all men to be saved and to come to a knowledge of the truth…". [361]

Dallas Willard says it with the following wise words "…We are enraptured by a well-done movie sequence or by a few bars from an opera or lines from a poem. We treasure our great experiences for a lifetime, and we may have very few of them. But He is simply one great and inexhaustible experience of all that is good and true and beautiful and right. This is what we must think of when we hear theologians and philosophers speak of Him as a perfect Being. *This is His life…*".[362] No matter how much we try, we will not be able to absorb the meaning of these things while we remain in this part of eternity.

8.7 God's Patience

Not only is God's love beyond description and limitless in depth and scope, it is freely available at all times – and to all people. That is to say, the love of God extends to us during every part of life – both when we feel close to Him and

[359] Paul David Tripp; A Quest For More; Pg 45; New Growth Press; 2007
[360] 1 Samuel 12:22
[361] 1 Timothy 2:4
[362] Dallas Willard; The Divine Conspiracy; Pg 73; William Collins; 2014

also when we don't feel so close. Thankfully, God does not treat us the way we treat Him – in fact "...as far as the east is from the west, so far has He removed our transgressions from us..."[363] and elsewhere we are reminded by God's words "...I, even I, am the one who blots out your transgressions, for My own sake, and remember your sins no more...".[364]

God perseveres with us to an extent beyond description. He persevered with the children of Israel when He brought them out of Egypt. His patience is also beyond description. The Lord tolerates the fact that even though humankind was created perfect in the Garden of Eden, we degenerated quickly to the point where Scripture tells that "...the heart is deceitful above all things, and beyond cure...".[365] How could this have happened?

Subsequent to 'the Fall' (Genesis 3), humankind has become more and more depraved throughout history and has increasingly turned against Almighty God. Consider how often God's people have rebelled against Him – starting with the Fall in the Garden of Eden when Adam and Eve chose to do the only thing God told them not to do. A bit further on in Genesis we read, "...The Lord saw how great man's wickedness on the earth had become, and that every inclination of the thoughts of his heart was only evil all the time. The Lord was grieved that He had made man on the earth and His heart was filled with pain...Now the earth was corrupt in God's sight and was full of violence ...".[366] I wouldn't be surprised if this is how God regards humankind today – since things have only deteriorated over the course of history. How disappointed He must be.

God rescued His people miraculously – from the oppression of the Egyptians and in the process, brought them safely through the Red Sea. Nevertheless, in Numbers 11, we read that they complained. They grumbled that they had been better off in Egypt generally – and in particular, they complained about the lack of food.[367] This moaning went on and on – "...All the Israelites grumbled against Moses and Aaron, and the whole assembly said to them, 'If only we had died in Egypt...'[368] God was merciful and fed them (Numbers 11:31-35) and brought them to Canaan (the promised land) in due course – but the behaviour of His

[363] Psalm 103:12
[364] Isaiah 43:25
[365] Jeremiah 17:9
[366] Genesis 6:5-6, 11
[367] Exodus 16: 2-3
[368] Numbers 14:2

people (for whom He had already done so much) displeased Him and – '…His anger was aroused…'"[369]

Humankind's degeneracy is described throughout Scripture because it knows no end. For example, the Book of Judges describes the consistent failure of God's people and the introduction of Judges (leaders or champions) as a result of which prosperity returned – but soon after – the Israelites failed God again – and the process restarted. No matter how many times God supported His people with forgiveness and blessing, they responded with sinful behaviour and rejection of Him and His way. God appointed Samuel as His prophet. Through Samuel, God made known His ways to His people – but God specifically told them He did not want a King to be appointed. It's no surprise that this is precisely what His people did.

It is only "…because of the Lord's great love we are not consumed, for His compassions never fail. They are new every morning; great is your faithfulness…". (Lamentations 3:22-23). "…God did not send his Son into the world to condemn the world, but to save the world through Him…".[370] We seem to have learned so little from those times when humankind turned its back on God and pursued its own way. It never worked out well in Biblical times and it continues to fail to this very day.

In this case, the stimulus was the disobedience of God's people – but God's attitude towards His people demonstrates His perseverance and long-suffering nature – only made possible by His indescribable love towards us. The Psalmist said "…But you, O Lord are a compassionate and gracious God, slow to anger, abounding in love and faithfulness…".[371] We have disappointed God from time immemorial but His patience and perseverance is reflected by the fact that He does not punish us in the way we deserve. How great is the God we adore?[372] In this respect, J I Packer points out that "…within the cluster of God's moral perfections there is one in particular to which the term 'goodness' points – the quality which God specially singled out from the whole when, proclaiming 'all His goodness' to Moses, He spoke of Himself as 'abundant in *goodness* and truth' (Exod. 34:6f.). This is the quality of *generosity*. Generosity means a

[369] Numbers 11:1
[370] John 3:17
[371] Psalm 86:15
[372] Hymn; Joseph Hart; 1759

disposition to give to others in a way which has no mercenary motive and is not limited by what the recipients deserve, but consistently goes beyond it'…".[373]

8.8 God's Grace

'Grace' can be considered as the gift of God's favour. One author has said "…Grace implies both gift and gift freely given. It also implies a gift bestowed beyond the powers of the recipient to claim or to demand. Grace is a freely given gift of exceeding worth…".[374] The critical factor is that grace is unmerited – it can't be bought or acquired – it is given freely to all humankind whether people are Christians or not. This is referred to as 'Common Grace'. Scripture tells us "…He causes His sun to rise on the evil and the good, and sends rain on the righteous and the unrighteous…".[375] It has been said that "common grace is seen in God's continuing care for His creation, His restraining human society from becoming altogether intolerable and ungovernable, His making it possible for mankind to live together in a generally orderly and cooperative manner, and maintaining man's conscious sense of basic right and wrong behaviour…".[376]

There is a second type of grace – referred to as 'Saving Grace'. Unlike 'Common Grace', 'Saving Grace' refers to the grace by which Almighty God redeems sinners through faith in Jesus Christ. Just like Common Grace, Saving Grace is available to all because Jesus said that "… God so loved the world that He gave His one and only Son, that whoever believes in Him shall not perish but have eternal life…".[377] However, Saving Grace can only be enjoyed by those who acknowledge Jesus as Lord. "…If we confess our sins, He is faithful and just and will forgive us our sins and purify us from all unrighteousness…". [378]

The important point is that God makes both types of Grace available in the first place – and this says so much about His providence and love towards His creation. The fact that so many reject His Saving Grace but He still loves them and treats them with common grace speaks volumes about our God and Saviour. One writer says that "…The biblical way of putting this distinction would be to say that God is good to all in some ways and to some in all ways…".[379]

---

373 J I Packer; Knowing God; Pg 183; Hodder & Stoughton; 2013
374 James W Fowler; Stages Of Faith; Pg 302; Harper One; 1981
375 Matthew 5:45
376 S Lewis Johnson; The Doctrine of Common Grace
377 John 3:16
378 1 John1:9
379 J I Packer Knowing God; Pg 184; Hodder & Stoughton; 2013

Regrettably, society is replete with people who have grown so accustomed to enjoying God's common grace that they are unable to recognise it for what it is – unmerited favour.

Naturally, if we do not approach these sacred truths in an attitude of humility and gratitude, we will not even begin to comprehend their eternal significance.

8.9 Summary

It has been said that "…God's truthfulness and trustworthiness, His unfailing justice and wisdom. His tenderness, forbearance and entire adequacy to all who penitently seek His help, His noble kindness in offering people the exalted destiny of fellowship with Him in holiness and love – these things together make up God's goodness, in the overall sense of the sum total of His revealed excellences…"[380] Perhaps a good way to conclude these thoughts on God's person and plan is to consider some words from an old hymn by Joseph Hart that summarises the attitude we should adopt in considering these matters:[381]

How good is the God we adore,
Our faithful unchangeable friend;
His love is as great as His power,
And knows neither measure nor end.

My God is beyond description – His ways are infinite and His knowledge is beyond our comprehension. Perhaps, the inadequate prompts above might point us in the right direction as we worship and glorify Him. It has been said that "…when we consider that Jesus not only taught and acted out the ethics of the kingdom of God as spelled out in the Sermon on the Mount but also embodied those principles as the God-man, through the indwelling Holy spirit, so too should the Christian…".[382]

This chapter sits at the core of the text – because it provides the answer to the question – as to why attitude is important. The answer is since our God is the awesome Deity – whose love and providence are so comprehensive that our

[380] J I Packer; Knowing God; Pg 183; Hodder & Stoughton; 2013

[381] How Good Is The God We Adore; Joseph Hart; Hymns Composed On Various Subjects; 1759; Music – Celeste

[382] C Marvin Pate; From Plato To Jesus; Pg 281; Kregel Publications; 2011

finite minds do not have adequate capacity to comprehend Him – or to describe them, it is incumbent upon us to adopt appropriate attitudes in His service.

I have attempted to comment on who God is – and to describe His deity and purity in this chapter. Naturally, I have failed miserably in both respects – because it is beyond the capability of this writer to formulate adequate words despite experience, intellect and lexicon of vocabulary. As second best, I have attempted to provide some food for thought by the hints I have written.

We move now to chapter 9 – where we consider the status of humankind before the Almighty God we have considered in this chapter.

Chapter Nine
The Attitude of Humankind in Context

9.1 Introduction

In light of all that we have considered so far about the nature of Almighty God and about His providence and common and saving grace towards humankind – at least one significant question arises – and this concerns the implications for our attitude towards Him?

We will tease out some answers to this question in this chapter and in doing so we will explore the status of humankind and make some comments upon some of the attributes that should be influencing our attitudes as Christians. Regrettably, because our lives are often so busy, we can easily forget to consider the normative view – and so we default to a diluted Christian approach – or worse still to the approach of those around us who have no relationship with Almighty God at all. Dallas Willard reminds us that "…for anyone who has a genuine knowledge of God, praise is the only appropriate attitude in which to live…".[383] Have you considered the extent to which praise is the most fundamental attitude in your life? In this chapter, (notwithstanding chapters 5,6 and 7) we will (inter alia) consider love, awe and faith as fundamental sacrifices of praise.

9.2 The Status of Humankind

In the last chapter, we considered a small number of the Lord's attributes. We saw how His plan for humankind has been frustrated throughout the ages by the incessant moves away from Him by those who should be closest to Him. We

---

383 Dallas Willard; The Divine Conspiracy; Pg 267; Harper Collins; 2014

begin this chapter by reminding ourselves about the status of humankind before Almighty God.

Firstly, God has made man in His own image.[384] This means that God made humankind as "...a free spiritual being, a responsible moral agent with powers of choice and action, able to commune with Him and respond to Him, and by nature good, truthful, holy, upright (cf. Eccles. 7:29); in a word, godly...".[385] However, this all changed with the Fall of humankind in the Garden of Eden – we must remember that our attitudes are not automatically good because we are religious people.[386] Rick Richter points out that now, "...every inclination of his [humankind's] heart is evil from childhood...It explains why it is 'human nature' to be rebellious and indifferent toward God and selfish and neglectful of our fellow human beings. It is not hard to sin. It is not just a weakness; there is an inclination to do so. One does not have to think 'Now I will think or do something that is wrong.' It comes naturally...".[387] This is precisely what Scripture warns us about when it says (as quoted above) "...every inclination of the human heart is evil from childhood..."[388] and that "...I was sinful at birth, sinful from the time my mother conceived me...".[389] In chapter one of his letter to the Romans Paul provides a graphic description of our fallen state – and a later verse in Romans says, "...the sinful mind is hostile to God..."[390] On this basis, it's hard to know why the Lord bothers with us at all – for we are certainly people "...without excuse...".[391] Thankfully, God does not treat humankind as we deserve to be treated.

9.3 What Does The Lord Expect of Humankind?

Scripture reminds us that God "...has showed you, O man, what is good. And what does the Lord require of you? To act justly and to love mercy and to walk humbly with your God...". [392] You might have questions about what this means – so Scripture provides substantial insight into how we should conduct

---

384 Genesis 1:27
385 J I Packer; Knowing God; Pg 111; Hodder & Stoughton; 2013
386 John C Maxwell; Attitude 101; Pg 24; 2003; Maxwell Motivation
387 Rick Richter; Comparing the Qur'an And The Bible; Pg 165; Baker Books; 2011
388 Genesis 8:21
389 Psalm 51:5
390 Romans 8:7
391 Romans 1:20
392 Micah 6:8

our lives – that is to say how the Lord would like us to live. For example, elsewhere, Scripture reminds us that God said "... If My people, who are called by My name, will humble themselves and pray and seek My face and turn from their wicked ways, then will I hear from heaven and will forgive their sin and will heal their land...". [393]

There is food for thought in these verses – but notice in particular, the central role of humility – the significance of humility for the Christian was discussed earlier (see Para 5.2). Humility is not to be underestimated – it takes a lifetime of effort and practice to have any meaningful understanding of what this means for everyday living. Acting justly and loving mercy represent humility in action. As we have seen already, attitude is a determinant of action – so it's important to consider what sort of an attitude is likely to lead to a life that is dedicated to glorifying and honouring Almighty God.

Earlier in this text, reference was made to Philippians 2:5 – the verse that tells us explicitly what our attitude should be – "...Your attitude should be the same as that of Jesus Christ...". [394] In one sense, this succinct statement leaves no doubt as to what is expected from each of us as Christians in principle – but the danger is that we read it too quickly and gloss over the significance of these words without taking time to mull over what this might mean on a day-to day basis? In C S Lewis' view this means that "...The first step is to recognise that your moods change. The next is to make sure that if you have accepted Christianity, then some of its main doctrines shall be deliberately held before your mind for some time every day. That is why daily prayers and religious readings and Church-going are necessary parts of the Christian life. We have to be continually reminded of what we believe. Neither this belief nor any other will automatically remain in the mind. It must be fed...".[395] The food comes from a number of sources – not least Holy Scripture – which helps us to grasp the application of these words. Help also comes from past experiences. It is good to remember that "...God chooses what we go through but we choose how we go through it...". [396] In the words of Epictetus "...It's not what happens to you, but how you react to it that matters...". While it is a truism for the Christian to believe that his/her attitude should reflect Christ's, we need the benefit of

---

[393] 2 Chronicles 7:14

[394] Philippians 2:5

[395] C S Lewis; Mere Christianity; Harper San Francisco; Pg 141; 1952

[396] John C Maxwell; Developing The Leader Within You; Pg 105; Thomas Nelson Publishing; 1993

experience to help us consider questions like – what would Jesus do in such circumstances. (This is a question that Christians were encouraged (some years ago) to ask themselves but which appears now to be less well used.) Some direct answers might be found in Scripture (do not steal, do not commit adultery) but other answers will not be there per se (should I marry this person). In such circumstances, it is wise to refer to the principles Scripture includes about the question in hand and what the Lord has taught us through our previous experiences that might relate to this matter. All this should be a part of prayerful advice seeking from our Saviour in an attempt to figure out what the Lord would have us do in the circumstances in which we find ourselves. In seeking the Lord's will, we should be humble, prayerful and energetic in researching Scripture and perhaps in taking advice from Christian friends when that is possible. Frequent attendance at public worship is another means of understanding God's will for us on an on-going basis. It's also important to think about our on-going experiences and what the Lord might be trying to teach us about our current situation by reference to our current experiences – sensitivity is once more the order of the day. If our attitude is not right, it is unlikely that we will be taking the steps that are necessary in determining what we should do in any particular circumstance.

As quoted earlier, the prophet Micah asked and answered an important question as follows – "…And what does the Lord require of you? To act justly and to love mercy and to walk humbly with your God…". [397] This should be a helpful starting point for Christians. How to apply this principle depends upon many variables – not least our attitude. If we were all to live in a way that glorifies God, our attitudes would reflect this – because in this case – we would try to avoid doing anything that would offend our God and simultaneously put more effort in doing things in a way that we believe is in accordance with Scripture. The questions it might be useful to ask ourselves include – am I living in a way that glorifies God – really? Do I act justly (fairly)? Am I merciful (willing to forgive)? Am I living humbly?

[397] Micah 6:8

9.4 The Status of the Non-Christian

If we are not Christians, our human spirit will make every effort to curtail the Holy Spirit's influence and thereby limit the Holy Spirit's prompts to behave in a way that will be acceptable to God. Until the point when we accept Christ's redemptive gift of salvation, humankind is unable to "...accept the things that come from the Spirit of God, for they are foolishness to him, and he cannot understand them, because they are spiritually discerned...".[398] This means that non-Christians default – naturally – to a style of life that prioritises their own well-being. Dallas Willard points out to anyone who might be in this position that "...you're a soul made by God, made for God, and made to need God, which means you were not made to be self-sufficient...".[399]

Regrettably, the consequence is that non-Christians are frequently de-sensitised to the status of people around them because "...They are darkened in their understanding and separated from the life of God because of the ignorance that is in them due to the hardening of their hearts...".[400] One author suggests that "...every non-Christian is living in tension with the realities he experiences. God points things out to us but we wilfully turn a blind eye...".[401] Non-Christians don't deliberately and directly create hardness in their heart – it's not premeditated. Instead, it is a consequence of moving further and further away from God and His ways. This happens through desensitised conscience and unwillingness to consider Christ's plans for them.

This is not to say that non-Christians are not good people nor uncaring people nor people who do not have integrity. Some non-Christians have much to teach those of us who claim to be Christ's disciples – because we often fall short of the standards set for us by Jesus Christ. The difficulty is that frequently, non-Christians have little outside of themselves to which they may aspire. Naturally therefore, the other influences to which they are subject, manifest themselves in human passions, affections and desires that are likely to be entirely different to those of Christians. We must be careful because attitudes are reinforced by beliefs – whether they are right or wrong.[402] In other words, the values and standards adopted by non-Christians emanate from the absence of the Holy

[398] 1 Corinthians 2:14
[399] Dallas Willard; As Quoted By John Ortberg; Soul Keeping; Pg 39; Zondervan; 2014
[400] Ephesians 4:18
[401] Peter May; The Search For God & The Path To Persuasion; Pg 139; Malcolm Down Publishing; 2016
[402] John C Maxwell; Attitude 101; Pg 31; 2003; Maxwell Motivation

Spirit's influence upon the spirit of mankind and in light of this vacuum, a character is formed that is different to what God wants it to be. This does not mean that Christians are somehow better than non-Christians – because Christians are sinners just the same as everyone else. Christians are no better people than non-Christians! The difference between Christians and non-Christians is that Christians are sinners saved by accepting God's grace – whereas non-Christians have rejected God's grace. However, the good news is that – as stated above – saving grace is available to everyone – no matter what their status. This is what the hymn writer meant when long ago he wrote the hymn "...Naught have I gotten but what I received – grace has bestowed it since I have believed. Boasting excluded, pride I abase, I'm only a sinner saved by grace...".[403]

9.5 The Significance of a Christian's Soul

We considered the essence of our Souls earlier in this text (Para 3.4) – but I would like to add a few more comments here. "...A deep soul has the capacity to understand and empathise deeply with other people – not just himself. A deep soul notices and questions and doesn't just go through the motions. A deep soul lives in conscious awareness of eternity, not simply to-day. It notices and observes and reflects in surprising ways ...".[404] How can Christians even understand or react appropriately to the blatant needs of the world around them in the absence of this sort of sensitivity? The quote from John Ortberg above suggests to me that this sensitivity comes from 'a deep soul'.

My experience suggests that those who do not yet know Christ as Saviour cannot have the same degree of sensitivity as a Christian. This is because in general – the soul of a non-believer is not attuned to the needs or to the circumstances in which other people find themselves. How can (s)he be if (s)he is unaware of the need of Christ as Saviour? Note that I am not thinking here about all those very self-sacrificing individuals who have devoted themselves (sometimes entirely – and for their whole lives) in serving the needs of others. These are exceptional people in my view – who, whether they are Christians or not, are showing exemplary Christ-like love. Such people are already sensitive to very practical matters of life and death in some cases – but unless they are in

[403] James Martin Gray; Moody Bible Institute; 1851-1935

[404] John Ortberg; Soul Keeping; Pg 57; Zondervan; 2014

a personal relationship with Jesus Christ, their practical sensitivity cannot be complemented with the sensitivity required to redeem their own soul and the souls of the people around them. **No matter how 'good' people may be, they must accept God's saving grace before they can be in a right relationship with Him.**

So, what are the factors that are most likely to sensitise the soul of a believer? Here are some for consideration.

9.6 Love

"...we must understand that God does not 'love' us without liking us – through gritted teeth – as 'Christian' love is sometimes thought to do. Rather, out of the eternal freshness of His perpetually self-renewed being, the Heavenly Father cherishes the earth and each human being upon it. The fondness, the endearment, the unstintingly affectionate regard of God towards all His creatures is the natural outflow of what He is to the core – which we vainly try to capture with our tired but indispensable old-world *love*...".[405] We must be careful to understand what love is – "...love in the Christian sense, does not mean an emotion. It is a state not of the feelings but of the will; that state of the will that we have naturally about ourselves, and must learn to have about other people...".[406]

Love is a fundamental theme in Scripture. In fact, as Christians, we are required to "...do everything in love...".[407] – so it is fitting that reference is made to it here. In Scripture (see Para 6.2) there are many guiding principles (see Para 1.6 above) that emanate from those rules. For example, Jesus said "...My command is this: Love each other as I have loved you..."[408] and again "...live a life of love...".[409] "...Above all, love each other deeply, because love covers a multitude of sins...". [410] We should be careful to note that love requires more than merely abstaining from wrongdoing – it requires positive action. Consider Jesus' instruction to "...Love your enemies, do good to those who hate you, bless those who curse you, pray for those who mistreat you. ...".[411] This is radical

[405] Dallas Willard; The Divine Conspiracy; Pg 74; William Collins; 2014
[406] C S Lewis; Mere Christianity; Pg 129; HarperCollins; 1952
[407] 1 Corinthians 16:14
[408] John 15:12
[409] Ephesians 5:2
[410] 1 Peter 4:8
[411] Luke 6:27-28

teaching – way beyond the capacity of humans working in their own strength. In this world, we have adopted a philosophy that is the direct opposite of this teaching – and we have been doing this for so many years that no one can remember when it started. Despite how clever and progressive and developed humankind has become, we have not yet learned that selfishness and pursuing a strategy of 'I, me and mine' does not work well for anybody other than me. It only makes the perpetrator selfish, insensitive and self-serving and antagonises others. At its worst, it produces loneliness, isolation, misery and unhappiness. Why do we pursue this route even though time and experience has shown it leads to disaster? One reason is that we do not behave rationally as human beings – maybe we are too proud to concede that Jesus' way is better – although much harder – to the extent that it is unthinkable for most people – or is it just too hard?

Jesus was once asked by a law expert to explain which is "...the greatest commandment in the law...?" ...Jesus replied: "Love the Lord your God with all your heart and with all your soul and with all your mind." This is the first and greatest commandment. And the second is like it "...Love your neighbour as yourself". All the Law and the Prophets hang on these two commandments...[412]. There is so much dependent upon observance of these two 'rules' – that if we managed to internalise them and embed them into our character, our attitude would be so much different – in fact, it would be "...the same as that of Christ Jesus ...".[413]

One description of love that I have found deeply helpful is that "...Love is the only way to grasp another human being in the innermost core of his personality. No one can become fully aware of the very essence of another human being unless he loves him. By his love he is enabled to see the essential traits and features in the beloved person; and even more, he sees that which is potential in him, which is not yet actualised but yet ought to be actualised. Furthermore, by his love, the loving person enables the beloved person to actualise these potentialities. By making him aware of what he can be and of what he should become, he makes these potentialities come true...".[414] We should be aiming to live lives based on love (1 Corinthians 13) and in doing so, we should adopt the style that Peter describes in 2 Peter 1:5-8.

---

[412] Matthew 22: 34-40

[413] Philippians 2:5

[414] Viktor E Frankl; "Man's Search for Meaning"; Pg 134; Washington Square Press; 1985

Much more could be said on this topic – but so much has been written about it already elsewhere – and more profoundly – that there is less need to dwell on it further here. Accordingly, only this brief reference to love has been provided to emphasise the fact that love is a determining factor in attitude – and to stimulate us to think more on these things.

9.7 Awe

In chapter 8, we considered God's Person. We looked at His perfection, His nature, His patience and His grace – and concluded that our God is truly awesome (in the proper sense of this word). It can be no surprise therefore that God expects His creation to treat Him with appropriate respect and reverence – "...in order that you may live a life worthy of the Lord and may please Him in every way: bearing fruit in every good work, growing in the knowledge of God...".[415] He is the Creator and we are His servants – the created. We are told "...just as He who called you is holy, so be holy in all you do; for it is written: 'Be holy, because I am holy'...".[416]

In this respect, God's requirement goes way back in time. For example, consider Samuel's words to the Lord's people in the Old Testament "...be sure to fear the Lord and serve Him faithfully with all your heart ...".[417] The word 'awe' captures the word 'fear' in this verse. This theme is continued in the New Testament where we read '...in your hearts set apart Christ as Lord'.[418]

In short, God wants us to emulate him – in our character, in our values and principles – and thereby in our attitudes – "...to be made new in the attitude of your minds; and to put on the new self, created to be like God in true righteousness and holiness...". [419] John Ortberg puts it like this "...Doing something in Jesus' name means to do it in His character. It means doing it as Jesus Himself would do it if He were in your place ...". [420] This fits with the instruction "...He must become greater; I must become less...". [421] This includes living according to the principles set out in the Beatitudes (Matthew 5:1-12) – so that our lives begin to reflect the fruits of the Spirit (Galatians 5:22-23).

---

[415] Colossians 1:10
[416] 1 Peter 1:15-16
[417] 1 Samuel 12:24
[418] 1 Peter 3:15
[419] Ephesians 4:23-24
[420] John Ortberg; The Life You've Always Wanted; Pg 201; Zondervan; 2002
[421] John 3:30

Scripture asks the question "...what does the Lord your God ask of you..." and answers "... to fear the Lord your God, to walk in all His ways, to love Him, to serve the Lord your God with all your heart and with all your soul...". [422] It is not possible to adopt the right attitude towards God unless we are not only humbled by His holiness but also hold Him in awe – in love. How great is our God! However, Scripture has made us aware that "...the sinful mind is hostile to God..." [423] and if nothing else, then this alone behoves us to point those who have not yet accepted Christ as the Lord of their lives to consider these eternal truths. If we find it difficult to do so in words – then we must do so through our example at least.

9.8 Faith

The word 'faith' has more than one meaning. For example, we use this word to refer to particular religions such as the Christian faith. Faith also means strong trust – and it is in this sense that faith is foundational to the Christian way. In this case, faith means confidence in God. Sometimes Christians refer to 'saving faith' by way of acknowledging that we need faith if we are to respond to God's offer of salvation "...for now we see through a glass, darkly; but then face to face: now I know in part; but then shall I know even as also I am known...".[424] Often we have to concede that there is so much about our relationship with our Saviour about which we are unaware and that we do not have the capacity to understand. This is an understandable difficulty if we happen to be sharing our beliefs with positivists (whose approach is to adopt 'the scientific method' – which requires verifiable facts to be presented to them before they can consider becoming Christians. Such an approach leaves no room for faith.) Positivists must be lovingly made aware that it is not possible to prove God because we need to exercise faith as part of our conversion to Christianity.

In his book, James Fowler (a respected writer in developmental psychology) provides a review of the conclusions of Wilfred Cantwell Smith as further summarised here as follows: "...Faith, rather than belief or religion is the most fundamental category in the human quest for transcendence...Each of the major religious traditions studied speaks about faith in ways that make the same phenomenon visible. In each and all, faith involves an alignment of the will, a

---

[422] Deuteronomy 10:12
[423] Romans 8:7
[424] KJV; 1 Corinthians 13:12

resting of the heart, in accordance with a vision of transcendent value and power, one's ultimate concern…Faith, classically understood, is not a separate dimension of life, a compartmentalized speciality. Faith is an orientation of the total person, giving purpose and goal to one's hopes and strivings, thoughts and actions…".[425] While Fowler distinguishes faith from religion and belief (he says "…faith is a generic feature of the human struggle to find and maintain meaning and that it may or may not find religious expression…"[426]), he says "…faith is an integral part of one's character…"[427] and faith and religion "…are reciprocal. Each is dynamic; each grows or is renewed through its interaction with the other…".[428]

In addition to 'faith' per se, in his book, Dr Fowler presents a very useful description of what he refers to as "…the structural development theory of faith stages…".[429] He explains that "…In the course of their [our] research into structural aspects of faith development, they [we] have identified seven categories in relation to which the dominant features of the stage of a person's faith may be identified…".[430] The value (not least with respect to this text) is that Dr Fowler's text clearly indicates how attitudes can be influenced by the faith 'stage' someone is in at a particular moment of human development. This is fascinating insight into the sorts of influences on our attitude that we might easily overlook.

How to define 'faith'? This is how the (unknown) writer to the Hebrews defined it – "…faith is being sure of what we hope for and certain of what we do not see. This is what the ancients were commended for…".[431] The 'ancients' were commended because they exercised faith – examples of which are provided in Hebrews "…By faith Moses' parents hid him for three months after he was born, because they saw he was no ordinary child, and they were not afraid of the king's edict. By faith Moses, when he had grown up, refused to be known as the son of Pharaoh's daughter… By faith he left Egypt, not fearing the king's anger; he persevered because he saw Him who is invisible. By faith he kept the Passover

---

425 Wilfred Cantwell Smith; The Meaning and End Of Religion, Belief and History and Faith and Belief; as quoted by James W Fowler; Stages Of Faith; Pg 14; Harper One; 1981
426 James W Fowler; Stages Of Faith; Pg 91; Harper One; 1981
427 James W Fowler; Stages Of Faith; Pg 92; Harper One; 1981
428 James W Fowler; Stages Of Faith; Pg 9; Harper One; 1981
429 James W Fowler; Stages Of Faith; Pg 199; Harper One; 1981
430 James W Fowler; Stages Of Faith; Pg 241; Harper One; 1981
431 Hebrews 11:1

and the sprinkling of blood, so that the destroyer of the firstborn would not touch the firstborn of Israel…”.[432]

Elsewhere, it has been suggested that “…For most of us, most of the time, faith functions so as to screen off the abyss of mystery that surrounds us…I want to affirm the largeness and mystery of faith. So *fundamental* that none of us can live well for very long without it, so *universal* that when we move beneath the symbols, rituals and ethical patterns that express it, faith is recognizably the same phenomenon in Christians, Marxists, Hindus and Dinka, yet it is *so infinitely varied* that each person's faith is unique. Faith is inexhaustibly mysterious…”[433]

9.9 Summary

In this chapter, we looked at some aspects of humankind – status, what God requires of us, the particular status of non-Christians and importantly, we emphasised the significance of a Christian's soul – building upon para 3.4 above. The second half of the chapter focused on three factors that are most likely to sensitise the soul of a believer – love, awe and faith.

Overall, the preceding text is a serious attempt to show us a better way – but make no mistake about it – the principles and rules are extremely difficult to apply in a full and meaningful way – on a daily basis. While all this guidance plays a role, it is no more than a part of a long process of learning and understanding – but therein lies the joy because it is a journey of continuous learning and application. Most importantly – the proof of the pudding is in the eating and so application tests the extent to which we have applied ourselves in seeking to honour God. Accordingly, these are on-going challenges – but the good thing is that the process is itself a teacher about the experiences that we will have along the way. One important point to consider is that while many of us find rules helpful in understanding what is required in certain circumstances, principles allow us to form our own rules to cover those situations in which we have no specific guidance. This is experience in action.

The next chapter (10), is the last in section 3. Having looked at God's person and plan (to the extent that we are able to do so), we then considered – by way of comparison, the dreadful status of humankind and its lack of devotion and awe

---

432 Hebrews 11:23-28

433 James W Fowler; Stages Of Faith; Pgs xii-xiii; Harper One; 1981

towards Almighty God. Chapter 10 explores what this means with respect to how we conduct our lives with our fellow human beings on a day-to-day basis.

(For further guidance, consider: Ephesians 4:17-32 and Chapters 5 and 6.)

Chapter Ten
Humankind's Attitude Towards Humankind

10.1 Introduction

In this chapter, we will focus on humankind's relationship with humankind. Right at the outset, we probably all agree that no matter where we look – whether globally, nationally, locally – or perhaps even in our personal environments – observations on humankind's relationship with humankind are far from encouraging.

In a global context, the world is experiencing conflict on all sides. It seems that humankind is more prone to being at war than in living in harmony and as if the death, suffering, bloodshed and grief arising therefrom is not enough, we cannot but despair at the collateral damage arising. The number of refugees and people fleeing for their lives from conflict zones continues to increase – the Rohingyas and the Yazidi causes are two blatant cases in point (although there are many more than these two). The sheer brutality and violence together with all the attendant misery, grief and despair point to the total brokenness of humanity. The problems have become so large in terms of human suffering that we have difficulty in absorbing the cumulative trauma and its effects in terms of human grief. "...The world has unwittingly created a hierarchy of suffering...".[434] The physical and mental trauma being experienced by those who have escaped must make us wonder about the horrific status of those who have been unable to leave, Afghanistan being a case in point. Whether – and to what extent – people are able ever to get over such traumas – remains to be seen.

Even in countries where there is no war per se, there is often conflict – arising from all sorts of social problems – not least in inner cities where there is obvious

---

[434] Genocide Prevention – Never Again, Again And Again; The Economist; Pg 66; 08 December 2018

decline and decay. Health Services can no longer cope demonstrated ever so clearly by the covid 19 pandemic. As if this was not already far more than enough, we are taking inadequate action to save our environment with the clear implication that further global damage is inevitable. Knife attacks are increasing continuously – not least in UK. Prisons are frequently too small to accommodate all the offenders. We are used to hearing statistics that summarise the number of assaults, robberies killings and rape that happen annually in cities around the world. ("...The number of murders in Mexico increased by 27% last year to a record 31,174, according to the country's statistics institute...".[435] This is equivalent to 85 murders every day – 1 every 20 minutes. It is difficult to absorb the implications of this single statistic.) Note that this is the type of metric used to identify whether there has been any progress year on year! If these statistics are falling this infers greater societal cohesion. It's not easy to reconcile fewer murders with social cohesion – but that is what the metric is used to measure. It is not possible to imagine the cruelty and barbarity involved in human trafficking – nor the irreparable ensuing physical and mental trauma. How is it possible that one human being can have so much disdain, so little empathy and a complete lack of sensitivity towards another to allow such wickedness? Why do we find it so difficult to live in harmony? Why is there so much brutality and violence? How can such wickedness exist? How can humankind be so depraved?

Even at a personal level, the story is not dissimilar. On an on-going basis, our newspapers are full of stories of physical attacks, sexual abuse (in some cases going back years and years), fraud, verbal abuse and all sorts of examples of people who are unable to live peaceably alongside others. We often put this down to ethnicity or to religion – but in fact, the people carrying out attacks in the name of religion appear often to understand little about what their religion says concerning violence and respect for others. The force that drives these types of behaviour is not religion – it is pure evil – what the Christian calls the propensity to sin. One of our Lord's instructions is that we should "...Let the peace of Christ rule in your hearts...".[436] We have failed to the uttermost in this respect – to the extent that we are now focusing on not being "...overcome by evil, but overcome evil with good...".[437]

[435] The World This Week; The Economist; Pg 5: 04 August 2018
[436] Colossians 3:15
[437] Romans 12:21

At first sight, it is overwhelming to consider issues such as these (and only a very few examples out of the plethora that are available have been given), we risk despairing in light of the fact that there is little or nothing (physically) that we can do about it. Is this correct? While most of us are not empowered – nor have the capacity – to intervene in such matters in a way that will bring them to an end, we are not entirely helpless either. Generally speaking, when we want things to change, we have to start with ourselves. Maybe one thing that we could do is to ask questions of ourselves such as – what can I do to improve those areas over which I have the power and capacity to exert influence for change? "...Nothing is more difficult to accomplish than changing outward actions without changing inward feelings...".[438] Maybe this seems very superficial compared to what we have been considering in this paragraph – but maybe even the smallest changes will gain enough cumulative momentum over time to influence positive change. (The seat-belt example and the no-smoking example cited above indicate that change is possible.) I think it's worth trying – and seemingly innocuous actions such as increasing praying may be the place to start.

10.2 Insensitivity

We considered 'sensitivity' in an earlier paragraph (4.3) – but now I want to add a few words about 'insensitivity' – especially with respect to how we speak – because what we say comes from the heart – and it is at that point we must strive to change attitudes.

Many of us live in environments where even making eye contact with another person can be problematic. In such circumstances, people tend to wonder whether they are being considered as a possible victim. We tend not to think that the other person is merely trying to be friendly – because this is how our society is likely to mould our thinking. Probably, it's most noticeable on underground trains when it seems that everyone is making determined efforts to avoid eye contact with other people. We certainly would never dream of embarking upon a conversation! We live in an age that is hallmarked by suspicion – where the norm is to be suspicious of strangers. We expect people to demonstrate that they are not suspicious and we believe they are or might be suspicious until they prove themselves otherwise. It might be reasonably argued that the media provides ample evidence every day to demonstrate that this is a prudent way to behave –

---

[438] John C Maxwell; Attitude 101; Pg 35; 2003; Maxwell Motivation

and often it is – but not always. Sometimes, our suspicions arise from bias at worst – or misunderstanding at best. We need to be careful in our assessments.

Naturally, we cannot make contact with – or speak to everyone we meet – but there are occasions (for example when we are walking or in a park or somewhere else where we pass by someone else) when saying 'hello' is – or should be – a natural acknowledgement of the presence of another human being. On some such occasions and in the right circumstances, it might be quite easy to acknowledge the presence of someone else. Often, we fail to take such opportunities. Is this a safety mechanism, a cultural influence or is that just a stick we lean upon because we don't want to bother trying to be friendly? My experience is that people respond (although not always it has to be said) when greeted by someone else. Even when we don't speak, our body language often says a great deal. Recently, an older woman in our local village shop was taking more than a little time to pay for her meagre shopping – talking all the while to the shop assistant. When the lady finally left, the shop assistant apologised to me for keeping me waiting. She explained that the older lady likes to come in and have a chat – for as long as possible – because she has no one else to talk with. With respect to older people about whom I am aware, I asked myself whether I am sufficiently sensitive to their needs in general – and to their loneliness in particular? Have you ever considered these types of questions?

Worse than ignoring someone else is to overhear one person berating another – or speaking insensitively to or about someone else – in the absence of the subject person. Do I do this I ask myself? It's so easy to fall into this trap – but it's insensitive and not good practice – especially for Christians – see quotations below.

Communication is a great gift – one that distinguishes human beings from animals. That said, communicating effectively is a skill – and as such, it takes time to learn the rudiments – that is to say when to speak and when to be silent. It is also important to know what words to use – but just as important – which of all the words that could be used are the most appropriate in the circumstances. Then there is the tone we adopt. Sometimes a quiet word spoken empathically achieves much more than a reprimand spoken loudly and vehemently. In short, when we speak (because speaking is the main way we communicate), we have some options. It is frequently better not to speak at all than to do so in a way that is negative or demeaning – or even overcharged. I am going to try to remember this next time I am on the point of expressing myself – especially when I am in the car! Remember the 'I don't like your attitude' examples considered in chapter 1? Our attitude will determine when we speak and what we say and how we say it – and to whom.

Scripture has some things to say about speaking. For example, we are told "…The tongue also is a fire, a world of evil among the parts of the body. It corrupts the whole person, sets the whole course of his life on fire, and is itself set on fire by hell…".[439] Scripture warns us that "…The tongue, has the power of life and death…"[440] and that "…whoever would love life and see good days must keep his tongue from evil and his lips from deceitful speech…".[441] The Psalms contain similar warnings – "…Set a guard over my mouth O Lord; keep watch over the door of my lips…".[442] Clearly, Scripture includes a number of precautions about speaking so it is important to exercise control over what we say – but Christians have added responsibilities in this respect.

Moving on from exercising control over what we say and how we speak, we shouldn't lose sight of the value of communicating positively. For example, it does not take much effort to give someone a compliment – but we often find it easier to withhold compliments and indeed all positive words or encouragements – even when we know how appropriate and important it can be to say a few meaningful words to someone. Sometimes we withhold a compliment because we are inwardly a little bit jealous and we feel the need to avoid making the other person feel a little bit better about him/herself. It's almost as if there is not enough goodwill to go around and if I make someone feel good, there won't be enough left for me (see below). Encouragement is not restricted to acknowledging really important achievements – it can also be applied in so many everyday scenarios. For example – "thank you for coming", or "I appreciate your support" or "I know it must be difficult for you at the moment – but I really admire you for coping so well" – or "that meal was delicious" – or "you are looking happy". The permutations are endless – all it takes is a little empathy and a big heart to eradicate insensitivity! "…Therefore encourage one another and build each other up, just as in fact you are doing…".[443] Further, "…let us consider how we may spur one another on toward love and good deeds. Let us not give up meeting

---

[439] James 3:6
[440] Proverbs 18:21
[441] 1 Peter 3:10
[442] Psalm 141:3
[443] 1 Thessalonians 5:11

together, as some are in the habit of doing, but let us encourage one another – and all the more as you see the Day approaching…".[444]

Stephen Covey refers to what he calls the scarcity mentality [445] – the view that I cannot applaud you or your efforts because if I do, there will not be enough kudos left for me. Consider what sort of a difference it might make to someone else if you acknowledged them or managed to strike up a conversation with them – or even complimented them. Consider what sort of difference it might make in your life if you were able to do such things on a regular basis – and if others treated you similarly. (Sometimes, we refuse to say positive things to other people because no one says positive things to us. Is this a mature Christian attitude I ask myself?) What is the cost benefit ratio here? It seems to me that the ratio is skewed heavily towards making people feel better where and when we can. There is probably very little risk involved and a whole lot of positive potential.

I don't believe that we are naturally callous – I think we have to learn to be so. However, we learn really quickly – often as the result of hard knocks and disappointment arising from how other people treat us. It is not easy to turn the other cheek but it might be helpful to remember that "…people do things for their reasons…And those reasons are emotional, aroused by the ways they feel…".[446] It is one of our responsibilities as Christians to try to break through the hard exterior that many people surround themselves with – because beneath that outer veneer, there is a heart that our Saviour loves – and whom we as Christians are called upon to love as well. We don't have to like everyone we meet – or even to like everyone we work with or even all those who go to the same Church – but we are required to love them. More strongly than trying to love those whom we do not like particularly, Jesus has even told us to "…Love your enemies, do good to those who hate you…".[447] What a challenge!

On the human plane, and in referring to Tennessee Williams, Lady Maria St. Just said "…I wanted people to see the real Tennessee, who was a gentle, loving, kind, incredibly sensitive, marvellous human being," she continues. "He was always concerned about the person who had the least chance in life, the least

---

[444] Hebrews 10:24-25

[445] Steven Covey; The 7 Habits Of Highly Effective People: Pg 230; Simon & Schuster; 1989

[446] From "Be A People Person"; John C Maxwell; Cook Ministries; 1994 as quoted by Bob Conklin; How to Get People to Do Things

[447] Luke 6:27

chance of making a success. He was always for the underdog." That concern, as Williams himself said, became the basic premise of his work: "The need for understanding and tenderness and fortitude among individuals trapped by circumstance."

"... He had X-ray eyes, and they went right into situations. He felt so deeply about everything. He was just so passionate, and he understood the smallest detail that would be in anybody's heart, the tiniest desire, the tiniest rejection, the tiniest affection. He would just sense it." [448]

As considered earlier (Para 4.3) sensitivity exposes us as human beings to a vast range of opportunities to add value to the life of those around us and to the communities within which we exist – and the quote above testifies to this. However, in so doing it also exposes us to a degree of hurt and is therefore not to be taken lightly. The more sensitive you are, the more keenly you will feel the insensitivity and insults and sleights of others. The corollary is that the more sensitive you are the greater you will enjoy the sheer depth of love and beauty and everything positive around you. Each one of us must choose what our attitude should be to sensitivity – what will your decision be?

10.3 Duplicity

We considered honesty in a previous paragraph (para 6.4.2) – but I just want to add a comment from the perspective of duplicity – because being honest means there is no room for duplicity – the truth, the whole truth and nothing but the truth is the required standard. Many of us have been taught that 'honesty is the best policy'. While that still remains the case (and always will be), the honest to goodness truth is that in our society, this is often regarded as an extreme – not the norm. (I recently handed over to someone a £5 note that he had pulled out of his pocket inadvertently – without realising it. Not a lot of money – but more than any of us would want to throw away. The man was really pleased – as pleased as if I had handed him back a lot more. He was surprised he had lost the money – but even more surprised that someone had returned it. This says a lot about the society in which we live.) Shouldn't we be living our lives as honest people?

---

448 "Remembering Tennessee Williams as a Gentle Genius of Empathy"; Mervyn Rothstein;30May1990https://archive.nytimes.com/www.nytimes.com/books/00/12/31/specials/williams-empathy.html

You may have heard the expression 'you are too honest'. What does that mean? Is it possible to be too honest? Surely a person is either honest or dishonest? Can there be anything in between? Our whole world seems to be hallmarked by a propensity to be less than totally honest. Even those in the highest office find it expedient to be less than totally honest. The regrettable fact about being dishonest is that the more dishonest we become, the more difficult it is to be honest about the extent to which we are dishonest or indeed about anything in the future. It is much easier to lie than to tell the truth – at least at first – but once we start telling lies there is no end to the mischief that we can create – deliberately or otherwise. As lying increases, it becomes harder to separate fact from fiction. Politicians are very exposed in this respect. It's not good enough to add deliberately a 'half-truth' or an outright lie as a response to a question.

Once upon a time people had a sense of self-respect and were able to genuinely affirm that their word was their bond. They meant that when they said something, it was true and they stood by it. If they committed to do something, they could be relied upon to do it. Generally, speaking we find that in the society in which we live, we cannot rely on too many people to be honest or to tell the truth or to honour their commitments or to behave with integrity. Why should this be? Where have all the old values gone? Why have we lost our self-respect? Sadly, the attitude of integrity is rarely seen in action.

As Christians, we are called upon to be 'salt and light'.[449] We are called to maintain standards and values that are appropriate to our status as sinners who have been saved by God's overwhelming grace. It makes me think what the world would be like if there was less duplicity in it and more integrity and personal discipline. None of this is easy – naturally – otherwise it would not be a challenge. In addition, we must allow for the fact that "…People treat you according to how they see themselves rather than how you really are…" [450] – and so a huge effort is required by we Christians to tilt that balance back in the direction in which the Lord expects it to be in the first place.

---

[449] Matthew 5:13-14

[450] John C Maxwell; Be A People Person; Cook Ministries; 1994

10.4 Indifference

Another type of behaviour that we often display as Christians is indifference or apathy – a blatant lack of concern or interest – or maybe a better definition is a blatant failure to take any action because we are unwilling to exert ourselves to do so. In this respect, Theodore Roosevelt has said "...In a moment of decision, the best thing you can do is the right thing to do, the next best thing is the wrong thing, and the worst thing you can do is nothing...". Apart from this, when there are matters about which we should be speaking out, we often defer to those who speak more vociferously – or more often. It's not that they are right and we are wrong, it's just that they believe more strongly than we do that they are right – and we are not prepared to stand up and to be counted. Whether this is because we are too shy or whether our attitude is not to rock the boat or whether we just couldn't care less is irrelevant. We need to keep reminding ourselves that nothing changes if nothing changes. "...The only thing necessary for the triumph of evil is that good men do nothing...".[451] On the other hand, there are some people who just like to speak out because of the attention doing so brings to their ego. Christians need to exercise sufficient strength of character to speak out when it is necessary for them to do so – and to exercise self-restraint when doing so – to avoid seeking attention because of what it does for our ego.

It's not that others have different rights than we Christians have or that we Christians have more rights than anyone else. It is more the case that others exercise their rights and we frequently do not. We are so afraid of offending others that sometimes we are not true to what we believe. We are required "...in your hearts set apart Christ as Lord. Always be prepared to give an answer to everyone who asks you to give the reason for the hope that you have. But do this with gentleness and respect...".[452] It must be said that in standing up for what we know to be right, we should not be aggressive or intolerant. On the contrary, as Christians we have a code of behaviour that complements our attitude – and it is to this that we must be true if we are to have any chance in influencing those who may disagree with us.

The inevitable result is that we risk being drowned by the flood of non-Christian influences that permeate our society – to the extent that non-Christians no longer know what we Christians stand for. Is this being the salt and light referred to above? Our standards have slipped so much that it is sometimes hard

[451] Edmund Burke; Bartlett's Familiar Quotations; 1968

[452] 1 Peter 3:15

to demonstrate by our lives just what we believe. We just never get around to acting in the way we know we should in order to uphold what we believe in. In this respect, Charles Dickens pointed out that "... procrastination is the thief of time...".[453] We need to be careful about waiting too long in case we do not have another opportunity.

As Christians, we cannot be impervious to what is going on around us – whether personally, locally, nationally or globally.

10.5 Indiscipline

When we considered integrity earlier (see Para 6.4.1), we saw that integrity and discipline go hand in hand. It takes discipline to live according to the Christian way (see Footnote 144) that is to say living in a way that is in accordance with how Jesus has specified and thereby glorifying God. The first step in doing so is to make ourselves aware how we should live as Christians. We can pursue this by: (1) active communication with Him – in prayer and reflection, (2) in researching His word – and (3) in meeting with and learning from other Christians. Some comments on each of these three activities are included in chapter 12 but for the time being, do not underestimate that all this requires discipline – with respect to time and effort. The difficulty is that undisciplined living is much easier accomplished than disciplined living – as we all know already. Indiscipline has a lot to do with why many people find it hard to take exercise or to lose weight or to give up smoking or to read more – or whatever. It seems that many of us aspire to what discipline might achieve (whether that is physical fitness or a degree or any one of a myriad of things) but we are not willing to pay the price. In this respect, one author [454] has researched just how much effort it takes to be the absolute best (not just an expert) at whatever discipline interests you. The answer is 10,000 hours practice. The question I ask myself is – based on my life thus far, how many hours am I likely to spend on prayer, reflection, study of God's Word and meeting with other Christians – all being well? The honest answer is probably a lot less than 10,000 hours. So then, if I am not prepared to devote all those hours to a discipline with eternal consequences, what about becoming an expert – am I willing to devote sufficient hours to that aspiration – whatever number of hours that entails? If the

453 David Copperfield; Charles Dickens

454 Malcolm Gladwell; The Outliers – The Story of Success; Little, Brown and Company; 2008

answer to that is negative, what number of hours am I prepared to devote? Is the answer enough to read the whole Bible – even once – for example? These few brief comments are enough to make it clear that our lives can easily be overly influenced by indiscipline.

This is only one example of how indiscipline can influence our lives – but there are many others. Indiscipline is one reason why we find it difficult to control what we say and how we say it; we are insincere; we harbour grudges; we find it difficult to forgive; we give grudgingly; we are sometimes jealous of others – what they are, what they have, how they look, their gifts etc., etc. There is food for thought here. Consider whether and to what extent, the Christian way that you follow is hallmarked by indiscipline – and what options are available to you to change that. What is your attitude towards indiscipline?

10.6 Behaviour

We have learned already that attitude does not just happen – it is the result of the effect of some event – external to ourselves – that stimulates our attitude – which then leads to an internal response – which response might take the form of action or might lead to no action at all. So – behaviour emanates from our attitude – which underscores the importance of having an appropriate attitude at all times. In this respect, Scripture tells us that "…Whatever happens, conduct yourselves in a manner worthy of the gospel of Christ…". [455] Naturally, this applies to each of us as individuals – and not simply to those of us who may be VIPs or Pastors or those of us who may have a public persona. Every one of us – irrespective of our individual profile is required to "conduct [y]ourselves in a manner worthy of the gospel of Christ". In addition, this instruction applies to young and to old. In a toddler, bad behaviour is sometimes (just) tolerable – taking account of the toddler's age, understanding and experience. Even for a young person, a degree of tolerance will be allowed. As people become older however, bad behaviour is increasingly unacceptable. We older people should know better therefore than to behave in an 'unseemly' way.

Generally speaking, what does behaving appropriately mean in practice? Jesus was once asked to specify which was the greatest commandment (see above). (Perhaps the person asking the question meant which was the most important to satisfy.) Scripture tells us that Jesus replied: "…Love the Lord your

---

[455] Philippians 1:27

God with all your heart and with all your soul and with all your mind. This is the first and greatest commandment. And the second is like it: Love your neighbour as yourself. All the Law and the Prophets hang on these two commandments…".[456] At first sight, this might not appear to answer the question at all – so it is worth pondering whether or not this is the case. Jesus' answer means firstly that <u>if we are to conduct ourselves appropriately, we must first give God His rightful place.</u> That is to say, we must approach Him in awe and with respect – as befits Almighty God. Anyone who fails to treat our Lord in the way that He deserves to be treated lacks understanding. Secondly, these verses mean that we are required to treat other human beings as fellow 'pilgrims' who like each of us, are subject to life's circumstances and weaknesses. None of us is better than any other. We are all just as vulnerable as each other. <u>We are all equally dependent upon God's grace – the only difference between us is that some of us do not yet know it.</u>

The implication is that we need adequate maturity to understand certain things that are fundamental. For example – as discussed earlier – our lives are finite and all those resources that we strive to amass during our lifetime are finite too. Actually, they count for nothing in the long run. The book of Ecclesiastes has much to say about the meaningless of many things and influences that surround us and which delude us into believing they are important. <u>We must stop taking ourselves so seriously and rid ourselves of our pride and overbearing egos.</u> We need to stop thinking that I, me and mine are my areas of responsibility and I must look after myself because there is just not enough to go around and if I am not in there first, someone else will grab my share – in which case, it is gone for good. In fact, there is enough to go around – and we need to accept this and behave more maturely. Max Lucado has written a book entitled 'It's Not About Me' – I think these words sum up neatly what I am trying to say.

However, when bad behaviour is manifested, it is often less obvious than a toddler stomping his or her feet in bad temper. As we get older, we learn to behave badly in a more subtle way – and some of us are experts at this. For example, we are very quick to judge others. Scripture tells us that we must not do this.[457] We are prone to speak about people behind their back. We take action – which might be good in itself – but with an ulterior motive (think of Ananias and Sapphira who sold their property and retained some of the proceeds for

---

[456] Matthew 22:36-40
[457] Matthew 7:1-5

themselves but made it out that they had contributed all they had received to the common purse.).[458] We are sometimes wronged but grapple with the need to extend genuine forgiveness – despite being told that we are to "...Bear with each other and forgive whatever grievances you may have against one another...". [459] Just because bad behaviour is not obvious, we must remember that behaviour does not need to be obvious to be bad!

If we want to know what good behaviour looks like – consider Holy Scripture. In this respect, you might care to start with the references in this text that describe the life of our Lord on earth. Scripture contains other useful examples – such as the parable of the Good Samaritan.[460] What does my behaviour say about me?

10.7 Summary

In the first chapter of section three (chapter 8), we reminded ourselves of God's Person and Plan. In chapter 9, we explored the status of humankind and made some comments on some of the attributes that should be influencing our attitudes as Christians – and in chapter 10, we focused on humankind's attitude towards humankind – in the light of which – we considered our behaviour as Christians. We concluded that we must behave with the sort of rigour that Christ adopted as He lived His life on earth – and that we must act as if we are under constant scrutiny – because that is not too far from the truth. We must live in such a way as to make it very difficult for anyone to accuse us justifiably of any wilful or deliberate wrongdoing. This is part of what having an appropriate attitude means in practice. As Scripture advises "...Be very careful, then, how you live – not as unwise but as wise...".[461]

This section has been a chilling reminder of how far we have wandered away from the norms expected by Almighty God. While we considered only some of what it means to live in a broken world, the extent of humankind's fall from grace is obvious from our everyday experiences. It is difficult to comprehend and to absorb how far we have come from the perfection that defined the Garden of Eden. Our Lord can only be disappointed that despite His grace and mercy

[458] Acts 5:1-11
[459] Colossians 3:13
[460] Luke 10:25-37
[461] Ephesians 5:15

and goodness and provision, we have failed so badly in understanding and putting His ways into practice.

However, the good news is that there is a better way – and the next section (4) points to some suggestions for action.

Section Four
Application

Chapter Eleven

Where Do We Go from Here?

11.1 Introduction

One commentator has suggested that "…As religion and faith are being driven out of the public square, the Judeo-Christian ethical foundations that have sustained our country since its beginning, are being lost and are being replaced with a humanistic amorality, a self-centred pragmatic indifference that will ensure that our moral compasses will fail to point us in the right direction in the future…". [462] One warning provided by Scripture to Christians is that we are required to "…Be very careful, then, how you live – not as unwise but as wise, making the most of every opportunity, because the days are evil. Therefore, do not be foolish, but understand what the Lord's will is…". [463] How can we know what the Lord's will is? Scripture provides guidance that includes – ask "…God to fill you with the knowledge of His will through all spiritual wisdom and understanding…".[464] This is where understanding how to apply the truths that we have been considering comes into play – and this is why application is the focus of this last section of the text.

As part of that process, we will firstly remind ourselves what we set out to achieve at the beginning of the text. In the preface, we identified four objectives as follows:

1. to increase awareness of the universality, potency and the multiple forms in which attitude manifests itself. This was the focus of section 1;
2. to explain the dynamics of attitude – demonstrating (inter alia) how body, soul and spirit combine with all the 'components' which they comprise (such as conscience, sensitivity and discipline) to produce character. These matters were addressed in section 2;

[462] Archie B Carroll
[463] Ephesians 5:15-17
[464] Colossians 1:9

3. ‘to ground’ the entire discussion – by reference to the central role of Almighty God – and then to consider how far humankind has removed itself from God’s plan of salvation. Section 3 sets out the analysis that was conducted; and
4. to suggest the types of action that might be taken to help compile a plan designed to develop attitudes that will culminate in making positive things (with transformational effects) happen in individual lives. How this objective might be fulfilled is considered in this section (4).

By way of context, section 3 concluded that humankind is entirely lost and broken. This is the result of humankind having been fooled into believing that an individual’s ego is the only meaningful driver in a person’s life – and to satisfy that ego, humankind believes that it only needs to direct all its strength and effort to what brings pleasure and comfort with least effort for me. Accordingly, humankind has been distracted from its original purpose and has lost its way – choosing attitudes that move it – each day – further away from God’s plan.

Chapters 11, 12 and 13 explore the sorts of steps that are necessary to recalibrate our individual compasses to enable us to identify what changes are necessary in our attitudes to get us pointed in the right direction. Chapter 11 begins the process by considering some fundamentals that are important in helping us understand where we are right now – and this will be our starting point for what is to follow. So, we must ensure that first things are actually first in our lives – and we must recognise attitude for what it is.

Chapter 14 ends the section with a crucial, meaningful step – the formation of a plan of action – the aim of which is to satisfy objective 4 above.

11.2 First Things First

This paragraph is directed to any non-Christians who may be reading this text – because the very first step that any individual must take in learning how to adopt the right attitude – is to place his/her life on a meaningful foundation. The result of not taking this initial step was described in a parable Jesus told – the core of which is that “…everyone who hears these words of Mine and does not put them into practice is like a foolish man who built his house on sand. The rain came down, the streams rose, and the winds blew and beat against that house, and it fell with a great crash…".[465] In other words, unless and until a non-Christian accepts the sovereignty of Christ in his/her life, (s)he can have no meaningful foundation on which to build experience and to develop attitude. Non-Christian – I urge you to recognise the Lordship of Christ in your life – by asking God for His forgiveness for your past sin and acknowledging Christ as Lord of your life from this moment. Scripture tells us "…Do not conform any longer to the pattern of this world, but be transformed by the renewing of your mind. Then you will be able to test and approve what God's will is – His good, pleasing and perfect will…".[466] Unless you take this step, you will never be able to discern what for you is the correct attitude in making all the decisions and taking all the actions necessary to make your life the way God intended it to be.

One writer says that "…When we see Jesus as He is, we must turn away or else shamelessly adore Him…"[467] – which will it be for you? Somewhere else, Dallas Willard reminds us that "…It is the inner life of the soul that we must endeavour to transform, and then behaviour will naturally and easily follow. But not the reverse…".[468] On this point, C S Lewis says "…We might think that God wanted simply obedience to a set of rules: whereas He really wants people of a particular sort…".[469] This is summarised succinctly by John Ortberg who says "…What matters most is not what you accomplish; it is who you become…".[470]

Please consider the implications of failing to do what you need to do to follow the Christian way.

11.3 Recognising Attitude for What It Is

As we have seen, attitude is a potent force – which can be used for good or otherwise. We have discovered that attitude does not just happen out of the blue. Attitude is a reaction to a stimulus and the result of the overlap and inter-connection between many factors that influence our lives. Some influences in life arise outside what we ourselves control – e.g. where we have been born, the language we speak, the family of which we form a part. Other influences are a product of our own choice – where we live, career, friends, what we read and so on. For the latter, we are totally responsible.

---

[465] Matthew 7:26-27

[466] Romans 12:2

[467] Dallas Willard; The Divine Conspiracy; Pg 27; William Collins; 2014

[468] Dallas Willard; The Divine Conspiracy; Pg 161; William Collins; 2014

[469] C S Lewis; Mere Christianity: Pg 80; HarperCollins; 1952

[470] John Ortberg; The Me I Want To Be; Pg 20; Zondervan; 2010

All these influences combine together with our experiences – including for example – education, how we communicate, our peers and whom we choose as friends. Note that acquaintances, neighbours, friends, colleagues and people with whom we are or were at school or University can influence us markedly. Being in the company of groups of people such as these exposes us to their attitudes. The frequency of that exposure might be regular – and so this on-going exposure may have a cumulative effect. Often, the indirect permission we give to people to affect our attitude is passive – we may not even realise the extent to which we tolerate the influence of some people – or some factors/beliefs in our lives.

The important point is that we act and re-act in particular ways in particular circumstances in accordance with the influences that we 'allow' to affect our attitudes.

If we don't object, we passively reinforce the influence of another person – or of something else. One writer has said "…the ultimate freedom we have as human beings is the power to select what we will allow or require our minds to dwell upon…".[471] However, while we might imagine that we are aware of all the influences to which our decisions are subject – that need not necessarily be the case. For example, consider the following views with respect to subtle influence upon adolescents "…This is not to deny that adolescents make choices or that they develop strong feelings and commitments regarding their values and behavioural norms. It is to say however, that despite their genuine feelings of having made choices and commitments, a truer reading is that their values and self-images, mediated by the significant others in their lives, have largely chosen them. And in *their* (the youths') choosing they have, in the main, clarified and ratified those images and values which have chosen them…".[472] (For readers who may want to probe this further, consider Carl Jung's comments on the collective unconscious – which Jung believed has profound influence on individuals – "…who live out its symbols and clothed them in meaning through their experiences…".[473]) This is another indication why we need to examine our attitudes – because otherwise, we may be unaware of their existence. Elsewhere, the same author points out an additional matter that refers when he says "…Tacit means unexamined; my tacit knowing – as Michael Polanyi calls it – is that part of my knowing that plays a role in guiding and shaping my choices, but of which

[471] Dallas Willard
[472] James W Fowler; Stages of Faith; Pg 154; Harper One; 1981
[473] Wikipedia; Collective Unconscious

I can give no account. I cannot tell you how I know with my tacit knowing…".[474] This is not the only thing we need to be aware of – because – as Donald Rumsfeld has pointed out – "… There are known knowns; there are things we know we know. We also know there are known unknowns; that is to say we know there are some things we do not know. But there are also unknown unknowns – the ones we don't know we don't know…".[475] The point is that it is a useful discipline to stop and to consider what and who affects us – and then to pursue this by considering who or what affects us most – and whether the conclusions of that consideration are acceptable.

If we ask ourselves to account for the attitude we have adopted at any time, we may realise that our attitude is neither objective nor mature. This might be an uncomfortable exercise but if we do not examine ourselves, how can we ever know whether we are subject to improper or adverse influences? Alternatively, we might wait for someone to say something such as "I don't like your attitude" – but in this case, most of us are unlikely to respond positively – which fact alone reduces the possibility of people we know pointing out anything adverse they see in us. That being so, self-analysis might be a catalyst in pointing us in a different direction. Often, a wrong attitude or an attitude that is less than optimal leads to wrongful or sub-optimal action.

It has to be said that even if and when we recognise all the interactions described in the model considered in earlier chapters, the pace of life will not allow us to consider them as we go about our daily lives – making the decisions and taking the actions that this entails on an on-going basis. Probably, the core message of this text is to recognise that all these influences exist and that two choices arise – either act on your attitude (ACTIVE) or alternatively let your attitude be acted upon by all the experiences and influences for good or evil that you will encounter in life (PASSIVE).

11.4 The Christian's Attitude

With respect to attitude, the Christian has a huge responsibility. This is because our Christianity must be seen in action – and if our actions (and re-actions for that matter) do not conform to what we say when we speak, then what we say is unlikely to influence anyone for good. "…It is easier to be smart than

[474] Michael Polyani; The Tacit Dimension; Doubleday; 1966 as quoted by James W Fowler; Stages Of Faith; Pg 161; Harper One; 1981

[475] https://en.wikiquote.org/wiki/Donald_Rumsfeld

to be good. You don't need to know more from the Bible; you just need to do what you already know…".[476] It couldn't be more clearly explained. Meanwhile, it is so easy to be a hypocrite (which word is used only infrequently nowadays) – sometimes we don't even have to try – it's almost as if it is natural. Well – to an extent it is natural – but only as far as the 'old self' is concerned – it's not natural for the 'new self'. By way of clarification – 'old self' refers to the status of humankind before accepting Christ as Saviour while 'new self' refers to people who have accepted Christ as their Saviour and who are now trying to live their lives in accordance with His standards. In this respect Scripture says: "…You were taught, with regard to your former way of life, to put off your old self, which is being corrupted by its deceitful desires; to be made new in the attitude of your minds; and to put on the new self, created to be like God in true righteousness and holiness…".[477] The prophet Ezekiel passed on God's word to His people "…I will give you a new heart and put a new spirit in you; I will remove from you your heart of stone and give you a heart of flesh. And I will put my Spirit in you and move you to follow my decrees and be careful to keep my laws…".[478] One author has pointed out "…Francis of Assisi became the patron saint of relational evangelism with the oft-quoted saying, '…Preach the gospel at all times; and if necessary, use words'. There is apparently no good evidence that he ever said that – but it captures the postmodern mood succinctly…If we apply the dictum attributed to St Francis to Jesus, we find that Jesus demonstrated the love of God in action by caring for people. But He also used words to teach compassion and was Himself described as the Logos – the Word made flesh. Deeds alone were not enough for Him. They had to be interpreted using language. He proclaimed the kingdom of God in speech and action – and that is the balance that we have to find…".[479] What a challenging mandate for those of us who claim to be sinners saved by grace! Here is how another writer puts it – "…ordinary Christians must live in a way that differs from the surrounding cultures or our message will never get a hearing. Herein lies the most solemn challenge facing Christians who want to communicate their faith: if we do not live in a way that draws others to the faith rather than repels

---

[476] John Ortberg; The Me I Want To Be; Pg 47; Zondervan; 2010

[477] Ephesians 4:22-24

[478] Ezekiel 36:26-27

[479] Peter May; The Search For God & The Path To Persuasion; Pg 123/125; Malcolm Down Publishing; 2016

them, none of our words will matter…".[480] John puts it like this "…Whoever claims to live in Him must walk as Jesus did…".[481]

Living in accordance with our Christian tradition and principles is the responsibility of each Christian. As one author has observed "…Everything can be taken from man but one thing: the last of human freedoms – to choose one's attitude in any given set of circumstances, to choose one's own way…".[482] This is a very powerful, liberating statement – and Frankl's story places it in context. Bereft of everything – and subjected to horrendous treatment as a prisoner in a Nazi concentration camp, Frankl still enjoyed freedom of mind even though he was deprived of liberty. Amongst the lessons to be learned is that the only person who is responsible for our individual attitude (and the consequent action/reaction) is oneself. There is no point – or validity for that matter – in trying to make some set of circumstances or events the reason for our actions. As practising Christians, we must take responsibility for our actions and for our inaction. This is another reason why discipline is so important.

11.5 A Strategy for Development

One writer believes that "…Spiritual transformation cannot be orchestrated or controlled, but neither is it a random venture…we need a plan…".[483] Cultivating appropriate attitudes and rejecting attitudes that are inappropriate is a process that we need to practice. This is not something that can be achieved quickly – because it takes the experiences of life to understand and then to refine our attitudes. The permutations of experiences and events in life are so many – and the influences so many and potentially so delicate that to make any progress requires a lifetime of practice. The good news is that each victory has a cumulative experiential effect. There is a synergistic benefit in successfully adjusting incrementally. One writer points out that "…to be a real person of faith we cannot view or attempt things from a human point of view. We have to see things as God sees them and allow Him to work through us to accomplish that which in human terms is impossible! This is the essence of supernatural living –

---

[480] Philip Yancey; Vanishing Grace; Pg 68; Hodder & Stoughton; 2014
[481] 1 John 2:6
[482] Victor E Frankl; Man's Search For Meaning; Pg 86; Washington Square Press; 1984;
[483] John Ortberg; The Life You've Always Wanted; Pg 200; Zondervan; 2002

hearing God and living in obedience to Him, even when it doesn't make logical sense...". [484]

John Ortberg provides some very practical examples of actions he takes even before getting out of bed – which actions doubtless help him to approach his day in the right attitude. He says: "...I have made it a point recently to take a few moments before I get out of bed to greet God. I tell Him that my day belongs to Him. I invite Him to go through it with me. I believe that is one way to wake up in 'Jesus' name'. How we greet the people closest to us is critical. The first fifteen seconds that we spend with them really sets the tone for an entire day. How would Jesus greet our spouse, or children or our roommate? What words would He use, in what tone of voice, with what expression on His face..."? [485] This seems like good advice to me.

"...In a sense, each of us chooses a 'spiritual strategy' whether or not we are intentional about it. We can choose it by default...". [486] We have heard it said that a certain person is just the way (s)he is. They have always been like that and they are not going to change now. This approach seems to be an attempt to excuse what otherwise might be considered as an unacceptable approach. It seems to exonerate the person displaying inappropriate behaviour as if that is something outside their control. This is not their fault – they can't help it sort of thing. This is not a persuasive argument. Changing our attitudes may be difficult – but it is not impossible. "...The command 'Be ye perfect' is not idealistic gas. Nor is it a command to do the impossible. He is going to make us into creatures that can obey that command...".[487] We reminded ourselves earlier (see para 6.5) about what happened when seat belts first became mandatory, and when the suggestion was made that smokers would no longer be permitted to smoke in bars, planes, restaurants, and all sorts of public places. People now automatically 'belt up' before starting to drive and smoking is no longer allowed (or even tolerated) in public places. Change is possible – even where attitudes seem to be entrenched. Naturally, change requires cooperation, goodwill and effort – but it remains possible.

"...Many times, people who have suffered adverse conditions in their lives become bitter and angry. Over time their lives will be negative and hardened

---

[484] Andrew White; Faith Under Fire; Pg 43; Monarch Books 2011
[485] John Ortberg; The Life You've Always Wanted; Pg 202; Zondervan; 2002
[486] John Ortberg; The Life You've Always Wanted; Pg 204; Zondervan; 2002
[487] C S Lewis; Mere Christianity; 1952; HarperCollins

toward others. The tendency for them is to point back to a difficult time and say 'that incident ruined my life'. What they do not realize is that the incident called for an attitude decision...a response. Their wrong attitude choice, not the condition, ruined their lives...". [488] One writer has commented that "...Romans 12:9-21 describes a life of brotherly love, honour, service, prayer, charity, hospitality, blessing, rejoicing, sympathy, harmony, humility, peace and compassion. In short, the Godly life is not overcome by evil but overcomes evil with good. This beautiful and inspiriting description of the Godly life might well be read in every Christian worship service and be put to memory by every believer in Christ...".[489]

11.6 Good Deeds

"...Altruism is the belief that it's bad to be self-serving and good to be other-serving, or put another way, that our greatest happiness comes in selflessly giving to others, even when this involves self-sacrifice... The Bible refers to 'doing good works'. For example, we are told that '...we are God's workmanship, created in Christ Jesus [490] to do good works, which God prepared in advance for us to do'...".[491] We need to be clear what this means. Christians cannot earn their salvation – whether by doing good deeds – or for that matter in any other way. Salvation is beyond price – its value cannot be quantified – it cannot be bought, earned or achieved. Scripture makes it clear that "...it is by grace you have been saved, through faith – and this not from yourselves, it is the gift of God – not by works, so that no one can boast...".[492] That said, we are told also that "...remembering the words the Lord Jesus himself said: 'It is more blessed to give than to receive.'... "[493]

Christianity differs from religions that believe doing good deeds from which other people will benefit will enhance their chances of being admitted to heaven. While sharing (especially sacrificially) is a truly worthy thing to do per se – and something that Christians should emulate – giving money for charitable and

---

[488] John C Maxwell; Developing The Leader Within You; Pg 105; Thomas Nelson Publishing; 1993

[489] Rick Richter; Comparing The Qur'an And The Bible; Pg 126; Baker Books; 2011

[490] David Keirsey; Please Understand Me II; Pg 132; Prometheus Nemesis Book Company; 1998

[491] Ephesians 2:10

[492] Ephesians 2:8-9

[493] Acts 20:35

religious purposes and doing good deeds does not grant access to heaven. To be generous and kind in this way is very creditable – but for the Christian, it is a natural reaction to saving grace – not a means to an end. While this is true, we need to remember what we are told in Scripture – "...faith by itself, if it is not accompanied by action, is dead. But someone will say, "You have faith; I have deeds." Show me your faith without deeds, and I will show you my faith by what I do...".[494] If our attitude is appropriate, we will 'do good' automatically – because our DNA has been altered by God's grace. That is to say, we will not do good things for other people because we have been told we must – or because we think we can gain something from doing so – rather, we will do good things for other people because that is what is natural for us. (If that is not our experience, we need to consider why.)

Another writer puts it like this "...For love awakens love in return; and love, once awakened, desires to give pleasure; and the revealed will of God is that those who have received grace should henceforth give themselves to 'good works' (Eph. 2:10, Titus 2:11f.), and gratitude will move anyone who has truly received grace to do as God requires...".[495] The same author clarifies elsewhere that the important thing about good deeds "...is not that they ever merit an award from the court – they are too short of perfection to do that – but that they provide an index of what is in the heart – what, in other words, is the real nature of each agent...".[496]

11.7 Summary

If I want something to change – I have got to take action to make that happen. With respect to my attitude this rule applies – which means that my attitude will remain as it is right at this moment unless and until I take steps to alter it. "...Above all else, guard your heart, for it is the wellspring of life...".[497]

The conclusion reached in section 3 was that humankind has lost its direction. Humankind's original purpose has been obfuscated and diverted. The purpose of section 4 is to consider whether by changing our attitudes, we can improve things. This first chapter of section 4 has begun to consider what we need to do to recalibrate our compass to enable us to understand the direction

---

[494] James 2:17-18
[495] J I Packer; Knowing God; Pg 155; Hodder & Stoughton; 2013
[496] J I Packer; Knowing God; Pg 164; Hodder & Stoughton; 2013
[497] Proverbs 4:23

that was always intended for us. Accordingly, we have tried in this chapter to make sure that the first thing is in fact the first thing. We reminded ourselves what attitude is in effect and we posited what was described as the core message of the text. We considered what the Christian's attitude might look like if it is to conform more closely to that of Christ. A strategy for development has been presented demonstrating the long-term nature of attitude enhancement – whilst clarifying the relevance but also the limitations of good deeds.

We can now begin to take a closer look at the practical significance of what we have been considering – which will be the focus of chapter 12.

Chapter Twelve
Suggested Action Points

12.1 Introduction

In the introduction to section 4, we proposed using chapters 11, 12 and 13 to explore the sorts of steps that are necessary to recalibrate our individual compasses to enable us to identify what changes are necessary in our attitudes to get us pointed in whatever new direction is necessary. As a starting point, chapter 11 considered some fundamentals that are important if we are to understand where we are right now. Having passed the starting point on the road to self-discovery, chapter 12 continues to set out the groundwork necessary – to move us to a position where we can be confident about the direction we need to take. This step must precede planning.

So, we begin this chapter by teasing out what our attitudes are in respect of certain fundamentals – such as with respect to how we communicate. In doing so, we need to remember that as Christians we are sinners saved by grace and so we face very strong daily challenges as we try to live our lives in an environment totally influenced by humankind's evil and selfish pursuit of one's own ends. Sadly – to many people this is the norm because it is all they have ever known and more sadly still, they aspire to nothing more. So, one of the first and most obvious ways that we can make people aware of these matters is by communicating with them – which is where chapter 12 begins.

We continue by looking at some scriptural guidance on attitude addressing some basic questions such as what our attitude to attitude is? This is followed by an invitation to consider a number of fundamental disciplines that will help us along the way: prayer, reference to Scripture and meeting with other believers.

12.2 Communication

Scripture tells us that we are "fearfully and wonderfully made". [498] One of the (many) ways in which this truth manifests itself is our ability to communicate. Often, we don't think about this or about how important it is – probably because we communicate so much that we take it for granted. Imagine for a moment what it would be like if communication as we understand it was not possible for some reason. For example, going to a country where the language is different from the language we speak and understand is not an entirely adequate comparison – but it gives a flavour of the point being made. Note that as with so many other things in life, this privilege brings with it some responsibilities. Regrettably, most of us are less careful about how we communicate than we should be.

In the Preface, reference was made to how people sometimes speak to each other. It's so easy to be encouraging in what we say but it seems it's easier still to be thoughtless, unkind and even acerbic. This is not how the Lord expects us to communicate with each other. For example, Scripture points out that whoever loves life and desires to see many good days, should keep his/her tongue from evil and refrain from telling lies. Turn from evil and do good; seek peace and pursue it.[499] Further Scripture says "...Let your conversation be always full of grace, seasoned with salt, so that you may know how to answer everyone...". [500]

None of us needs to be told how destructive hurtful words or a sarcastic tone can be. There is a good chance that we have all been in situations where we have been embarrassed because of the way in which other people have spoken to us – or situations when we have been embarrassed by the way someone has spoken to someone else in our presence. The closer our physical situation is to this type of exchange – the worse it is. Many of us possess an (untaught) ability to be volatile and vitriolic in our speech – which we can 'turn on' at a moment's notice. In addition, we can always find good reasons afterwards to justify our approach – 'he deserved it' or 'I can't help it – she brings out the worst in me' – or some other excuse for what amounts to downright rudeness, discourtesy and bad behaviour. Scripture recognises how difficult it is for us to control what we say. In fact, Scripture goes so far as to say "...If anyone is never at fault in what he says, he is a perfect man, able to keep his whole body in check...".[501] In addition,

---

[498] Psalm 139:14
[499] Psalm 34:12-14
[500] Colossians 4:6
[501] James 3:2

Scripture warns that even though "…the tongue is a small part of the body, [but] it makes great boasts. Consider what a great forest is set on fire by a small spark. The tongue also is a fire, a world of evil among the parts of the body. It corrupts the whole person, sets the whole course of his life on fire, and is itself set on fire by hell…".[502] Clearly, we should be aware of the potential of speaking improperly – despite the circumstances and we should be aware of the source of the motivation that prompts us to speak in a particular way (our attitude). Scripture makes it clear that "…a good man brings good things out of the good stored up in his heart, and an evil man brings evil things out of the evil stored up in his heart. For out of the overflow of his heart his mouth speaks…".[503] Note that <u>what we say is influenced by who we are in our innermost being – our soul – the source of attitude</u> (see Para 3.4). Our attitude is often revealed by what we say and how we say it.

Of course, we communicate in ways other than speech. Sometimes, it is by way of body language. A withering look, a raised eyebrow or a cynical smirk will do to convey what we are thinking – without the need to speak a word. There are yet more ways to communicate messages – e.g. through ignoring the other person – avoiding eye contact – or not paying attention or staring so coldly that the other person can read something unfavourable in our look. Besides speaking or communicating by way of body language, there is also the written word – and this can be the most corrosive of all methods of communication – because once written, the words are difficult to obliterate and may not be easily forgotten by those who read them. In this case, the words can be read and re-read and shown to others and end up in places where they were never intended to be and read by people who were never intended to read them. Thanks to technology, we have very powerful methods of communication at the tips of our fingers – literally. However, this facility is potentially dangerous. Probably, we are all aware of emails being sent to one or more people in error. Sometimes it is not significant – but if that email contains inappropriate remarks – the potential for lasting damage is greater. The 'reply to all facility' on our email software is very useful – but it can be very destructive at the same time. The capacity for wrongful communication is virtually limitless when you factor in a potential global audience through the web, television and radio. Naturally, bad news or embarrassing news spreads like wildfire – and some people like to be part of that

---

[502] James 3:5-6
[503] Luke 6:45 (compare Matthew 12:35)

process – enjoying in some perverse way the problems and difficulties caused to others. This is not how Christ intended our attitude towards communication to be.

It will be clear from what we have considered already that the manner in which we choose to communicate has much to do with our attitude – and this is another good reason to adopt the right attitude. In particular circumstances, there might well be value in asking ourselves whether our attitude at particular points in time reflects the love of our Saviour. What might Jesus say in this particular circumstance – and how might He say it? Why is my attitude what it is? Does my attitude reflect the best that I can attain? It is prudent to adopt a disciplined and loving attitude when we are communicating – especially if we are feeling emotional. It is never a good idea to communicate in anger.

12.3 Scriptural Guidance About Attitude

It will be clear from the discussion thus far that attitude comes into play in a plethora of circumstances in our daily lives. It affects what we think, how we think, what we say and our reactions to our experiences. Attitude permeates our whole being. It percolates through all sorts of filters and eventually manifests itself in behaviour – for good or ill. If this is true, then we should understand what Scripture tells us about attitude. Here is some Scriptural guidance on living with the right attitudes.

12.3.1 Attitude to Attitude

We have seen that the prevailing attitude of mankind is very selfish – looking after oneself is the norm – but Scripture tells we Christians not to "...conform any longer to the pattern of this world, but be transformed by the renewing of your mind...".[504] Further, "...You were taught, with regard to your former way of life, to put off your old self which is being corrupted by its deceitful desires; to be made new in the attitude of your minds; and to put on the new self, created to be like God in true righteousness and holiness...".[505] It may be that most of us have paid little or no attention to 'attitude' per se – we just don't think about it. (In preparing this text, I was not able to identify any other text on this subject – which suggests that this matter has not been given much attention generally.) We

---

[504] Romans 12:2
[505] Ephesians 4:22-24

need to remember that whether we are conscious of our attitude or not, it exists and it is potent – and we ignore it at our peril.

12.3.2 Attitude to Christ as Example

As has been noted already, scripture makes us aware that "...Your attitude should be the same as that of Christ Jesus...". [506] We are told also that we must be "...imitators of God, therefore as dearly loved children...". [507] Naturally, if we are to be imitators of Christ, we must know about Christ in the first place – which means that we must become familiar with Holy Scripture. There are many important characteristics that mark the life of Jesus – here are three: His humility, His selflessness and His service. As Christians, we are required to ensure that in following Christ our lives should reflect these characteristics. We must remember that "...Christ suffered for you, leaving you an example, that you should follow in His steps...". [508] In short, Christ prepared us for all that this entails by showing us how to live – the question is, whether we understand this? How much have we learned?

12.3.3 Attitude to Work

With respect to our attitude to what we do, Scripture contains a number of instructions. For example: "...Whatever you do, work at it with all your heart, as working for the Lord, not for men...It is the Lord Christ you are serving...".[509] This means working hard and working well – truly earning what we are paid and not trying to get off with as little as possible as often as possible. Similarly, "...whatever you do, whether in word or deed, do it all in the name of the Lord Jesus, giving thanks to God the Father through Him...". [510] In fact, "...Whatever your hand finds to do, do it with all your might...". [511] If we adopt this attitude in what we do, we will always be working at our optimum. It is really important to note that perfection is not expected – but working to the highest standard that we can attain is our reasonable service.

---

[506] Philippians 2:5
[507] Ephesians 5:1
[508] 1 Peter 2:21
[509] Colossians 3:23
[510] Colossians 3:17
[511] Ecclesiastes 9:10

12.3.4 Attitude to Others

With respect to our attitude to other people, the prayer of Paul in Romans has much to teach us. Paul says "...May the God who gives endurance and encouragement give you a spirit of unity among yourselves as you follow Christ Jesus..." [512] In the Gospel he wrote, Matthew provides an important precept to follow. He says "...in everything, do to others what you would have them do to you ...".[513] And in particular, "...do not judge, or you too will be judged...". [514] These are very clear guiding principles – leaving no room for misunderstanding or ambiguity. In fact, it doesn't get any clearer! Luke tells us to "...Love your enemies, do good to those who hate you, bless those who curse you, pray for those who mistreat you...".[515] More specifically, "...do not repay anyone evil for evil. Be careful to do what is right in the eyes of everybody...".[516] Again – "...Do nothing out of selfish ambition or vain conceit, but in humility consider others better than yourselves. Each of you should look not only to your own interests, but also to the interests of others...". [517]

How is it possible to live a life in accordance with these principles? The short answer is that it is probably impossible for humankind to live like this – "...So I say, live by the Spirit,...the fruit of the Spirit is love, joy, peace, patience, kindness, goodness, faithfulness, gentleness and self-control...".[518] We need to understand that non-Christians live as they do because that style is their default – it is the norm for them – and it is also the norm for us. So, <u>if we want to live according to the principles laid out for us in Scripture, we are going to need a lot of help.</u> That help is available – because each Christian is in-dwelt by God's Holy Spirit – our Advocate with the Father and our Helper (John 14:26). <u>Any serious attempt at living in this manner will only be possible through God's grace and through the intervention of the Holy Spirit.</u>

We should not delude ourselves about the needs of others – nor should we dilute their plight. There are limitless opportunities to share our resources with those who really need that share. Consider this example "...According to a recent World Bank study of seven sub-Saharan African countries, half of nine-year-

[512] Romans 15:5
[513] Matthew 7:12
[514] Matthew 7:1
[515] Luke 6:27-28
[516] Romans 12:17
[517] Philippians 2:3-4
[518] Galatians 5:16 and 22-23

olds cannot read a simple word and three quarters cannot read a simple sentence. The reason is terrible teaching. The same study found that only 7% of teachers had the minimum knowledge needed to teach reading and writing effectively. When classrooms were inspected to see whether a teacher was present, half the time the answer was no…".[519] Two questions arise: (1) what is my attitude towards these unbelievable statistics that reflect what is happening in the world today and (2) what will be the attitude of these children for the whole of their life as they mature? These figures are only an example – one metric – but they are sufficiently chronic to demonstrate that the attitude of Christians to figures like these should prompt concern at worst and action at best. Christians should be sufficiently sensitive not only to the circumstances of people closest to them but also to the circumstances of people in need – whatever their geographical location – and if we are unaware of these needs, we should take steps to remedy that. When one day, I have to account to Almighty God for my life and how I used all the resources He has placed at my disposal, I don't think He will expect me to say in my defence that I didn't know or wasn't aware of the needs of others.

12.3.5 Attitude About Self-Discipline

Despite the difficulties, our mandate is not to be "…overcome by evil, but overcome evil with good…".[520] This is increasingly difficult in the face of so much evil and corruption in our world – and as we read of events and circumstances that occur around the world, we are sometimes unable to process just how broken our world is. Nevertheless, the writer to the Ephesians said, "…I urge you to live a life worthy of the calling you have received…".[521] This is another clear instruction that complements what has been considered already but once again an instruction that requires a huge amount of self-discipline – not only to do what is 'right' – but in learning how to distinguish 'right' from 'wrong' in the first place. This is only possible through familiarity with the principles taught in Scripture and by walking in close proximity with our God.

---

[519] Click To Download Teacher; The Economist; Pg 20; 17 November 2018
[520] Romans 12:21
[521] Ephesians 4:1

12.4 Daily Living

Learning how to be a Christian takes a lifetime – because there is so much to learn if we are to equip ourselves adequately to deal with all the possible permutations that life throws at us. In addition, we need time to practice. We will not be successful at daily living in accordance with right attitudes overnight – we have to learn from our experiences and especially from our mistakes. Thus, personal discipline is required. "...Do your best to present yourself to God as one approved, a workman who does not need to be ashamed and who correctly handles the word of truth...".[522]

Scripture is quite clear about the fundamental principles we should adopt in ordinary day-to-day living. For example, "...this is what the Lord Almighty says: 'Give careful thought to your ways'...". [523] We have discovered already that our attitudes are not haphazard thoughts that come into our mind as situations develop. Accordingly, "...whatever is true, whatever is noble, whatever is right, whatever is pure, whatever is lovely, whatever is admirable – if anything is excellent or praiseworthy – think about such things...". [524] We need to remember this instruction if our attitudes are to benefit from such instruction. If we feed our minds with appropriate material, it is much more likely that our attitudes will be attuned to the principles set out in Scripture – and this in turn influences how we live. Scripture says "...make every effort to add to your faith goodness; and to goodness knowledge; and to knowledge self-control; and to self-control perseverance; and to perseverance godliness; and to godliness brotherly kindness; and to brotherly kindness love...". [525] In essence, the Christian way is to treat others in the way that we as individuals want to be treated. This should be sufficient to make us stop and think. We must avoid judging and/or condemning others – whether that takes the form of blatant anger or self-righteous behaviour.

Daily living inherently involves uncertainty, challenges and difficulties. In this respect, we have been told to "...Let the peace of Christ rule in your hearts..." [526] and to "...Be still before the Lord and wait patiently for Him; do not fret when men succeed in their ways, when they carry out their wicked

---

[522] 2 Timothy 2:15
[523] Haggai 1:5
[524] Philippians 4:8
[525] 2 Peter 1:5-8
[526] Colossians 3:15

schemes. Refrain from anger and turn from wrath; do not fret – it leads only to evil…". [527] In fact, we are to "…Live such good lives among the pagans that, though they accuse you of doing wrong, they may see your good deeds and glorify God on the day He visits us…". [528] Meanwhile, we are to "…Be on [y]our guard; stand firm in the faith; be men of courage; be strong. Do everything in love…". [529]

12.5 Scriptural Guidance on Living the Christian Way

In the last section, we considered some of the guidance provided in Scripture about attitude. In this section, we want to look at some practical implications about the guidance just considered. What are some of the things Scripture says about living the Christian way?

12.5.1 Prayer

With respect to prayer, the position from where we start can be summarised by two verses from Scripture – (1) "…Be joyful always, pray continually, give thanks in all circumstances; for this is God's will for you in Christ Jesus…" [530] and (2) "…What does the Lord ask of you but to fear the Lord your God, to walk in all His ways, to love Him, to serve the Lord your God with all your heart and with all your soul…". [531]

In Christian circles, we often hear it said that prayer is a great privilege – and indeed this is absolutely right. Why then is it so difficult to the extent that we do not give it the attention it merits? "…Somehow it seems that if we really love God, prayer should flow out of us without effort or discipline. In fact, this was not the case even with Jesus' first followers…". [532] In the Garden at Gethsemane the disciples couldn't even remain awake when Jesus asked them to be with Him at a very difficult time. Matthew tells us "…Then he returned to his disciples and found them sleeping. 'Couldn't you men keep watch with me for one hour?' he asked Peter. '…Watch and pray so that you will not fall into temptation. The

---

[527] Psalm 37:7-8
[528] 1 Peter 2:12
[529] 1 Corinthians 16:13-14
[530] 1 Thessalonians 5:16-18
[531] Deuteronomy 10:12
[532] John Ortberg; The Life You Have Always Wanted; Pg 95; 2002; Zondervan

spirit is willing, but the flesh is weak'…". [533] The weakness experienced by those closest to Jesus is the same weakness that Christians today experience with respect to prayer.

One author believes that prayer is "…turning any concern over to God when we feel it is the part we play in allowing the peace of God to stand guard over our mind…" [534] – Why should this be? The answer is that "…the peace of God, which transcends all understanding, will guard your hearts and your minds in Christ Jesus…".[535] John Ortberg says "…Prayer, more than any other single activity, is what places us in the flow of the Spirit. When we pray, hearts get convicted, sin gets confessed, believers get united, intentions get encouraged, people receive guidance, the church is strengthened, stubbornness gets melted, wills get surrendered, evil gets defeated, grace gets released, illness gets healed, sorrows are comforted, faith is born, hope is grown and love triumphs…".[536]

The fact is that very few of us treat prayer with the respect that it deserves – and that is precisely because so many of us find it such a difficult discipline. Perhaps this is why prayer is said to be character forming. We all know that anything that conforms to the 'character forming' discipline means hard work. One writer has pointed out that "…Prayer, it is rightly said, is the method of genuine theological research, the method of understanding what and who God is. God is Spirit and exists at the level of reality where the human heart, or spirit, also exists, serving as the foundation and source of our visible life. It is there that the individual meets with God 'in spirit and in truth'…".[537]

Prayer gives us access into God's immediate presence – through the righteousness imputed to us through Christ's sacrifice on the cross at Calvary. This is communication at its zenith – at its most pure and at the optimal point for human understanding. Can we be surprised that it is not easy? We must remember that God knows all about us – because He created us – so He already knows our circumstances before we pray to Him. The thing is, He wants us to humble ourselves and to worship Him in prayer as we present our praise, our prayers and our petitions to Him. Not too much to ask considering all we have pondered so far. We are told to "…Devote yourselves to prayer, being watchful

---

533 Matthew 27:40-41
534 John Ortberg; The Me I Want to Be; Pg 124; 2010; Zondervan
535 Philippians 4:7
536 John Ortberg; The Me I Want to Be; Pg 180; Zondervan; 2010
537 Dallas Willard; The Divine Conspiracy; Pg 214; William Collins; 2014

and thankful..."[538] and elsewhere "...Be joyful in hope, patient in affliction, faithful in prayer...".[539]

We should note that prayer is not tantamount to a lengthy mini-sermon – or presenting a long list of needs and requirements as quickly as possible and then waiting for those requests to be delivered. On the contrary, Scripture reminds us that "...when you pray, do not keep on babbling like pagans, for they think they will be heard because of their many words...".[540] Instead, our approach should be based on Scripture's advice "...This is the confidence we have in approaching God: that if we ask anything according to His will, He hears us...".[541] Further, "...Sometimes we are to pray privately. It is good to pray with people, but when I am praying and other people are listening, the fact that I am aware that they are listening changes how I pray. Being alone with God, however, I can fully be myself...".[542] This reflects what Scripture says – "...But when you pray, go into your room, close the door and pray to your Father, who is unseen. Then your Father, who sees what is done in secret, will reward you...".[543] When praying with others, we must try to eradicate any thought that the others around us are listening to see how well we pray, how eloquent we are or how pious we seem. In all these respects, it's as if no one is there. We are addressing God – and it is on Him we should be concentrating.

Prayer firstly involves worship and gratitude. We must "...remember the Lord [y]our God, for it is He who gives you the ability to produce wealth...". [544] We are often so wrapped up in ourselves that we forget to thank God for His mercies and grace. We have nothing apart from what the Lord has loaned to us (see below). As David prayed when he was handing over the gifts that he had prepared for the temple to be built by Solomon his son "...But who am I and who are my people, that we should be able to give as generously as this? Everything comes from You, and we have given You only what comes from Your hand...as for all this abundance that we have provided for building You a temple for Your Holy Name, it comes from Your hand, and all of it belongs to You...".[545] C S Lewis puts it like this "...If you devoted every moment of your

---

[538] Colossians 4:2
[539] Romans 12:12
[540] Matthew 6:7
[541] 1 John 5:14
[542] John Ortberg; The Me I Want to Be; Pg 172; Zondervan; 2010
[543] Matthew 6:6
[544] Deuteronomy 8:18
[545] 1 Chronicles 29:14 and 16

whole life exclusively to His service you could not give Him anything that was not in a sense His own already...".[546] Scripture says "...Yours, O Lord, is the greatness and the power and the glory and the majesty and the splendour, for everything in heaven and earth is yours. Yours, O Lord, is the kingdom; you are exalted as head over all...".[547]

(The word 'loaned' used above is an appropriate word for three reasons. Firstly, as we discovered earlier in this text, these things are mortal – that is to say temporary. They will fade away – they will not last forever. Despite the quantity, quality and value of all the preparatory materials that (we read about in 1 Chronicles), David had collated to build the temple, they were all finite and had no eternal significance. Secondly, using what has been loaned for my needs and for the needs of others reminds us that they are finite – and we must not lose sight of this fact. Lastly in this respect, as David recognised, what we have, we have been given – and someday, we will be asked to give account as to how we have used such things. We must approach these matters in the right attitude.)

Secondly – with respect to prayer involving worship and gratitude – prayer includes our confession of all those occasions when we have failed to live in accordance with the Christian way and an expression of sorrow for those failures. Thirdly, prayer includes petitions with respect to the needs of both others and ourselves. It is a matter of great wonder that Almighty God is willing to give us a hearing at all – but this is not the end of the matter – because He will attend to our prayers whenever we seek to address Him (see below). Scripture encourages us as follows: "...Then you will call upon Me and come and pray to Me, and I will listen to you...".[548] One author reminds us that the times when Jesus prayed included: (1) when His life was crowded and draining; (2) when He faced important choices; (3) when He was sad or frightened; (4) when He needed strength for His work; (5) when He was worried about people He loved; and (6) when He faced an insurmountable problem. [549] Clearly, Jesus prayed a lot!

In addition, He not only listens to all our prayers, He also answers them. In this respect, we need a mature attitude to accept that God knows better than we know and so He responds to some prayers precisely as we have asked – but to other petitions, He says no – and to yet others He says, yes but not yet – or

---

[546] C S Lewis; Mere Christianity; Pg 143; HarperCollins; 1952
[547] 1 Chronicles 29:11
[548] Jeremiah 29:12
[549] John Ortberg; The Me I Want to Be; Pg 174; Zondervan; 2010

perhaps yes but not quite the way we anticipated. "…Let us then approach the throne of grace with confidence, so that we may receive mercy and find grace to help us in our time of need…".[550]

We need to make time to pray, to know more about our faith and to worship God and to get to know Him better. As we communicate with people in life, we get to know them better – and in the absence of meaningful communication, we will not get to know them at all. If we need to communicate on a human level, our need is much greater at a divine level. We need to pray individually, in our marriages, in our families, amongst our friends and in meetings with other believers.

Praying is not an easy discipline – but it is infinitely powerful. In the part of eternity in which we are now living, we are unable to comprehend prayer fully – but we know that it works. It's perverse isn't it that – in general – despite how potent prayer is, we are so reluctant to devote the time and energy to it that would be sensible? Could this be Satan's way of keeping us from this discipline – because if we treated it seriously, it could wreak havoc amongst his plans? It's really easy for Satan to discourage us from praying isn't it? It's just too demanding for most of us despite our Lord's teaching and despite prayer's innate benefits.

Apart from needing absolutely to bring our prayers and petitions to Almighty God, we are encouraged to do so in order to benefit from God's blessings. God told His people of old "…if my people, who are called by My name, will humble themselves and pray and seek My face and turn from their wicked ways, then will I hear from heaven and will forgive their sin and will heal their land…". [551] Apart from our prayers needing an answer, how much does our world need God's forgiveness and healing? We have been told what we must do – we cannot say we are unaware. The ball is in our court.

So much has been written about prayer. Regrettably, we often fail to give God His rightful place in our lives. We should never forget what the Lord requires of us in respect of daily living. Christian – have you absorbed this?

Lastly in this respect, prayer should include a time of silence to see what God will put into our minds as we wait upon Him – "…Call to me and I will answer you and tell you great and unsearchable things you do not know…".[552] We

[550] Hebrews 4:16
[551] 2 Chronicles 7:14
[552] Jeremiah 33:3

should not expect to hear the Lord address us audibly – but we can reasonably expect that in our meditation, the Lord will direct our thoughts and attention. One of the problems with prayer is that it not only requires effort – it also requires time. As we considered elsewhere – time is just what most of us believe we do not have. (It's perverse to think that we feel we have no time to talk to God – without whom we would have no time at all.) There are at least two problems with this approach. Firstly, we need to distinguish between what is urgent and what is important. If we fail to devote sufficient attention to what is important, everything in our lives becomes urgent. Secondly, if we do not have enough time to reflect on matters pertaining to our calling and to our eternal significance, then we are just too busy! A superficial approach will deprive us of blessings that otherwise might be ours.

Sometimes, we need to get away from all the activities that fill our lives every day – despite how good those activities may be per se. We need to stop sometimes – so we can reflect upon our God and to ponder what God is trying to tell us about what is happening in our lives and to compare that with what we believe should be happening in our lives. "...Be still, and know that I am God...".[553] We run the risk of glossing over the significance of Scripture if we read it too fast or if we fail to absorb what we are reading. Simultaneously, we run the risk of missing signals God is using to try to influence us if we fail to consider sufficiently deeply what our prayers are really about. In order to maximise the value of communication to and from God, we need to allocate sufficient time to reflect upon what God is trying to say to us.

12.5.2 Holy Scripture

Holy Scripture is Divinely inspired – "...All Scripture is God-breathed and is useful for teaching, rebuking, correcting and training in righteousness, so that the man of God may be thoroughly equipped for every good work...".[554] In addition, Scripture is infallible. The Bible has survived for such a long time and has been a source of great learning, influence, encouragement and comfort to so many people over many, many years. Wikipedia says that estimates of total sales and annual sales respectively are over 5 billion and 100 million copies.[555] Scripture includes the Old Testament and the New Testament. The Bible

---

[553] Psalm 46:10
[554] 2 Timothy 3:16-17
[555] en.wikipedia.org

contains 66 books – 39 of which are in the Old Testament while the remaining 27 books are in the New Testament.

Being a disciplined Christian means knowing and learning Scripture – because that is the way to increase our knowledge about the Christian way. This is how Christians are aware of Scripture's instructions for living. How can we expect to know about God's way if we don't take steps to learn and understand what Scripture says? Anyone who is serious about anything wants to know as much about it as possible. We need to know Scripture if we are to have any idea how to apply what it teaches to every-day living.

John Ortberg quotes Eugene Peterson as follows "...Christians feed on Scripture. Holy Scripture nurtures the holy community as food nourishes the human body. Christians don't simply learn or study or use Scripture: we assimilate it, take it into our lives in such a way that it gets metabolised into acts of love..." [and Mr Ortberg continues] "...Yet consumer researchers say that the average Bible owner possesses 9 Bibles and is looking for more. Something is lacking...".[556]

The quotes contained in this text give some idea of the depth and width of Holy Scripture. While Scripture does not contain specific insights into many of the matters that pertain to life today (e.g. same sex marriage), it definitely includes principles (as stated elsewhere) to provide a road map to guide us in those specificities.

12.5.3 Meeting with Other Believers

It's not fashionable to go to Church any more, even in the absence of COVID restrictions – and people can suggest many reasons why they feel there is no need to do so. Fundamentally it's too much effort for most people – which is why many say it is not relevant. Not so for the Christian. Christians are told not to give up "...meeting together, as some are in the habit of doing, but let us encourage one another – and all the more as you see the day approaching...".[557] Going to Church and meeting in Church groups are excellent ways to learn about Scripture and what is has to say about daily living. Not only that – going to Church presents us with an opportunity to learn from the experiences of others –

[556] As quoted by John Ortberg; The Me I Want To Be; Pg 105; Zondervan; 2010
[557] Hebrews 10:25

just like you and me. It could be that some folks don't attend Church because they do not like the challenges they are faced with there.

We should be clear that Christians should not feel that going to Church provides an opportunity to earn some kudos. Nor do Christians go to Church because they are good people. On the contrary, our need arises because we realise that we are not good people and we need continuous help from God and from other Christians to learn – and to understand what we don't already know (or what we do know but do not yet know how to apply). All this requires humility, tenacity and strong discipline.

Being disciplined affects so many aspects of day-to-day living – but fundamentally it is important to remember that doing the right thing requires much more than simply doing the easiest thing. Doing the right thing often costs us. Adopting the Christian way implies that we are called upon to reject the line of least resistance despite how much easier that would be. On the contrary, as Christians, we are asked to behave in a way that may make us appear weak – because we refuse to exploit people or opportunities that will adversely affect other people. In fact, this requires strength of character – which is the total opposite of weakness. The discipline involved in loving other people and in treating them better than they treat us is very demanding. Sometimes, it's very difficult to love people who to all intents and purposes make this as difficult as possible. Discipline means on-going effort – to do what is right and to avoid doing what is wrong. In turn, this requires us to develop character and to live according to principles that reflect our values and standards. This is what is required if our attitudes are to conform to the Christian way.

You may be thinking as you read this that it's all too much – that it's beyond you. One of the decisions that every individual makes for him or herself is the extent to which we allow ourselves to become victims of our own circumstances. Invariably, the only positive way forward is to accept our circumstances for what they are in the meantime – and try to improve them to the extent that we are able. The negative way forward is to blame everything on someone or something else. I am responsible for me. It is not helpful to delude oneself into thinking that if only I had this job or earned this much or could afford the other thing that life would be different. If only I was more outgoing, or had more skills. If only I could speak another language. If only I could do whatever. If all those 'ifs' became realities – what then? Would everything be perfect? I doubt it. Accordingly, our aim should not be perfection – but rather to do the best that we can with the resources that are available to us – and our Lord will do whatever else is necessary.

Being a Christian requires a lot of learning 'on the job'. Accordingly, we need the right mind-set because we often get it wrong – and we must learn from our mistakes and keep going. We must remember that God is not seeking perfection from us. Instead, God wants us to adopt the right attitude as we grow in grace – because in doing so – we will optimise our opportunities to learn, to grow and to be more like Him. This type of dependence upon God is pleasing to Him.

12.6 Conclusion

In this section, we have considered some of Scripture's teaching for our daily living according to the Christian way. This teaching includes both rules and principles. Rules are specific – while principles are generic guidelines – sufficiently generic (by definition) that they apply to myriad scenarios. They will influence our attitudes and prompt the sort of action that God has made it clear that He expects. We have looked at rules and principles that show us a better way – because as Christians, we must remember that non-Christians take an interest in how we live. This should prompt us to do everything within our power to live in such a way as to make it very difficult for anyone to accuse us justifiably of any wilful or deliberate wrongdoing. In addition, living in this way may assist non-Christians with whom we rub shoulders daily to see that there is a better way – which simultaneously – works and is effective when ordinary people accept what God is offering. This is part of what it means to have an appropriate attitude.

In the next chapter (13), we consider our attitude to some matters that affect every human being – Christian or otherwise – and which in turn are foundational to our attitude to other matters. The extent to which these matters are influential in our lives depends upon our attitude towards them.

Chapter Thirteen

Attitude to Some Foundational Matters in Life

13.1 Introduction

At this point, we would do well to remind ourselves of one matter in particular that was first raised in an earlier chapter (5) when we considered the many decisions and actions that we make every day. Accordingly, we have on-going opportunities to act as if we believe what we say is true – because every decision and every action is affected by our attitude at the time. Our attitude at decision points is critical. In this respect we should remind ourselves what has been repeated several times already – inaction is not merely the absence of action – it is a decision to do nothing in the circumstances.

With respect to decision-making (where attitude has perhaps most potential to influence our lives) there are a few 'drivers' in every individual's life that are very potent forces (because of their myriad implications). This chapter focuses on three of those drivers that have to do with how we spend: (1) time, (2) energy and (3) money – resources over which we all have control – and about which attitude is a determining factor. This chapter refers also to another important area about which attitude is deeply important and concerns what makes life worth living for each of us as individuals. (Let's call the attitudes dealt with in this chapter – 'foundational attitudes' – so named because the attitudes adopted concerning these areas ('foundational matters') impinge upon many ancillary decisions.)

13.2 My Attitude to Spending My Time, My Energy and My Money

There are at least 2 common threads that connect time, energy and money. The first is that everybody has them and the second is that they are all in limited and finite supply. This means that there are implications in how we spend them – that is to say we have to make choices as how to use them because they are scarce and the more scarce they are, the more valuable they become.

Firstly, with respect to time, we have distinguished already that mortality is probably the most significant factor in life. We reminded ourselves that our lives are finite – and relative to eternity, they are very brief. Scripture says "…You have made my days a mere handbreadth; the span of my years is as nothing before You. Each man's life is but a breath…".[558] We are unable to add even a moment of time to our life span. Once a moment is spent, it cannot be reclaimed or spent again – it has gone forever. One writer has commented "…The Bible teaches that time and life are tied together. It seems that the whole universe is organized for measuring time. Nature is like a huge clockmaker's shop in which thousands of timepieces are ticking. Pulse beats indicate the fleeting moments; the rotation of the earth marks the passing of day and night; the phases of the moon, the moving on of the months; the revolutions of the planets, the march of the years. Geology studies the wrinkles written by time on earth's brow. Astronomy studies the clockwork of the heavens. Archaeology, peering about among the relics of the ancient past, traces the footprints of time in the ages gone by. Approaching a new year, we speak of Father Time and visualize an old man with a long white beard who is holding a scythe in one hand and an hourglass in the other hand. But time is a thief. Time steals strength from our muscles and youth from our faces. Time robs us of our health and strips us at last of everything that we have…".[559] What more needs to be said to underscore how important it is to use our time carefully and avoid taking it for granted. It is always a valuable exercise to consider how we use the time available to us. This is a critical test for all of us – but especially for Christians.

There is general recognition of the value of time – for example, Wikipedia makes us aware that "…Time-use research is an interdisciplinary field of study dedicated to learning how people allocate their time during an average day…". Notwithstanding this, we don't always treat time with the respect it deserves. For example, while it has to be said that the permutations available as to how to use time are limited only by our imagination – we often waste many of the opportunities available to us by failing to use any imagination or discipline in

[558] Psalm 39:5

[559] Billy Graham; Three Ways to Use Time Wisely; Billy Graham Evangelistic Association; July 2004

deciding how to make use of our time. Possibly, many of us disregard the value of time – not even considering whether we are using it productively or unproductively. This may be an indication why so much time is wasted. Worse still, sometimes this happens deliberately. Sometimes, we say we just can't be bothered – and by this, we mean that we allow time to fritter away without doing anything productive with it. I do not mean to suggest that relaxation is a waste of time – because we all need time for that purpose – but deciding to relax is a conscious decision – whereas behaving like a lazy slob achieves no useful purpose and infers a total lack of discipline.

Time wastage often happens because we are aimless and undisciplined in our thinking. The difficulty is that all too often, this can become a way of life. On the other hand, trying to use every moment as productively as possible may be good as a general principle – but it shouldn't become a paranoia. I am advocating something in between. (By way of anecdote, I really dislike having to join a queue to have my haircut! I accept this is necessary because it will grow too long otherwise but I recognise also that those who are in a line before me deserve to have their turn before me. My objection is not taking my turn – it is having to waste time waiting. My life clock is ticking away while I wait and wait – and wait some more. [In some parts of the world, the concept of a queue has not yet proven to be popular – so the first person to get to the front irrespective of how they got there or whether they have been waiting longest or not – gets attention first!] To avoid wasting time in a line, I walk away sometimes because I don't have the patience to wait but when I wait, I always make sure that I have a book to hand. At least I am not wasting time.

Scripture tells us that "…there is a time for everything, and a season for every activity under heaven: a time to be born and a time to die, a time to plant and a time to uproot, a time to kill and a time to heal, a time to tear down and a time to build, a time to weep and a time to laugh, a time to mourn and a time to dance, a time to scatter stones and a time to gather them, a time to embrace and a time to refrain, a time to search and a time to give up, a time to keep and a time to throw away, a time to tear and a time to mend, a time to be silent and a time to speak, a time to love and a time to hate, a time for war and a time for peace…".[560] There is so much to think about in these few short verses – sad in some senses of that word – perhaps because they are so true to life.

---

[560] Ecclesiastes 3:1-8

In looking back at your attitude at particular points in time in particular circumstances, do you believe that your attitude has always been appropriate? Do you recognise some of the 'times' mentioned above in the quote from Ecclesiastes and if so, do you believe you responded appropriately? Elsewhere, Scripture reminds the non-Christian "...In the time of my favour I heard you, and in the day of salvation I helped you...".[561] The King James Version of Scripture refers to 'redeeming the time' – reminding Christians to treat time with the respect that it deserves. Make no mistake, <u>what we choose to do with the time available to us is our choice</u> – and once we make our decision, we cannot go back and change our mind – there is no re-run or second opportunity to use our time differently.

All that said, we often hear the words "I can't help you – I don't have enough time". In fact, this means we are saying that within the time we have available to us, we don't believe there is any room left to include that particular task or meeting – or whatever is being referred to. Sometimes, this is merely a trite excuse – and at other times, it is a true and valid reason for not taking a particular action. There are so many demands upon time for most of us – how can we tell the difference between being unable to add even one more task to our schedule and just being unwilling to put ourselves out by re-arranging our schedules to exclude one or more activities that are merely ancillary or otherwise superfluous and trivial to enable us to fit in something that is meaningful and worthwhile? It is often said that when you want something done – ask a busy person – because they will always manage to fit it in for you. Fitting in more and doing more do not come naturally to many of us. What is your attitude with respect to spending your time?

Secondly, with respect to energy, we don't need to be reminded that like time, energy is limited in supply also. We considered earlier how marvellously we are made – and how meticulous our Creator has been in creating humankind. We recognise however that our bodies do not exist in a vacuum – and in fact, demand a great deal of care and attention to keep them healthy and functional. Our bodies are slowly wasting away and lack of appropriate care and attention will speed up that process. Accordingly, we must eat, sleep, exercise and keep our bodies clean in providing them with nutrition, care and rest to protect us as far as possible from risk of damage, infection or disease. All this requires energy and discipline. Surrounding all this, we might easily forget God's timetable in

[561] 2 Corinthians 6:2

creation. He gave us the example that we should rest our bodies – "...By the seventh day God had finished the work He had been doing; so, on the seventh day He rested from all His work. And God blessed the seventh day and made it holy, because on it He rested from all the work of creating that He had done...".[562] God did not rest because He was physically tired – but unlike God, we are physical beings and we become tired so we need rest to regenerate energy to keep living.

We cannot help but recognise the need for rest – because we are all too familiar with how tired we become if we are deprived of sleep for whatever reason – but it seems that the business of living demands an increasing amount of energy. Working adds to that need – and exercise and maintaining friendships add even more energy absorbing activities to it – but we all need to work, to exercise and to spend time with friends and family – but how can we fit in everything? No one needs to be persuaded that energy is an integral part of living. We know also that we can only do so much before our internal reservoir of strength runs out. If our usage of energy exceeds what is reasonable in the circumstances – we can easily cause problems for our bodies. So, we need to eat, hydrate and rest properly to replace lost energy before we try to use more of it. The point is that since energy is in such short supply, our attitude as to how we expend it is important.

As with the allocation of time, there are so many demands upon our energies that we often (genuinely) feel exhausted and in dire need of rest. There is something called saturation point that needs to be taken into account – this means <u>there is a point in time when some activity has to be sacrificed because our current schedule is unsustainable.</u> I want to distinguish here between people who are living flat out – and those who merely think they are living flat out. People may be in the former group because of demands in the home and especially with young children – or because someone has to work incredibly hard just to retain their job – or because someone needs to have more than one job just to make ends meet. On the other hand, people who believe they are living flat out – but in fact are not – comprise people whose life experience does not expose them to the same sort of pressures as those in the first group. Have you ever asked a colleague if they are busy and been told "No – I'm not busy – can I help you with something?" If you have had this experience, treasure it! There are so many demands upon time for most of us – that we find it difficult to fit in everything –

562 Genesis 2:2-3

but since energy is such a critical part of life, it behoves us to consider carefully how we use it. What is your attitude to expending energy?

Thirdly, if we didn't need to be reminded that time and energy are in short supply, most of us certainly do not need to be reminded that money is in short supply too. In the same way that Scripture speaks about time, Scripture also has some important things to say about money. For example, "…the love of money is a root of all kinds of evil. Some people, eager for money, have wandered from the faith and pierced themselves with many griefs…".[563] It's perverse that people without money often crave to have lots of the stuff while some who have more than their fair share seem to be no happier as a result. It's a salutary reminder to think of those amongst big winners in lotteries etc. – some of whom are on record as saying that they wished they had never won it in the first place. Most of us might find this difficult to understand unless we have seen some of the complications that can develop with having too much money. It's difficult to reconcile the wealth of some people with the obvious need of others who literally have next to nothing. It's virtually impossible for those of us with less money to imagine the type of difficulties that can arise for people with too much – but those difficulties are real and are not to be underestimated.

Note that there is no suggestion here that money itself is wrongful – although it might be if our attitude towards management of our resources is influenced by wrongful attitudes. For example – Scripture tells us that we should "…Bring the whole tithe into the storehouse, that there may be food in My house. Test Me in this," says the Lord Almighty, "and see if I will not throw open the floodgates of heaven and pour out so much blessing that you will not have room enough for it…". [564] (Tithing simply means allocating 10% of our income to the Lord's work.) Leaving aside the 10 % quantum for the time being [remember the story in Scripture of the widow's mite? [565] – the amount one gives is less significant than the amount one has left], I wonder how many of us give regularly to the Lord's work and to people in need? It has to be said that many non-Christians give sacrificially to people in need so the recognition of the need of others and the consequent responsibility for action is not restricted to Christians.

Scripture also reminds us of Paul's example. He said "…In everything I did, I showed you that by this kind of hard work we must help the weak, remembering

[563] 1 Timothy 6:10
[564] Malachi 3:10
[565] Mark 12:41-44

the words the Lord Jesus himself said: 'It is more blessed to give than to receive.'…".[566] Think about it, do you feel more blessed when you give – or when you receive? "…But my sense of freedom always increases when I give because giving is a declaration that my security rests someplace other than the bank. Giving is an act of confidence in God…".[567] What is your attitude with respect to spending your money?

Christians have hard decisions to make in adopting the right response to these fundamental attitude scenarios. How much time, energy and money need to be devoted to the Lord's work? There is no easy answer to this – and Scripture is not prescriptive. Each of us must be motivated by our conscience (see Para 4.2). The point is that as Christians, we should be testing our attitudes regularly – and especially with respect to these fundamental questions. We should compare the extent to which we spend time, energy and money on Christian activity (that has immortal consequences) with the time, energy and money spent on non-Christian activity – that is finite by nature.

13.3 My Attitude to Those Things That Make Life Worth Living for Me

One writer has asked "…On what or whom do you set your heart? To what vision of right-relatedness between humans, nature and the transcendent are you loyal? What hope and what ground of hope animate you and give shape to the force field of your life and to how you move into it…"?[568]

Many writers and commentators agree on the value of living for something bigger and outside of ourselves. For example, one writer has said "…There is woven within each of us a desire for something more – a craving to be part of something bigger, greater, and more profound than our relatively meaningless day-by-day existence…In a fallen world there is powerful pressure to constrict your life to the shape and size of your life…".[569] In addition, it has been said "…Man's search for meaning is the primary motivation in his life…".[570] The same author said that "…being human always points, and is directed, to

[566] Acts 20:35
[567] John Ortberg; When The Game Is Over It All Goes Back In The Box; Pg 89; Zondervan; 2007
[568] James W Fowler; Stages Of Faith; Pg 14; Harper One; 1981
[569] Paul David Tripp; A Quest For More; Pgs 18 and 22; New Growth Press; 2007
[570] Viktor E Frankl; "Man's Search for Meaning"; Pg 121; Washington Square Press; 1985

something, or someone, other than oneself…the more one forgets himself – by giving himself to a cause to serve or another person to love – the more human he is and the more he actualises himself…We can discover this meaning in life in three different ways; by creating a work or doing a deed; by experiencing something or encountering someone; and by the attitude we take toward unavoidable suffering…”.[571]

Another writer has taken up the same theme in saying “…This is the true joy in life, the being used for a purpose recognized by yourself as a mighty one; the being thoroughly worn out before you are thrown on the scrap heap; the being a force of Nature instead of a feverish selfish little clod of ailments and grievances complaining that the world will not devote itself to making you happy. I am of the opinion that my life belongs to the community, and as long as I live, it is my privilege to do for it whatever I can. I want to be thoroughly used up when I die, for the harder I work, the more I live. Life is no ‘brief candle’ to me. It is a sort of splendid torch which I have got hold of for a moment, and I want to make it burn as brightly as possible before handing it on to the future generations…”.[572]

With respect to the potential of a life, J I Packer says “…What makes life worth living is having a big enough objective, something which catches our imagination and lays hold of our allegiance; and this the Christian has, in a way that no other person has. For what higher, more exalted, and more compelling goal can there be than to know God…”? [573]

All these quotes prompt us to think on a higher level. Clearly, there is room for deep consideration here. <u>What does life mean to me?</u> Regrettably, for most of the people in this world we live in, the only purpose in life is survival – getting by from one day to the next is an all-consuming task. For many people, there are inadequate monetary resources – so all energy and time has to be devoted to getting enough food and the necessities of life to survive for one more day. The rest of us – who are so well of that often we are complacent – have responsibilities towards such people. In Mr Packer’s words, for us Christians this is surely a big enough objective to catch our imagination and lay hold of our allegiance in getting to know our God? If we are to take these words seriously, then they will be a fitting context in which to re-examine what we called our

---

[571] Viktor E Frankl; “Man’s Search for Meaning”; Pg 133; Washington Square Press; 1985

[572] George Bernard Shaw – no other information on source of quote

[573] J I Packer; Knowing God; Pg 36; Hodder & Stoughton; 2013

‘fundamental attitudes’ with respect to how we spend our time, our energy and our money.

The key question is – for what thing that is bigger and outside yourself are you living? Maybe, you have pondered these things already and have devoted your time, energy and money to the Christian way – or perhaps you are so involved in pursuing your own ends that these matters have not crossed your mind – or if they have – you have swept them away quickly before you realise that pondering them further will activate your conscience. In this case, you might be concerned that you will be forced to take these matters more seriously than ever before. In which category would you say you fall? Do you need to do something about this?

13.4 Summary

This has been an introspective chapter – that is to say a chapter where some ‘soul-searching’ has been provoked. If life is as short as has been pointed out earlier and if we need something bigger that is outside ourselves to ‘self-actualise’, this may be an appropriate time to re-consider our attitudes to certain fundamental matters in life.

This chapter has brought us to the end of the preparations recommended – before starting to collate an action plan. We should now know a lot more about attitudes in general – and about our own in particular. We have been prompted to carefully re-examine all those attitudes – that combine to make us who and what we are. We know about the influence that conscience, sensitivity and discipline have on our character – and how humility plays such a critical role in character formation and decision-making. Further, we are aware of a number of qualities of character – together with those other influences – that can influence our attitude very greatly. After opening our minds to all these matters, we grounded sections 3 and 4 of the text in a chapter that focused on God’s attitude towards humanity. We took a candid look at how broken mankind is and analysed this with reference to humankind’s attitude towards humankind. This raised the question – where do we go from here? The answer is that probably, we need to alter direction if we are to be pointed towards where God wants us to head. At this stage, we tried to make an objective assessment of where we are now by examining the attitude of humankind in practice and in particular our attitude to what makes life worth living for each of us as individuals – considering how we spend our time, energy and money – all this en route to the compilation of an action plan – the subject of chapter 14 – the final chapter of the text.

Chapter Fourteen

Action Plan

14.1 Introduction

In trying to understand what attitude is and where it comes from, we have gained some insight into its prevalence and how it impinges upon every aspect of our being whether we realise it or not. We have seen that it affects how we think, how we act, how we interface with others, how we deal with difficulties, how we live, how we manage success and so on. One writer has said that "...The longer I live, the more I realize the impact of attitude on life. Attitude to me is more important than facts. It is more important than the past, than education, than money, than circumstances, than failures, than successes, than what other people think or say or do. It is more important than appearance, giftedness or skill. It will make or break a company, a church or a home. The remarkable thing is that we have a choice every day regarding the attitude we will embrace for that day. We cannot change our past. Nor can we change the fact that people will act in a certain way. We also cannot change the inevitable. The only thing we can do is to play on the one string we have and that is our attitude. I am convinced that life is 10 per cent what happens to me and 90 per cent how I react to it. And so it is with you. We are in charge of our attitudes...".[574]

If this is true, we have no reason to blame our attitude on anyone or anything else but ourselves. We are responsible for the decisions we make – and those decisions include the attitudes we adopt. When pressed about actions or inaction, we have considered that sometimes people defend themselves by saying, "...It's just the way I am..." Clearly, this is merely a crutch since the way we are is how we choose to be. The way we are is not because of anything outside our own decision-making. John Maxwell has said "...The greatest day of your life and

[574] "Attitude"; A Poem By Charles Swindoll

mine is when we take total responsibility for our attitudes. That's the day we truly grow up…".[575] Taking, total responsibility is difficult – it's much easier to protest "It's not my fault" – than it is to say "I accept responsibility – and all the implications that follow…". When will we grow up?

As we approach the end of this text, I want to consider some very practical applications of all that has been presented in earlier chapters. If all that has been written is true – and if it represents reasonable food for thought and action – and if the text is anything like as significant as what I have made it out to be – we must know how to apply it if it is to have any relevance in our lives in the 21st century. It has been said "…We don't believe something by merely saying we believe it, or even when we believe that we believe it. We believe something when we act as if it were true…".[576] <u>The question is whether you believe what you have read in the previous chapters to the extent that you think it is worth acting upon.</u>

Since "…Jesus is the only one with authoritative wisdom about how to live…",[577] I have quoted Holy Scripture extensively in what I have written – and it is these texts that must inform any practical action arising from the text. James admonishes us "…Do not merely listen to the word, and so deceive yourselves. Do what it says…".[578] My personal comments are ancillary to the importance, veracity and significance of Scripture.

Further, since attitude affects everything we think and do, this text has invited you to consider the implications of adopting the 'right' attitude in all environments, in all decisions and in all circumstances because "…sin has damaged everything, [so] God calls us to be concerned about everything…".[579] The text has explored what constitutes 'right' in certain circumstances and has dwelt at some length on 'right' principles.

Is all that has been described earlier possible for you? The answer probably depends to a large extent upon your personal credo. For example – non-Christians may be of the view that it is reasonable to treat others the way others treat you – but Jesus' teaching differs. He says – <u>don't treat others how they treat you</u> – instead treat them better! How on earth is it possible to have an attitude

---

575 John C Maxwell; Developing The Leader Within You; Pg 103; Thomas Nelson Publishing; 1993

576 Dallas Willard

577 John Ortberg; The Me I Want to Be; Pg 47; Zondervan; 2010

578 James 1:22

579 Paul David Tripp; A Quest For More; Pg 37; New Growth Press; 2007

like the attitude promoted by Jesus? The answer is that it is only possible if our heart and soul are attuned to believing what Jesus believed – and what He demonstrated about how to live life during His life on earth. It's our choice – Jesus does not compel us – instead He has given us free will. Someone wise has reminded us that when you pick up a stick, you pick up two ends – so exercising free will means that we must accept the consequences. So, if all that we have considered is relevant to you in any way, you may now want to consider what changes this implies for you to get you pointed in the right direction. If so, an action plan may facilitate you – to help you achieve an attitude of mind that has the potential to change you – and all those around you.

14.2 Reviewing the Text

Before starting your plan, you may want to review the text quickly to remind yourself on some areas. If so, there are three options for you to consider. Firstly, if you are short of time, you may want to focus on the overview set out in para 14.2.1 below. The overview summarises the focus of each section of the text. Alternatively, if you have a little more time and you want to drill down a little further without having to read the whole text, a summary of the key sentences is set out in para 14.2.2. Finally, if you want to refresh your mind, a summary of the whole text is set out in Appendix One.

14.2.1 A Quick Overview

Section 1 of the book comprises the 'The Platform' – so called because it provides the introduction to the text that follows and is aimed at helping us to begin to think about two important matters: (1) the importance of attitude and (2) why it is worth further consideration.

The Platform initiates discussion on how attitude works and how it arises. The word 'stimulus' is introduced. When a stimulus combines with an attitude, there is a response. Stimulus is the catalyst, attitude is the 'driver' and action is the output. Section 1 refers to what we know about attitude – based on both personal and general experiences. Attitude defines who I am. Therefore, to understand who I am, I need to understand my attitudes – and to be able to distinguish my real attitudes from what I think my attitudes are. Understanding one's attitude involves a journey of self-discovery.

Section 2 looked at the composition of humankind – and in doing so, provided important information that placed all the text that follows in context.

Firstly, we reminded ourselves that we need to distinguish mortality from immortality because this sole distinction is the only context that really matters. Humankind's body and mind are mortal but Spirit and Soul will last forever. While we need to take care of our bodies, we need to take much greater care of our Spirit and Soul.

Our bodies last for only a relatively short time – and although wondrously made, they are relatively fragile. Accordingly, discipline is required if we are to treat our bodies with the care and respect they deserve. More wonderfully, if our human spirit is linked to the Holy Spirit, the linkage will enhance the work of conscience and if our conscience is sensitised as a result of the umbilical cord that joins spirit and soul, our foundation in God will be secure.

Before a building is erected, the foundations must be laid – and the higher the building, the deeper the foundations must be. The Christian way is similar. If we are to make any impression on non-believers with whom we are surrounded day by day, we must be able to demonstrate that our faith has significance. Note that God does not demand that we need to become experts or masters in anything. We do not need to be rich or poor or to have had little education or a lengthy education or that we are leaders or followers or indeed that we are anything special as defined by the society in which we live. God requires that we recognise the eternal importance of spirit and soul and that we devote our mortal bodies in service to Him recognising His Lordship of our lives. This discussion brought us to the end of chapter 4.

The next part of Section Two (chapter 5) dealt with how to begin training our bodies to reflect – in life – the eternal nature of our spirit and soul.

Chapter 6 presented some qualities of character – and chapter 7 looked at some other influences on attitude.

Section 3 comprises chapters 8-10 – and in some ways represents the core of what the text is all about. Chapter 8 talks about God's person and plan – while Chapter 9 looked at humankind's attitude in general. This section ended with chapter (10) – which dealt with humankind's attitude to humankind. In short, Section 2 describes the eternal perspective of humankind's role and function while Section 3 provides more detail on the context in which our life's work has to be accomplished.

Section 4 gets down to the 'nitty gritty' – describing how to think about accomplishing what needs to be done. This Section includes some reflections on areas the text has covered thus far that are relevant to Christian living and includes comments on communication and scriptural guidance on attitude. Some further thoughts on living daily as a Christian are included – with particular reference to prayer, Scripture per se and meeting with other believers. Chapter 13 is an introspective chapter that invites readers to do some 'soul-searching' in considering their attitude towards certain fundamental matters in life – how we use our time, energy and money. Chapter 13 addresses the question – what is my attitude to the things that make life worth living for me? These matters are considered to be amongst the most important for consideration in anticipation of preparing a plan of action.

14.2.2 An Analysis of Key Sentences from the Text

So much has been condensed into the pages that precede this one that there might be value in re-stating some key sentences (underlined in the text) that in turn, might be useful in reviewing the text before starting to formulate the plan described above. As it turned out, deciding what to exclude was such a formidable task that I ended up with a much larger number of key sentences than I had intended. I felt that all were worth retaining. I hope you will feel similarly as you review them.

- Attitude is multi-faceted and ubiquitous – it exists everywhere human beings exist – and the permutations are myriad.
- Attitude is sensitive. It reflects not only who we are but sometimes also who we would like others to think we are. Attitude is very powerful.
- The question is whether or not we are sufficiently sensitive in our behaviour to even begin to think about the attitudes we adopt in the process of living?
- Only those things that have eternal significance have meaningful value.
- Our souls pre-date our birth and will exist after our mortal lives expire.
- What more has the Almighty God to do to get our attention?
- Attitude impinges upon the way we live – the way we think and what prompts us to think, the way we act – what we choose to do and which actions we will find unacceptable, whether we speak or whether we remain silent – and if we speak how we will do so.
- The significance of our heart/soul is that it defines our whole being and is the source of every attitude and behaviour pattern that we exhibit.

- As soon as the spirit within humankind is influenced by the Holy Spirit, then the focus of the human soul veers God-wards and this in turn has an absolute influence on our passions, feelings and desires.
- If we have not accepted the Lordship of Christ in our lives, our soul's eternal purpose is diverted from its original purpose.
- The more one ignores conscience, the less sharp it becomes until ultimately it is virtually ineffective and no longer inhibits or even influences adverse behaviour or action.
- As Christians, we need to be sensitive to our calling to glorify God and to enjoy Him forever. In addition, we need to be sensitive to the people around us – that is – those whom we are called to serve. How can we serve any person if we are insensitive to their needs or condition?
- Lord – help me to be as sensitive as I need to be to live effectively for You.
- Frequent communication with our Lord will help us: to glorify Him, to mature as Christians, to encourage the development of sensitivity towards others – and to remember whose we are and whom we serve.
- Humility is an attitude of mind.
- We are not masters of our own destiny – we control nothing – and we have only what we have been given.
- It has to be said that no matter how humble we are or might become, humility will neither replace nor become a substitute for acknowledgement of Jesus Christ as Lord of our lives.
- Character is intrinsically linked to attitude.
- Attitude is a fundamental part of every human being – not least because it affects our choices/decisions – which in turn affect whether – and if so, how we act and/or react in every circumstance in which we find ourselves throughout our lives.
- Scripture is not a rulebook. Instead, Scripture provides us with more of what we might describe as 'principles'.
- Notice the inter-play between conscience, character, behaviour, decisions and principles. They are all complementary.
- Human behaviour can be changed – if there is a willingness to change it.

- The types of principles and traits and qualities considered in the text are transformational catalysts in adopting attitudes that have potential to change individuals and societies – not only locally but globally as well.
- The narrower our experiences in life, the smaller our frame of reference will be in interpreting events as they unfold around us.
- One of the ways that God speaks to His people is through His Word.
- If we are right in what we believe we don't need to talk down to any other person – and if we are wrong – we have no right to do so.
- We need to remember that two people can react entirely differently to the same scenario – and both can be correct simultaneously.
- Attitude is a pattern of thought that arises through the interaction of spirit, soul and body. It involves the operation of conscience, character and principles – combining to persuade an individual in a particular environment to think, behave or to react in a particular way.
- We choose who we are – and we must accept responsibility for that.
- Our Creator has allowed us great latitude in deciding how we should live our lives – but that latitude is based on certain fundamental principles – including accountability and consequences.
- The attitude of Christ towards humankind is demonstrated in His supreme sacrifice.
- Understanding the awesome purity and majesty of our Creator and the utter wretchedness of our own sinful state are amongst the first steps in the process of becoming holy.
- The only hope we have begins with the realisation that it is God's wish that every human being should be in a right relationship with Him.
- Since our God is the awesome deity – whose love and providence are so comprehensive that our finite minds do not have adequate capacity to comprehend Him, the least we can do is adopt appropriate attitudes in His service.
- God has chosen not to set out a plethora of rules – presumably because we might be misled into thinking that adherence to such rules would guarantee us a place in His kingdom.
- God wants us to emulate Him – in our character, in our values and principles – and thereby in our attitudes.
- It is so easy to be a hypocrite – sometimes we don't even have to try – it's almost as if it is natural.

- Salvation is beyond price – its value cannot be quantified – it cannot be bought, earned or achieved.
- My attitude will remain as it is right at this moment unless and until I take steps to alter it.
- Perfection is not expected – but working to the highest standard that we can attain is our reasonable service.
- If we feed our minds with appropriate material, it is much more likely that our attitudes will be attuned to the principles set out in Scripture – and this in turn influences how we live.
- One of the decisions that every individual makes for him or herself is the extent to which we allow ourselves to become victims of our own circumstances.
- Every decision and every action are affected by our attitude at the time.
- The way we are is how we choose to be.
- Scripture is the principal guide to attitude – the platform from which appropriate attitudes emanate.
- Good intentions are not enough – action is what is required.
- God is good!

14.3 A Step-by-Step Guide to Compiling an Action Plan

"…The greatest discovery of my generation is that people can alter their lives by altering their attitude of mind…".[580] The word 'plan' as used in the title of this paragraph needs some explanation. By 'plan', I do not mean in the style of a research proposal for a PhD (but it can be if you so choose). Remember this is not an academic exercise – it is a tool that will help spiritual growth. Accordingly, by 'plan' I mean a thoughtful approach to constructing some form of logical review of your attitude as you perceive it to be currently – and how you might enhance it – if you consider that necessary. Your 'plan' need not even be in writing – but my suggestion is that it will be much more helpful if you spend time writing it out. There are four reasons for this: (1) writing a plan brings discipline to formulating it; (2) the original written draft can be amended and over time – refined – by reference to what was written before; (3) if the plan is not written, reference to previous drafts (of which there may be a few) will not

[580] William James – as quoted by John C Maxwell; Attitude 101; Pg 46; 2003; Maxwell Motivation

be possible; (4) you can access a written plan easily – so there will be no need to try to remember it.

Note that it is the purpose of the plan that is the critical point – not the method you use to construct it – and not the style in which you draft it. In short, the content of this paragraph is not prescriptive. If you find these comments useful – then please use them – but if you prefer a different approach – please use that instead. The point is to apply what you have been prompted to consider as you read the preceding text. Note also that this is not an exercise in isolation – it is a means to try and turn theory into practice. In making a plan, it is essential to remember why you are doing so. The purpose is to glorify God. An action plan might include the sort of steps that could be taken in order to help train our attitudes to work in accordance with the way we believe God expects.

The action plan is based upon the premise that (as repeated often in the text), attitudes do not just happen. Instead they are the result of myriad interactions – about which we may be more – or less aware (chapter 1). You will remember that whether we are aware of them or not, attitudes are active at all times – so the important lesson is to remind ourselves on an on-going basis that this is the case. Therefore, we should bear in mind the types of interactions that may be going on in our individual lives – and make sure that they do not control us but that we control them. In considering a plan:

The first step is absolutely essential – because it is acceptance of Christ as Lord of your life. This was explained at some length in Para 11.2. No progress can be made until this point has been reached. First steps are often critical – and this one is no exception.

The second step is to remind oneself about how we humans have been created. We have a finite existence (chapter 2) and we comprise spirit, soul and body (chapter 3). We have a conscience (chapter 4) that either complements our Christian life or grieves it because it challenges us – unless and until it becomes almost redundant through non-usage. In addition, we can decide how sensitive we want to be in life (chapter 4). That choice and the implications arising from it are our responsibility – and we must discipline ourselves to exercise that responsibility (chapter 4).

The third step is preparation for enhancing character. As the text has demonstrated, it is not possible to adopt an appropriate attitude without humility (chapter 5) and it is important to recognise this earlier rather than later. Humility precedes learning – and learning is essential if we are to approach all the decisions we need to make in life – with discernment (chapter 5).

These decisions per se lead to character – the means by which our spirit and soul connect with our physical body and mind in living the Christian way (see for example Paras 4.3, 5.2, 5.3 etc). A number of these qualities of character were described in chapter 6.

Naturally, the more qualities one has, the greater the probability that they will lead to enhancement and refinement of one's character. Consider the breadth of qualities that were described in the chapter (remembering that the list is not exhaustive). Conduct your own self-assessment to determine whether you have any bad attitudes. The objective is to try to identify what is preventing you from becoming the sort of person you believe God wants you to be. It is imperative that you specify your objectives clearly – and preparing a written plan will help you clarify your thoughts – and enable you to consider your objectives regularly and simply. So, consider the detail provided about each of the qualities considered earlier and decide which you think you aspire to. The hard part is to begin the process of adopting them in your life. For example, if you believe that integrity is of fundamental importance in the Christian life, you may want to think about how your life reflects that belief currently – and whether there are opportunities to refine your character by behaving with even more integrity – and if so, how that might be achieved. Take honesty as another example. You may want to think about your approach to honesty currently. Maybe (or maybe not) you will find it valuable to think about how you can demonstrate an even more refined approach to honesty than you do currently. (Note that there is no suggestion that an individual is currently dishonest (for example).) The same approach can be applied to all the qualities that you believe combine to produce a character that reflects the principles set out in Scripture – and which you consider reflect the life of someone who takes their relationship with God seriously. John Maxwell recommends identifying which attitudes make you feel negative about yourself – and then identify what attitudes create problems in dealing with other people. This is followed by thinking about whatever thought processes control your mind. Consider what Scripture says about all the matters you identify – and then determine a course of action that will lead to living in a new way.[581]

---

[581] John C Maxwell; Attitude 101; Pg 45; 2003; Maxwell Motivation

Note that qualities of character are not mutually exclusive. If you 'adopt' one quality, that does not mean that you cannot adopt another – they have a cumulative value as well as individual value – and they are not mutually exclusive. The suggestion is to review your character and to consider whether and how it might be strengthened as part of the process of underpinning all you do and say – with an attitude that emanates from a supportive character.

Then there are the other influences –some of which are set out in chapter 7. Consider to what extent the environments in which you live and move are influencing your life and how positive they are in helping you to adopt appropriate attitudes. Are your experiences helping you in this respect? Are your perceptions fair and reasonable? Consider your behaviour and the effect that your attitudes have on your behaviour. Is this effect acceptable – and if so, is there some way to enhance that effect? If the effect is unacceptable, what sort of changes do you think might improve that situation?

The fourth and final step is to use the 'infrastructure' just described to construct your own personal plan to consider your attitude and how to enhance it.

Careful consideration of who God is and reflection on His attributes will contribute to your planning (chapter 8) – which will be improved if you take a little time to remember the status of humankind as part of the process (chapter 9) – together with a review of just how far short we have fallen from God's original plan for us as described in Genesis (chapter 10).

Chapter 11 tries to give us some grounding for the way forward and together with Chapters 12 and 13 acts as an introduction to the themes for action presented in this last chapter (14).

With or without a plan, I encourage you to use whatever may have prompted you in the preceding text to make a difference in your life and in the life of others around you – in serving our Creator.

14.4 Contemporary Attitude in Action

A salutary warning has been provided by Mahatma Gandhi as follows – "...There are seven things that will destroy us: Wealth without work; Pleasure without conscience; Knowledge without character; Religion without sacrifice;

Politics without principle; Science without humanity and Business without ethics…”.[582]

In order to help those readers who may like to consider further how attitude might be brought to bear on how we live, a very brief summary of two books is provided below. (It should be noted that ‘personal development’ and matters arising therefrom are not new – for example Marcus Aurelius – who was a Roman Emperor wrote Meditations (on Stoic philosophy) between 161 and 180AD. Accordingly, there are many texts that can be used to stimulate thoughts on attitude.)

Each of these books has much to say about the effects of different attitudes. Summaries are provided here to help those formulating an action plan to see the potential that arises from the right sort of attitude. The objective of including them is to enable them to act as catalysts to those considering their own attitudes. The number of copies of each of the books that have been sold since they were first published testify to their value.

In general, summaries serve a purpose but in so saying, it is good to remember that reading a summary cannot be as valuable as reading the whole text. Accordingly, paragraphs 14.4.1 and 14.4.2 should be regarded merely as summaries of the text of which they form a part.

14.4.1 The 7 Habits of Highly Effective People [583]

The sub-title of this book (‘Powerful Lessons In Personal Change’) hints at its value in considering changes in personal attitudes that are replete with potential for positive changes in how we live our lives. The foreword to the 25th anniversary edition of the book says “…I think the most important aspect of *The 7 Habits* – what makes it not just practical, but profound – is its emphasis on *building character* rather than ‘attaining success’. There is no effectiveness without discipline, and there is no discipline without character…”.[584] The character ethic requires alignment between a person’s values (internal [subjective] drivers that govern behaviour) and principles (the laws of nature) that by definition are timeless and unchanging. This means that even though the book was written some years ago, its application is as timely now as it was when

---

[582] Mahatma Gandhi

[583] Stephen R Covey; The 7 Habits of Highly Effective People; Simon & Schuster; 1989

[584] Jim Collins; Foreword – The 7 Habits Of Highly Effective People; Pg 3; Simon & Schuster; 1989

the book was first published. The character ethic has universal applicability. The author (Dr Covey), presents 7 Habits in his model that take the reader through three progressive stages of growth – starting with Dependence – moving through Independence – and culminating in Interdependence.

Dependence involves: being proactive (Habit 1), beginning with the end in mind (Habit 2) and putting first things first (Habit 3). Independence means thinking win/win (Habit 4), seeking to understand first and then to be understood second (Habit 5) and creating synergy (Habit 6). Lastly, Interdependence means sharpening the saw (Habit 7).

This book is instructive because adopting the Habits on an on-going basis requires continuous improvement in creating the attitude required to optimise effectiveness in building a person's character.

14.4.2 How to Win Friends and Influence People [585]

Like The 7 Habits of Highly Effective People, *How to Win Friends and Influence People* is not a new book. The reason the text has survived since it was first published in 1936 is that its foundational principles are timeless. The text contains 30 Principles spread over 4 parts.

Part 1 concerns Fundamental Techniques in Handling People – covered by 3 Principles: (1) Don't criticise, condemn or complain; (2) Give honest and sincere appreciation and (3) Arouse in the other person an eager want.

Part 2 describes Six Ways To Make People Like You – and this is considered under 6 Principles: (1) Become genuinely interested in other people; (2) Smile; (3) Remember that a person's name is to that person the sweetest and most important sound in any language; (4) Be A good listener. Encourage others to talk about themselves; (5) Talk in terms of the other person's interests; (6) Make the other person feel important.

Part 3 is about Winning People To Your Way Of Thinking. The 12 principles in this part include: (1) The only way to get the best of an argument is to avoid it; (2) Show respect for the other person's opinions. Never say, "You're wrong." (3) If you are wrong, admit it quickly and emphatically; (4) Begin in a friendly way; (5) Get the other person saying "yes, yes" immediately; (6) Let the other person do a great deal of the talking; (7) Let the other person feel that the idea is his or hers; (8) Try honestly to see things from the other person's point of view;

---

[585] Dale Carnegie; How to Win Friends And Influence People; Simon & Schuster; 1936

(9) Be sympathetic with the other person's ideas and desires; (10) Appeal to the nobler motives; (11) Dramatize your ideas; and lastly (12) Throw down a challenge.

Part 4 is about Being A leader: How To Change People. There are 9 principles as follows: (1) Begin with praise and honest appreciation; (2) Call attention to people's mistakes indirectly; (3) Talk about your own mistakes before criticising the other person; (4) Ask questions instead of giving direct orders; (5) Let the other person save face; (6) Praise the slightest improvement and praise every improvement. Be "hearty in your approbation and lavish in your praise"; (7) Give the other person a fine reputation to live up to; (8) Use encouragement. Make the fault seem easy to correct; and finally (9) Make the other person happy about doing the thing you suggest.

Even though it is not possible to go into too much detail about the text, these headings will give readers some idea of what the author is trying to promote.

14.5 Transformational Change

The first few words of the Preface said "...The reason why it is worth considering attitude at all is because of the quantum of potential for empowerment that arises. The thesis of this book is that the person who understands and controls the influences that shape his/her attitude will be empowered to make positive things happen not only in his or her own life – but also in the life of others...". I call this 'transformational' change because it reflects how Scripture describes what happens when people stop conforming to "...the pattern of this world...".[586] One writer has said that "...If you and I will inspire the people with whom we come in contact to a realisation of the hidden treasures they possess, we can do far more than change people. We can literally transform them...".[587] The same author refers to someone else who said "...Compared with what we ought to be, we are only half awake. We are making use of only a small part of our physical and mental resources. Stating the thing broadly, the human individual thus lives far within his limits. He possesses powers of various sorts which he habitually fails to use...".[588]

---

[586] Romans 12:2

[587] How To Win Friends And Influence People; Dale Carnegie; Pg 236; 2006; Vermilion

[588] William James – as cited in How To Win Friends And Influence People; Dale Carnegie; Pg 236; 2006; Vermilion

Considered from a higher 'spiritual' perspective, the potential arising as a result of adopting the types of attitudes described in Scripture beggars belief – because the consequences are eternal in nature. Consider the extent to which your life would change if you adopted the correct attitude at the appropriate time – and then – to the extent that you are able – consider what the changes in your life could lead to in the lives of family, friends and others around you. The implications are staggering for those who want to accomplish much, much more than they are experiencing currently – and who are prepared to make the huge effort required. Remember, "...When we change ourselves, we change how others see us and respond to us. When we change ourselves, we change the world...".[589] Changes in attitude have a cumulative effect.

Even a cursory glance at the brief overview of the two books cited in the previous paragraph will indicate – at the most mundane level – what can be achieved as a result of adopting an appropriate attitude. As recommended in the text, the full impact of doing so will only be achieved by considering the text of each book in full.

14.6 Conclusion

This text contains some transformational concepts – because what Christ taught is radical by its very nature. However, this is the Christian way and the Christian way is not part of standard human practice. The many preceding references to Scripture indicate that Scripture is the principal guide to attitude – it is the platform from which appropriate attitudes emanate. Thinking about one's attitude opens up our minds to all sorts of experiences and possibilities – but this type of exercise is no panacea per se. To adopt meaningful attitudes is much easier said than done – and while adopting such attitudes will not correct all that is wrong in our world, it will certainly make a positive contribution. The pre-condition is application – prodigious effort is required. Good intentions are not enough – action is what is required! It's good to remember that "...As people begin to act differently and to feel differently, they become different...".[590]

---

[589] Robert Quinn; Building The Bridge As You Walk On It; as Quoted In Shannon Polly & Kathryn Britton; Character Strengths Matter; Pg 208; Positive Psychology News LLC; 2015

[590] Shannon Polly & Kathryn Britton; Character Strengths Matter; Pg 9; Positive Psychology News LLC; 2015

In concluding this book, I want to remind you of the text of Philippians 2:5 – "...Your attitude should be the same as that of Christ Jesus..." and in doing so, my prayer for you replicates that of St Paul: "...May the God who gives endurance and encouragement give you a spirit of unity among yourselves as you follow Christ Jesus, so that with one mind and one heart and mouth you may glorify the God and Father of our Lord Jesus Christ...". [591]

---

[591] Romans 15:5-6

Section Five
Appendices

Appendix One

A Summary of the Text

Introduction

We have covered a wide area in the previous chapters. That being so, there might be some value in recording key points by way of a summary of the whole text. Accordingly, I have re-visited each chapter in turn and highlighted what I consider to be the key points for review.

Firstly, here is the Model to help guide you through the summary that follows:

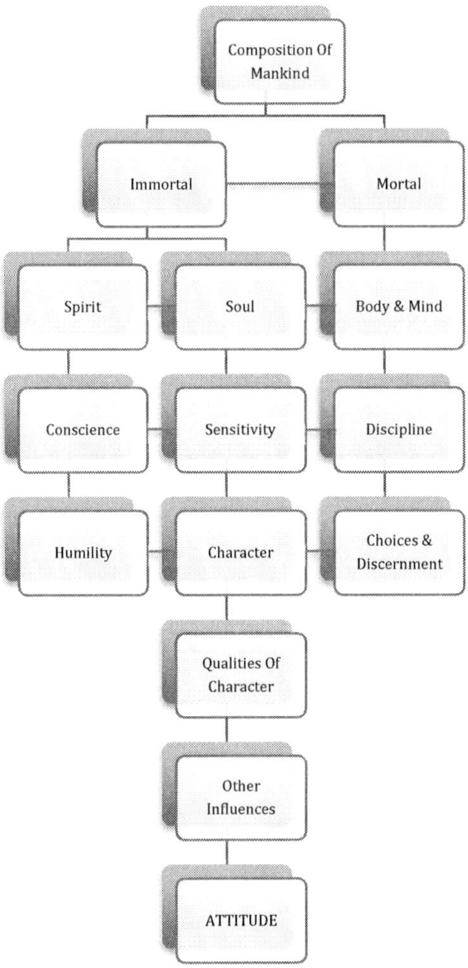

Chapter One

1. When you speak, do you consider not only what you are saying but the tone of voice you are using – and what your body language is saying in addition to the words you are using?
2. Attitude is multi-faceted and ubiquitous – it exists everywhere human beings exist and the permutations are myriad.
3. We should never underestimate the sensitivity and vulnerability of attitude to adverse influence.
4. While attitude is neither tangible nor measurable – it may or may not be visible.
5. Sometimes people make conscious efforts to hide their attitude and thereby who they really are.
6. An attitude need not only be displayed in what is said or done – but also by what is not said or not done – and in addition, consequential action (or words) might be deferred.
7. Attitude is sensitive. It reflects not only who we are but sometimes also who we would like others to think we are. Attitude is very powerful.
8. Something amongst a myriad of external possibilities has stimulated an internal part of us as human beings – and this stimulus gives rise to an attitude – from which a response follows.
9. The attitude created by the stimulus reflects our character.
10. Our nature leads us to believe that when something is amiss, it is the fault of someone else.
11. Jesus Christ is **THE** role model for all Christians.
12. Attitude is influenced by saving grace.
13. The question is whether or not we are sufficiently sensitive in our behaviour to even begin to think about the attitudes we adopt in the process of living?
14. 'Attitude' might be described initially as a pattern of thought that stimulates or prompts an individual to think, act or to react in a particular way – in a particular set of circumstances.
15. Attitude is a complex phenomenon – activated by a vast number of external 'triggers'.
16. As individuals we adopt attitudes – but we are not always aware that we have done so.

17. Holy Scripture tells us explicitly what our attitude should be "…the same as that of Jesus Christ…".

Chapter Two

1. Human beings are mortal.
2. Christians understand that the time allocated to us human beings on earth is only a part of eternity – death is not the end.
3. Only those things that have eternal significance have meaningful value.
4. God is infinite – existing before what we recognise as time (but which is actually part of eternity) – and will continue living forever.
5. Our souls pre-date our birth and will exist after our lives expire.
6. What more has Almighty God to do to get our attention?
7. Scripture distinguishes body from soul.
8. Life is eternal – and does not end with death. Death is merely a stepping-stone in the journey of immortality.
9. Attitude impinges upon the way we live – the way we think and what prompts us to think, the way we act – what we choose to do and which actions we will find unacceptable, whether we speak or whether we remain silent – and if we speak how we will do so.

Chapter Three

1. Humankind comprises: (1) spirit, (2) soul and (3) body.
2. The spirit within mankind may be considered as the umbilical cord between the Holy Spirit and the intrinsic nature of mankind.
3. The spirit is part of our human framework and controls the mechanism that we call our conscience.
4. It is when the Holy Spirit convicts men and women of their sin that the spirit within each of us human beings, has the opportunity to respond and to accept the redemption offered to us.
5. Our soul is of inestimable value.
6. If Satan controls our soul/heart, he controls us entirely.
7. The significance of our heart/soul is that it defines our whole being and is the source of every attitude and behaviour pattern that we exhibit.

8. As soon as the spirit within humankind is influenced by the Holy Spirit, then the focus of the human soul veers God-wards and this in turn has an absolute influence on our passions, feelings and desires.
9. Even though our minds should be under the control of our will, that does not always happen and the consequence is that we do not choose life-giving, truthful thoughts and healthy desires. Our bodies do not always submit to our minds and our habits are not always congruent with our values.
10. We need to exercise extreme care over what and who we allow to influence our minds.
11. Our character links up with our mind, our conscience and with our sensitivity to determine the attitudes that underlie the actions and words that we consider appropriate in daily life. When all these attitudes are collated in our mind, they represent our personal credo.
12. We need faith to believe that beyond the finite existence of our body/corpus and mind, our soul and spirit will continue to exist – throughout eternity.
13. The significance of our immortal soul and spirit cannot be over emphasised.
14. Everything we do emanates from deep within our being – from our everlasting soul.
15. If we have not accepted the Lordship of Christ in our lives, our soul's eternal purpose is diverted from its original purpose.
16. The Holy Spirit in-dwells every believer.
17. We need to be aware of the affinity between the Holy Spirit and the spirit that resides within each of us as human beings.
18. When an individual accepts the Lordship of Christ in their life, that person's physical body is imbued by the Holy Spirit – and everything changes.
19. The soul of a non-Christian is separated from the Holy Spirit's direction and influence – and instead, defaults to serving the needs and whims of the body that contains it.
20. Humankind cannot optimise its potential by merely accumulating assets – or indeed by accumulating anything that can be bought.

Chapter Four

1. Simply stated, conscience helps us to determine whether something is right or wrong according to our moral code.
2. Conscience is not something recognised by the Christian faith exclusively – it is inherent in the psyche of all human beings whether we regard it as religiously significant or not.
3. Importantly, conscience influences our choices, our behaviour – and ultimately our actions – and it is therefore central to a discussion on attitude.
4. When we accept Christ as Lord of our lives – the point at which the Holy Spirit joins with our spirit, renders our conscience acutely sensitive to God's influence.
5. The more one ignores conscience, the less sharp it becomes until ultimately it is virtually ineffective and no longer inhibits or even influences adverse behaviour or action.
6. Conscience and sensitivity work hand in hand within our mind to produce our attitude.
7. The level of sensitivity that triggers conscience reflects our attitude to what is appropriate and what is inappropriate.
8. There are at least two lessons here. Firstly, we need to be sensitive to others and secondly if we live in this way, there will be opportunities to influence others to live similarly.
9. As Christians, we need to be sensitive to our calling to glorify God and to enjoy Him forever. In addition, we need to be sensitive to the people around us – that is – those whom we are called to serve. How can we serve any other person if we are insensitive to their needs or condition?
10. As Christians, we need to be sensitive to the needs of other people if we are to serve God by serving our fellow man.
11. We need to follow Christ's example. Sensitivity is enhanced by humility.
12. It is not only procrastination that is the thief of time – it is everything that keeps us from focusing on what is important.
13. Consider how much (or how little) you are affected by what you read and hear that is happening globally – but especially in war zones and in disaster areas.

14. The question is whether and to what extent we have become insensitive to the needs of others?
15. Anything worth doing takes time and effort.
16. We have (substantially) lost the ability to communicate sensitively with people in general – and with our nearest and dearest in particular.
17. As Christians, we must not be insensitive about sensitivity.
18. We must be sensitive to the fact that we serve Almighty God – and to treat our God with awe and deep respect. We must be sensitive also to the people around us – and use our time and other 'assets' carefully.
19. Lord – help me to be as sensitive as I need to be to live effectively for You.
20. Kindness merely means doing something for someone out of the goodness of your heart not because of any compulsion. Kindness gets to the heart of being human.
21. We have not lost the capacity to be kind but we need to practice continuously if we are to avoid losing it – as if we were learning a foreign language!
22. Like athletes, Christians are in training – which means certain preferences must be foregone – and certain physical and attitudinal regimes must be adopted.
23. The Christian is called to discipline his/her life – to not only do the right thing – but also to do the thing right.
24. It requires discipline to say and to do the right thing. This is because the right thing is often the hardest thing.
25. Jesus' life epitomised discipline.
26. Jesus prayed consistently and lengthily.
27. Frequent communication with our Lord will help us to glorify Him, to mature as Christians, to encourage the development of sensitivity towards others – and to remember whose we are and whom we serve.
28. Prayer is not easy – but often we tend to make it harder than it needs to be because of our attitude towards it.

Chapter Five

1. Humility is an attitude of mind.
2. The fact of the matter is that we do not deserve any of our Lord's bounteous mercies.
3. We are not master of our own destiny – we control nothing – and we have only what we have been given.
4. Our God can be truly described as The Awesome God.
5. Jesus is the epitome of humility.
6. Of ourselves, we are nothing – and yet Jesus Christ surrendered His place in Heaven to live amongst humankind to redeem us and to point us to Almighty God.
7. Christ behaved with utmost dignity and humility.
8. We do not expect to see humility on display – we are more acquainted with self-esteem and arrogance.
9. When we see humility in action, we are firstly surprised but then uplifted – and often challenged.
10. It is instructive to think what the world might look like if our attitude demonstrated more humility.
11. If we choose to live humbly, life will not be easy – and we should not under-estimate the effort required.
12. It has to be said that no matter how humble we are or might become, humility will neither replace nor become a substitute for acknowledgement of Jesus Christ as Lord of our lives.
13. God expects us to emulate Christ's example in our daily lives.
14. Humility is a foundational element of the Christian way.
15. If we think we are humble, then we may have a problem.
16. There are just some people around who radiate positive vibes. These are the people who make us feel better when we meet them.
17. We are in danger of reading Scripture too quickly and thereby glossing over fundamental truths and lessons – and depriving ourselves of a proper understanding of what the words are really telling us.
18. The application of our world-view is a function of character – and character formation is ultimately a function of our soul – and the foundation for action.
19. Character is intrinsically linked to attitude.

20. For the Christian, character is the result of the Holy Spirit working in the human soul to produce an approach to life based on the principles (standards, values, habits and choices) that our conscience and character tell us is appropriate.
21. Character formation is a process that requires time and experience.
22. Displays of attitude – whether in the form of decisions, behaviour, tone of voice, words or action – reflect not only the character of the person(s) manifesting the display – but also the character of the person(s) reacting.
23. Discernment not only points in the direction of what is best – but warns us why we should avoid other courses of action.
24. Attitude is a fundamental part of every human being – not least because it affects our choices/decisions – which in turn affect whether – and if so, how we act and/or react in every circumstance in which we find ourselves throughout our lives.
25. Although we tend to make fewer important decisions than minor decisions in life, we should not lose sight of the fact that the cumulative effect of small decisions impacts our lives materially – because those decisions say so much about who we are.
26. The best decisions are those based on knowledge, previous experience, wisdom and discernment.
27. One of the ways that we can honour God is by referring all matters to Him whether large or small.
28. Obedience is one way we can demonstrate humility to our God.
29. It is pleasing to God when we humble ourselves before Him and pray for guidance and direction – for discernment from the Holy Spirit.
30. In this case, the Lord's answer to our request for discernment is to remind us to apply the experience, knowledge and common sense He has given us to do whatever is honouring to Him and in accordance with our Christian character.
31. Choice belongs to each of us.
32. Often, we are prone to blame other people for the consequences of our own decisions.

Chapter Six

1. Scripture is not a rulebook. Instead, Scripture provides us with what we might describe as 'principles'.
2. Principles are foundational to attitude.
3. Where principles are informed by traits such as honour and decency, the value of standards in the formation of character will be optimised.
4. Virtue might be considered as doing the right thing and avoiding doing the wrong thing.
5. If we can exercise adequate control over those actions that are repeated most often then our attitude will be influenced by a good character.
6. A positive disposition is an extremely effective backdrop to living a principle centred life.
7. One of the implications in adopting a negative approach is that it is cumulative. Soon, we risk seeing everything with a jaundiced eye.
8. Integrity is not easy to define – but it has much to do with morality and is a pillar of character.
9. Integrity means doing the right thing.
10. Character is at its finest when to act with integrity is not to a person's advantage and yet that person does the right thing.
11. Notice the inter-play between conscience, character, behaviour, decisions and principles. They are all complementary.
12. Doing the right thing often means the thing that is not easiest – which infers a personal cost.
13. Being honest includes not misleading people.
14. Whatever form it takes, cheating constitutes dishonesty.
15. Honesty and integrity go hand in hand.
16. Christians must be honest.
17. If honesty has implications for us as individuals – it has even more impact on communities as a whole.
18. Why have we lost sight of the old values of probity, candour, honesty and integrity?
19. We should never give our word lightly (especially to a child) – because we must expect to be held to it. Our word must be our bond.
20. Trust is a fundamental factor in the Christian experience.

21. The difference between a Christian's trust and that applicable amongst human beings in general is that with Christ, there is no chance whatsoever that our trust has been misplaced or that we are in jeopardy or at risk that we will be disappointed or let down.
22. It is not possible to express gratitude in the absence of humility.
23. Each day should begin with thanking God for all that He has done for us and each day should end with a similar expression of gratitude.
24. Take every opportunity to thank those around us for all they do for us – even if it is just opening the door.
25. Let's try to cultivate an attitude of gratitude in worship of our loving Saviour and in service of our fellow men and women.
26. Human behaviour can be changed – if there is a willingness to change it.
27. The fundamental criterion for success is that there must be willingness to change.
28. If I want things to change – that change process must begin with me in my environment – and you in yours!
29. When people see the changes brought about by someone living a principle centred life, they will want some of the same.
30. The types of principles and traits and qualities considered are transformational catalysts in adopting attitudes that will change individuals and societies – not only locally but globally as well.

Chapter Seven

1. The narrower our experiences in life, the smaller our frame of reference in interpreting events as they unfold around us.
2. A degree of tolerance is required in being open to explore the views of others – based on their respective background and circumstances.
3. Our mind must be sufficiently receptive to allow experience to affect our attitude.
4. Speak less and listen more.
5. We should not underestimate the worth of being a good listener.
6. For the Christian, reading Holy Scripture should be an imperative.
7. One of the ways that God speaks to His people is through His Word.
8. We Christians need to absorb Scripture.

9. Our attitudes cannot be Christ-like by accident.
10. We should never lose our capacity to learn and absorb and to review.
11. You might find considering your personal experience a valuable exercise.
12. We are all affected by the variables in the geographic environment where we live and spend our time.
13. Some people are deeply affected by nature.
14. The people with whom we mix, all have potential to influence our attitude.
15. The way we perceive the influence of others has substantial potential to affect our attitude.
16. As human beings, we are all vulnerable.
17. We all can exercise choice concerning which environments are conducive for us.
18. Sometimes, we need to sacrifice the good for the very best.
19. The perceptions of what other people may find acceptable should not be taken for granted.
20. Frustration means unmet expectations.
21. We are more inclined to expect other people to behave in a way that we expect – and fail to think what the other person might expect of us.
22. If we are right in what we believe we don't need to talk down to other people – and if we are wrong – we have no right to do so.
23. Could our expectations reflect our own prejudices?
24. Why is it always easier to see faults and weaknesses in other people than to see any weakness in ourselves?
25. Perceptions influence attitude.
26. Once we have reached certain conclusions, we do not often question whether our perceptions remain valid.
27. We need to remember that two people can react entirely differently to the same scenario – and both can be correct simultaneously.
28. So, we must teach ourselves to distinguish between how things are and how we expect things should be.
29. Our perception of ourselves is a fundamental determinant of attitude.
30. The lesson is to keep challenging our own perceptions.
31. Attitudes are adopted as reactions to a stimulus.
32. A 'trigger event' could be almost anything.

33. The tone and style of behaviour adopted by one person is very likely to affect how others involved react to that tone or behaviour.
34. One of the reasons why attitude is so significant is because of the intrinsic link between attitude and behaviour.
35. An optimistic or a pessimistic outlook has a great deal to do with outcomes.
36. We choose who we are – and we must accept responsibility for that.
37. Our soul uses our sensitised conscience to formulate character.
38. Attitude is a pattern of thought that arises through the interaction of spirit, soul and body. It involves the operation of conscience, character and principles – combining to persuade an individual in a particular environment to think, behave or to act in a particular way.
39. Our attitude cannot be right before God, unless our conscience, character and the principles by which we live are all attuned to the way that Scripture anticipates.
40. 'Success' in this respect is not a one point in time achievement – it is a process.
41. Attitude does not just happen – it arises as the result of complex interactions between all the variables described in the text – producing innumerable variations in the patterns of behaviour we exhibit as human beings.

Chapter Eight

1. While Almighty God has indicated how He would like us to conduct ourselves in the life He has given us, He does not force us to conform.
2. Our Creator has allowed us great latitude in deciding how we should live our lives – but that latitude is based on certain fundamental principles – including accountability and consequences.
3. God's patience and perseverance are seen throughout Scripture.
4. Jesus' trust in God was absolute.
5. Jesus was in continuous communication with His Father – to whom He humbly and unendingly remained faithful.
6. We often read of the compassion of our Saviour.
7. Scripture also tells us that there can be no forgiveness without the shedding of blood.

8. At Calvary, Christ died once – for all humankind.
9. What more could He give?
10. Jesus has done all that is necessary to save us from the punishment rightly due to us.
11. Sin was created through the actions of Adam and Eve – and through them it was passed on to the rest of humankind.
12. The attitude of Christ towards humankind is demonstrated in His supreme sacrifice.
13. God loves every one of us with a love that is so pure that it is impossible to comprehend it in this part of eternity.
14. We can experience it – all day every day.
15. Holiness involves understanding who our God is and who and what we are as we stand before Him.
16. God is unique.
17. God requires His holiness to be respected.
18. It should never cease to amaze those of us who love Him that in all His holiness, Almighty God deigned to stoop down to love us.
19. We could never have bridged the gap that exists between His purity and our sinfulness.
20. He is so holy that sinful humankind cannot look at Him and live.
21. Humankind is unholy – in fact humankind was born in sin.
22. It's so much easier to identify sin in others than in ourselves.
23. We fall so far short of the example set by Jesus Christ that we should be prompted to take action.
24. Either our view of God is too small or our view of ourselves is too big.
25. Understanding the awesome purity and majesty of our Creator and the utter wretchedness of our own sinful state must be amongst the first steps in the process of becoming holy.
26. Holiness is a process that continues throughout the lifetime of a Christian.
27. God wants His people to: acknowledge Him as Lord and to be: moral, upright and all things good – but these emanate from holiness – gradually and progressively after entering into a relationship with Jesus Christ.

28. As God's own people, we will be set apart – not because we are better than anyone else – but because our approach to God and to our fellow human beings is different.
29. Fundamentally, holiness depends upon attitude.
30. We are in danger of losing sight of how humble we should be before our Creator.
31. God is perfect.
32. God created humankind in perfection and in the absence of sin.
33. Attitude is all-encompassing – affecting every aspect of our being.
34. The only hope we have begins with the realisation that it is God's wish that every human being should be in a right relationship with Him.
35. Not only is God's love beyond description and limitless in depth and scope, it is freely available at all times and to all people.
36. God does not treat us the way we treat Him.
37. God perseveres with us to an extent beyond description.
38. We seem to have learned so little from those times when humankind turned its back on God and pursued its own way.
39. We have disappointed God from time immemorial but His patience and perseverance is reflected by the fact that He does not punish us in the way we deserve.
40. 'Grace' can be considered as the gift of God's favour.
41. My God is beyond description – His ways are infinite and His knowledge is beyond our comprehension.
42. Since our God is the awesome Deity – whose love and providence are so comprehensive that our finite minds do not have adequate capacity to comprehend Him, the least we can do is adopt appropriate attitudes in His service.

Chapter Nine

1. God has made man in His own image.
2. It's hard to know why the Lord bothers with us at all.
3. It's important to consider what sort of an attitude is likely to lead to a life that is dedicated to glorifying and honouring Almighty God.
4. What would Jesus do in such circumstances?

5. If our attitude is not right, it is unlikely that we will be taking the steps that are necessary in determining what we should do in all circumstances.
6. Am I living in a way that glorifies God?
7. Our human spirit will make every effort to curtail the Holy Spirit's influence.
8. The values and standards adopted by non-Christians emanate from the absence of the Holy Spirit's influence upon the spirit of humankind and in light of this vacuum, a character is formed that is entirely different to what God wants it to be.
9. The difference between Christians and non-Christians is that Christians are sinners saved by accepting God's grace – whereas non-Christians have rejected God's grace.
10. In the absence of sensitivity, how can Christians even understand or react appropriately to the obvious needs in the world around them?
11. God has chosen not to set out a plethora of rules – presumably because we might be misled into thinking that adherence to such rules would guarantee us a place in His kingdom.
12. Once the Christian's heart dictates his/her attitude, the less the need for rules.
13. In Scripture there are many guiding principles.
14. Love requires more than merely abstaining from wrongdoing – it requires positive action.
15. Despite how clever and progressive and developed humankind has become, we have not yet learned that selfishness and pursuing a strategy of 'I, me and mine' does not work well for anybody other than me.
16. Love is a determining factor in attitude.
17. God expects His creation to treat Him with appropriate respect and reverence.
18. God wants us to emulate Him – in our character, in our values and principles – and thereby in our attitudes.
19. It is not possible to adopt the right attitude towards God unless we are not only humbled by His holiness but also hold Him in awe.

Chapter Ten

1. What can I do to improve those areas on which I have the power and capacity to exert influence for change?
2. Sometimes, our suspicions arise from bias at worst or misunderstanding at best.
3. Communicating effectively is a skill – and as such, it takes time to learn the rudiments.
4. Our attitude will determine when we speak and what we say and how we say it – and to whom.
5. Encouragement is not restricted to acknowledging really important achievements because it can also be applied in many everyday situations.
6. All it takes is a little empathy and a big heart!
7. I don't believe that we are naturally callous – I think we have to learn to be so.
8. Beneath that outer veneer, there is a heart that our Saviour loves – and whom we as Christians are called upon to love as well.
9. Being honest means there is no room for duplicity – the truth, the whole truth and nothing but the truth is the required standard.
10. Our whole world seems to be hallmarked by a propensity to be less than totally honest.
11. It's not that they are right and we are wrong, it's just that they believe more strongly than we do that they are right – and we are not prepared to stand up and to be counted.
12. We are so afraid of offending others that sometimes we are not true to what we believe.
13. As Christians we have a code of behaviour that underscores our attitude – and it is to this we must be true if we are to have any chance in influencing those who may disagree with us.
14. We risk being drowned by the flood of non-Christian influences that permeate our society.
15. 'Undisciplined living' is much more easily accomplished than disciplined living.

16. Based on my life thus far, how many hours am I likely to spend on prayer, reflection, study of God's Word and meeting with other Christians?
17. If we are to conduct ourselves appropriately, we must first give God His rightful place.
18. We are all equally dependent upon God's grace – the only difference between us human beings is that some of us do not yet know it.
19. We must stop taking ourselves so seriously and rid ourselves of our pride and overbearing ego.
20. Behaviour does not need to be obvious to be bad!

Chapter Eleven

1. The very first step that any individual must take in learning how to adopt the right attitude – is to place his/her life on a meaningful foundation.
2. We act and re-act in particular ways in particular circumstances in accordance with the influences that we 'allow' to affect our attitudes.
3. Consider what and who affects us – and then pursue this by considering who or what affects us most.
4. Act on your attitude (ACTIVE) or let your attitude be acted upon by all the experiences and influences (for good or evil) that we encounter in life (PASSIVE)
5. It is so easy to be a hypocrite – sometimes we don't even have to try – it's almost as if it is natural.
6. The only person who is responsible for our individual attitude (and the consequent action/reaction) is oneself.
7. Cultivating appropriate attitudes and rejecting attitudes that are inappropriate is a process that we need to practice.
8. Changing our attitudes may be difficult – but it is not impossible.
9. If our attitude is appropriate, we will 'do good' automatically – because our DNA has been altered by God's grace.
10. Salvation is beyond price – its value cannot be quantified – it cannot be bought, earned or achieved.
11. With respect to my attitude this rule applies – which means that my attitude will remain as it is right at this moment unless and until I take steps to alter it.

Chapter Twelve

1. Most of us are less careful about how we communicate than we should be.
2. It's so easy to be encouraging in what we say but it seems it's easier still to be thoughtless, unkind and even acerbic.
3. What we say is influenced by what we are in our innermost being – our soul – the source of attitude.
4. The manner in which we choose to communicate has much to do with our attitude.
5. It is never a good idea to communicate in anger.
6. We need to remember that whether we are conscious of our attitude or not, it exists and it is potent – and we ignore it at our peril.
7. Perfection is not expected – but working to the highest standard that we can attain is our reasonable service.
8. If we want to live according to the principles laid out for us in Scripture, we are going to need a lot of help.
9. Any serious attempt at living in this manner will only be possible through God's grace and through the intervention of the Holy Spirit.
10. The sooner we start – the better.
11. Learning how to be a Christian takes a lifetime.
12. If we feed our minds with appropriate material, it is much more likely that our attitudes will be attuned to the principles set out in Scripture – and this is turn influences how we live.
13. The Christian way is to treat others how we want to be treated.
14. Prayer gives us access into God's immediate presence.
15. The thing is, He wants us to humble ourselves and to worship Him in prayer as we present our prayers and petitions to Him.
16. It is a matter of great wonder that Almighty God is willing to give us a hearing at all.
17. It's perverse isn't it that – in general – despite how potent prayer is, we are so reluctant to devote the time and energy to it that it merits?
18. Regrettably, we often fail to give God His rightful place in our lives.
19. Lastly in this respect, prayer should include a time of silence to see what God will put into our minds as we wait upon Him.
20. Scripture is infallible.

21. How can we expect to know about God's way if we don't take steps to learn and understand what Scripture says?
22. Going to Church presents us with an opportunity to learn (inter alia) from the experiences of others.
23. As Christians, we are asked to behave in a way that may make us appear weak – because we refuse to exploit people or opportunities that will adversely affect other people.
24. One of the decisions that every individual makes for him or herself is the extent to which we allow ourselves to become victims of our own circumstances.
25. The negative way forward is to blame everything on someone or something else. I am responsible for me.
26. God wants us to adopt the right attitude as we grow in grace – because in doing so – we will optimise our opportunities to learn, to grow and to be more like Him.

Chapter Thirteen

1. Every decision and every action are affected by our attitude at the time.
2. Inaction is in fact a decision to do nothing in the circumstances.
3. Mortality is probably the most significant factor in life.
4. We don't always treat time with the respect it deserves.
5. What we choose to do with the time available to us is our choice.
6. There is a point in time when something has to give because our current schedule is unsustainable.
7. Scripture also has some important things to say about money.
8. Do you feel more blessed when you give – or when you receive?
9. How much time, energy and money need to be devoted to the Lord's work? There is no easy answer to this – and Scripture is not prescriptive.
10. What does life mean to me?
11. For what thing that is bigger and outside yourself are you living?

Chapter Fourteen

1. The way we are is how we choose to be.
2. God requires that we recognise the eternal importance of spirit and soul and that we devote our mortal bodies in service to Him recognising His Lordship of our lives.
3. Qualities of character are not mutually exclusive.
4. Scripture is the principal guide to attitude – the platform from which appropriate attitudes emanate.
5. Good intentions are not enough – action is what is required.
6. God is good!

Appendix Two

Diagrams

Appendix Three

Examples of Scripture Verses That Provide Explicit Instructions

Number	Verse	Reference
	Old Testament	
1	Be careful to obey all the law my servant Moses gave you;	Joshua 1:7
2	Do not turn from it to the right or to the left, that you may be successful wherever you go;	Joshua 1:7
3	Keep this Book of the Law always on your lips;	Joshua 1:8
4	Meditate on it day and night, so that you may be careful to do everything written in it. Then you will be prosperous and successful;	Joshua 1:8
5	Have I not commanded you? Be strong and courageous;	Joshua 1:9
6	Do not be afraid;	Joshua 1:9
7	Do not be discouraged, for the Lord your God will be with you wherever you go;	Joshua 1:9

	New Testament	
8	Therefore encourage one another and build each other up, just as in fact you are doing;	1 Thessalonians 5:11
9	Now we ask you, brothers and sisters, to acknowledge those who work hard among you, who care for you in the Lord and who admonish you;	1 Thessalonians 5:12
10	Hold them in the highest regard in love because of their work;	1 Thessalonians 5:13
11	Live in peace with each other;	1 Thessalonians 5:13
12	And we urge you, brothers and sisters, warn those who are idle and disruptive;	1 Thessalonians 5:14
12	Encourage the disheartened;	1 Thessalonians 5:14
13	Help the weak;	1 Thessalonians 5:14
14	Make sure that nobody pays back wrong for wrong;	1 Thessalonians 5:15
15	But always strive to do what is good for each other and for everyone else;	1 Thessalonians 5:15
16	Rejoice always;	1 Thessalonians 5:16

17	Pray continually;	1 Thessalonians 5:17
18	Give thanks in all circumstances; for this is God's will for you in Christ Jesus;	1 Thessalonians 5:18
19	Do not quench the Spirit;	1 Thessalonians 5:19
20	Do not treat prophecies with contempt but test them all;	1 Thessalonians 5:20
21	Hold on to what is good;	1 Thessalonians 5:21
22	Reject every kind of evil.	1Thessalonians 5:21

Please note – these are merely a few of the many, many examples that could have been chosen to demonstrate specific rules and instructions that Scripture contains. For example, consider the book of Proverbs. Space prevents inclusion of the book – but the following summary might give readers a taste for its focus.

"…In a variety of situations and relationships the reader is exhorted to honesty, integrity, diligence, kindness, generosity, readiness to forgive, truthfulness, patience, humility, cheerfulness, loyalty, temperance, self-control and the prudent consideration of consequences that flow from attitudes, choices and/or actions. Anger should be held in check, violence and quarrelsomeness shunned, gossip avoided, arrogance repudiated. Drunkenness, gluttony, envy and greed should all be renounced. The poor are not to be exploited, the courts are not to be unjustly manipulated, legitimate authorities are to be honoured. Parents should care for the proper instruction and discipline of their children, and children should duly honour their parents and bring no disgrace on them. Human observation and experience have taught the wise that a certain order is in place in God's creation. To honour it leads to known positive effects; to defy it leads only to unhappy consequences. All of life should be lived in conscious awareness of the unfailing scrutiny of the Lord of creation and in reliance on His generous providence…"[592]

---

[592] Proverbs; Introduction From The NIV Study Bible; Biblica; Biblica.com

Appendix Four

A Word About Kaizen

In para 1.6, reference was made to the Japanese doctrine of Kaizen. There are four parts – as described below.

- "...Unconscious Incompetence – there is no realisation as to what is incorrect;
- Conscious Incompetence – this is the stage where one realises what is wrong and takes steps to fix it;
- Conscious Competence – when one is doing what is correct but only with effort; and finally
- Unconscious Competence – when one does what is correct without thinking about it...". [593]

Interestingly, the source of this quote is the obituary of a well-known swimming coach who applied this concept in training swimmers. It seems to me that there might be some applications in using these principles in living the Christian way? Someone very clever has noted that education is what you remember when you forget all that you have been taught – in which case, education does not culminate in being awarded a degree – it is in fact an on-going process refined by experience, the application of principles and lessons learned in maturity. The definition of 'unconscious competence' described above is where education begins. One author believes that "...commitment to continual improvement is the key to reaching your potential and to being successful...".[594]

---

[593] Obituary – Terry Laughlin; The Economist; Pg 86; 18 November 2017

[594] John C Maxwell; Attitude 101; Pg 91; 2003; Maxwell Motivation

Appendix Five

Index

H

I

J

K

L

M

N

O

P

Q

R

S

T

V

W